Building the Life

K A I R O S

In ancient Greek philosophy, *kairos* signifies the right time or the "moment of transition." We believe that we live in such a transitional period. The most important task of social science in time of transformation is to transform itself into a force of liberation. Kairos, an editorial imprint of the Anthropology and Social Change department housed in the California Institute of Integral Studies, publishes groundbreaking works in critical social sciences, including anthropology, sociology, geography, theory of education, political ecology, political theory, and history.

Series editor: Andrej Grubačić

Recent and featured Kairos books:

Practical Utopia: Strategies for a Desirable Society by Michael Albert

In, Against, and Beyond Capitalism: The San Francisco Lectures by John Holloway

Anthropocene or Capitalocene? Nature, History, and the Crisis of Capitalism edited by Jason W. Moore

We Are the Crisis of Capital: A John Holloway Reader by John Holloway

Archive That, Comrade! Left Legacies and the Counter Culture of Remembrance by Phil Cohen

Re-enchanting the World: Feminism and the Politics of the Commons by Silvia Federici

Autonomy Is in Our Hearts: Zapatista Autonomous Government through the Lens of the Tsotsil Language by Dylan Eldredge Fitzwater

The Battle for the Mountain of the Kurds: Self-Determination and Ethnic Cleansing in the Afrin Region of Rojava by Thomas Schmidinger

Beyond the Periphery of the Skin: Rethinking, Remaking, and Reclaiming the Body in Contemporary Capitalism by Silvia Federici

Beyond Crisis: After the Collapse of Institutional Hope in Greece, What? edited by John Holloway, Katerina Nasioka, and Panagiotis Doulos

For more information visit www.pmpress.org/blog/kairos/

Building Free Life

Dialogues with Öcalan

International Initiative Edition

KAIROS

Building Free Life: Dialogues with Öcalan
© 2020 PM Press.

All rights reserved. No part of this book may be transmitted by any means without permission in writing from the publisher.

ISBN: 978-1-62963-704-4 (paperback)
ISBN: 978-1-62963-764-8 (hardcover)
ISBN: 978-1-62963-768-6 (ebook)
Library of Congress Control Number: 2019933010

Cover Image: Abdullah Öcalan by Jim Fitzpatrick
Cover by John Yates / www.stealworks.com
Interior design by briandesign

10 9 8 7 6 5 4 3 2 1

PM Press
PO Box 23912
Oakland, CA 94623
www.pmpress.org

Printed in the USA.

Published with International Initiative Edition
International Initiative
"Freedom for Abdullah Öcalan – Peace in Kurdistan"
P.O. Box 100 511
D-50445 Cologne
Germany
www.freeocalan.org
First Published in 2019 by Aram, Diyarbakir
Translation where necessary by International Initiative

Contents

Introduction

International Initiative

Human beings are not born once and for all on the day their
mothers give birth to them, but ... life obliges them over and over
again to give birth to themselves.
—Gabriel García Marquez, *Love in the Time of Cholera*

While most of us refer to our own birth as a certain date, the day of our physical birth, Abdullah Öcalan has frequently mentioned that he was born three times. The third birth—after his physical birth and the founding of the organization he is best known for, the Partiya Karkerên Kurdistanê (PKK: Kurdistan Workers' Party)—is his paradigm shift toward his concept of "democratic civilization." This book, published to mark his seventieth birthday, in a certain way, tells the story of this third birth.

The massive transformation that Kurdish society has undergone in the last forty years did not primarily happen through books. In a culture that relies heavily on oral literature, songs, conversation, and word of mouth, speeches and personal dialogue have been very important. Öcalan—although he authored several books in the 1970s and 1980s, and a total of more than sixty to date, twelve of them in prison—is mainly a man of the spoken word and of dialogue. This makes his prison conditions since 1999, the total isolation and absence of dialogue, all the harder. Dialogue became monologue, and his only way to communicate with an audience was to write court submissions, his so-called defenses or prison writings. In the face of a possible genocide, he did not formulate

1

an individual defense but acted as a spokesperson for his people—and eventually for all the oppressed peoples of the Middle East.

But, still, it is not fair to speak of a monologue. Abdullah Öcalan's writings, first addressed to various courts in Turkey and Europe and subsequently published, did initiate a form of dialogue. The essays communicate with storytellers from mythological pasts as well as with living intellectuals, with companions who know him personally and unknown readers on other continents, with supporters and opponents alike—even with his long deceased mother. His writings are being translated—some of them into as many as twenty languages—and are read and discussed by people all over the world.

The International Initiative and many others have taken up this dialogue and discussed his ideas with people/s who are also weaving and building a free life. In many countries and places, we tried to further the dialogue with and between the young, women, anarchists, libertarian socialists, social ecologists, autonomists, Indigenous peoples, workers, and all those whose hearts, minds, and praxis are dedicated to furthering the quest for a free life. This book is our attempt to reflect those discussions and dialogues and the process of learning from one another.

This book for the first time collects written reactions to Abdullah Öcalan's prison writings. It brings together a number of academics, writers, and revolutionaries who are interested in and inspired by his thought. Since it is going to appear in various languages, it is an attempt to deepen and broaden the existing dialogue. Hopefully it will also pierce through prison walls, since the severe isolation conditions in the İmralı Island prison allow for very little of that dialogue to get back to the author. As writing has become the means for Öcalan to overcome his isolation and communicate with a wider audience, we hope that this book will be a way for that very audience to reach back to him and contribute to his relentless and resilient effort to create a better world.

The essays span a period of twenty years, and you will be able to trace a certain development. The topics discussed broaden in scope as they move away from the confines of nationalism and security-related issues toward more far-reaching ideas about the history of civilization and the struggle between capitalist modernity and democratic modernity as the current expression of a conflict that stretches back eons.

What is constant throughout the essays is the excitement about Öcalan's attempt at writing a holistic history of all the oppressed and linking their different struggles to become free or remain free. New concepts arise, such as democratic modernity, democratic nation, democratic confederalism, and especially *jineolojî* as a form of knowledge that could bring about the transformation needed for our quest to build free life.

The book is divided into four sections. Section I, "Introductions, Backgrounds, Postscripts," consists mainly of writings that have been published as forewords or afterwords to translations of Öcalan's books. Some of these writings are by people who, already in 1999, the year of Öcalan's abduction, were familiar with his thinking and the Kurdish situation, among them Norman Paech and the late Ekkehard Sauermann, or who later entered this indirect dialogue, for example, Arnaldo Otegi and John Holloway. Others such as Immanuel Wallerstein, Antonio Negri, and Barry K. Gills became familiar with Öcalan after he commented on their work and how it influenced his thought. What is special about this chapter is that it shows how the engagement with Öcalan's thought initially started, and how, in the beginning, different aspects of his identity—such as his role as a revolutionary leader who mobilized millions, as a Marxist reevaluating his position in the post-Soviet world order, as a man in an intense learning process from feminism and ecological movements in the light of his own experiences in the PKK, where he consistently promoted autonomous women's organizations, and as a captive suffering severe human rights abuses—were the interpretative grid through which his thought was evaluated.

Section II, "The Origins of Civilization," engages with Öcalan's writings that give a comprehensive account of human history. Peter Lamborn Wilson finds a kindred spirit in Öcalan and his interest in Sumerian civilization as a point of reference for understanding the transformation from non-state communities to states that monopolize the means of production, reproduction, and violence. Donald H. Matthews and Thomas Jeffrey Miley, on the other hand, focus on the making of the monotheistic tradition and reflect upon the transformation of the organization of power in monotheism through a dialogue with Öcalan's take on the issue. Finally, in this section, Muriel Gonzáles Athenas critically engages with Öcalan's understanding of gender and history.

Section III adds a spatial and comparative perspective to Öcalan's thought and collects essays that evaluate perspectives and resonances from other parts of the world. We have called this section "Weaving and Linking," because the essays included here, while linking different movements, pasts, dreams, memories, and thinkers from around the world, also contribute to the making of a decolonized world history and politics. Radha D'Souza addresses this question explicitly when she situates herself as a South East Asian woman in her dialogue with Öcalan. Raúl Zibechi, on the other hand, shows the parallels between movements and ideas in Latin America and Kurdistan. Despite the fact that they would seem to be separated by a great distance, they share concepts and an orientation and contribute greatly to keeping revolutionary opposition lively. Andrej Grubačić comes nearer in terms of geography, while going back in time and reminding us how the goal of a Balkan confederation, along with the struggle against Ottoman colonization, formed the backbone of socialist mobilization in the Balkans at the turn of the past century.

Section IV, "Political Philosophy and Political Action," discusses practical aspects of Öcalan's methodology and theory. While David Graeber makes a compelling argument for the uniqueness of Öcalan's approach to issues of value and labor and foregrounds his writing style as a means by which he addresses certain real dilemmas regarding his position as a leader who opposes hierarchy, Mechtchild Exo reflects upon and discusses the theoretical and practical repercussion of jineolojî—women's science—as proposed by Öcalan and developed and deepened by the Kurdish women's movement. Nazan Üstündağ pursues the question of theology in Öcalan and how Öcalan's writing promotes a framework of revolutionary spirituality for answering questions of universe, existence, afterlife, truth, and freedom. Fabian Scheidler, on the other hand, in line with Öcalan's view of civilization and its structural crisis and collapse, looks at Rojava as the art of transition in a collapsing civilization. Patrick Huff addresses Öcalan's approach to history and shows that it is critical of linearity and progress without being nostalgic. Shannon Brincat and Damian Gerber, on the other hand, deeply engage with Murray Bookchin's influence on Öcalan's thought, while also pointing out that since the Kurdish movement cannot remain solely theoretical but must experiment with the real effects of applying these ideas in practice, it faces enormous challenges.

We are confident that this unusual form of intellectual exchange will provide interesting insight into the discourses and discussions inside and surrounding the Kurdish freedom movement. Hopefully, it will inspire many more people to join the dialogue and engage in the worldwide search for alternatives.

Abdullah Öcalan "celebrated" his seventieth birthday on April 4, 2019, if we can talk about a celebration at all. He has been in solitary confinement for more than twenty years now. Since 2011, he has not even been able to consult with a lawyer; since April 2015, apart from three brief visits from his brother, most recently in 2019, he has seen no one from outside the island prison. Nonetheless, he continues to inspire numerous people with his ideas, even if they cannot meet with him in person—yet.

Thus, this book also aims to contribute to the struggle to break the isolation and eventually secure Abdullah Öcalan's freedom—a crucial step on the way to peace and a political solution of the ongoing conflict.
March 1, 2019

Addendum to the English Edition
After months of hunger strikes against solitary confinement led by MP Leyla Güven of the Halkların Demokratik Partisi (HDP: People's Democratic Party) involving thousands of people in a number of countries, Abdullah Öcalan was able to consult with his lawyer several times from May to August 2019. Talks on a solution to the conflict have not yet resumed. The isolation continues, as does the war.

Shortly before the English edition went to press, we found out that the internationalist Michael Panser lost his life during a Turkish air raid in December 2018. His essay about the intersection of Foucault and Öcalan concludes the book.
August 2019

International Initiative "Freedom for Abdullah Öcalan—Peace in Kurdistan" is a multinational peace initiative for the release of Abdullah Öcalan and a peaceful solution to the Kurdish question. It was established immediately after Öcalan was abducted in Kenya, Nairobi, and handed over to the Republic of Turkey on February 15, 1999, following a clandestine operation by an alliance of secret services. Part of its activity is the publication of Abdullah Öcalan's works.

SECTION I
Introductions, Backgrounds, Postscripts

ONE

Jumping on the Bus

John Holloway

I write in a rush, because I have left it too late and I want to be there, I want to be in this book. I am jumping on the bus just as it leaves.

I have been invited to write a foreword to Öcalan's *Sociology of Freedom*, a very great honor. But I do not have it ready in time for it to be included in the Turkish edition of this book of dialogues with Öcalan. Nevertheless, I write this note quickly to express admiration for Öcalan and to say how important his ideas and the Kurdish struggle are for us.

First, the admiration. Sitting in the comfort of my professorial desk, I have enormous admiration for all those who go out and give their lives to make the world a better place, who spend years in prison or die in the process. So many thousands and thousands of people who have fought and fought against the horrors of a foul system. Through all political differences and theoretical debates that might exist, we have to say: that is something wonderful, to dedicate your life to making the world a better place.

In this case, it is more than that. The danger of taking a political stance is that we become rigid, that we can no longer think beyond that stance. This is all the more so in the case of people who become leaders. The marvel of Abdullah Öcalan is that, even as a leader, he has been able to turn his thinking around, to rethink the meaning and the possibility of revolution and to convince so many people to accompany him in this process. This shows an extraordinary flexibility and sensitivity to the winds of social change. The only parallel that I can think of is the Zapatistas, albeit in quite different circumstances. Already immersed in their struggle, they had the courage and openness to say, "We are wrong, that is not the way to

9

change the world. We have to think again and change direction." In both cases, the Zapatistas and the Kurds, the rethinking has been very profound, very articulate, and very effective. It has been so effective because they have been able to tune in to changes taking place in rebel thought and action around the world and articulate and develop those changes in theory and in practice.

We need those struggles so much at the moment. It is not a question of wanting a vanguard or a model of revolution. It is rather that in a night that is getting darker and darker, we need these great explosions of light in the night sky. That is why the Kurdish movement is so important to us. Our reaction is a reaction of solidarity, but it is much more than that. It is a reaction of thirst, of hunger, of longing. The Kurdish movement and the Zapatistas give us joy, because we are looking for something like that, we need the light that brightens the sky, the light of hope. The dynamic of capital is gathering speed, and it becomes harder and harder to imagine that we can ever stop it. The annihilation of humanity is more firmly on the agenda than ever before. Everywhere there are movements of resistance and experiments in creating the foundations of another world, but we also see many of those movements and experiments falling and being reintegrated into capitalism, and then we very easily lose confidence. It is desperately urgent to break capitalism and create something else, but it is very hard to see how we are going to do it. So when we see the Kurdish movement doing that in the most awful of circumstances, then we want to help, we want to say, "Thank you," and we want to shout out, "Yes, yes, yes, your movement is ours, and our movements are yours!"

That is why I want to jump on the bus, and now I must hope that the driver-editor will let me.

John Holloway is a professor of sociology at the Instituto de Ciencias Sociales y Humanidades in the Benemerita Universidad Autonoma de Puebla, Mexico, and honorary visiting professor at the University of Rhodes, South Africa. He has published widely on Marxist theory, the Zapatista movement, and new forms of anti-capitalist struggle. His books *Change the World without Taking Power* (London: Pluto Press, 2010 [2002]) and *Crack Capitalism* (London: Pluto Press, 2010) have stirred international debate and have been translated into eleven languages.

TWO

Öcalan, European Law, and the Kurdish Question

Norman Paech

A good three years after the death sentence handed down by the Turkish state constitutional court, the decision of the European Court of Human Rights is expected this autumn.[1] The former chairman of the—no longer existing—Partiya Karkerên Kurdistanê (PKK: Kurdistan Workers' Party), Abdullah Öcalan, had to go this route, not so much to escape execution but, rather, to bring the Kurdish question back to Europe, because by means of his abduction and extradition to Turkey politicians there had tried to consign it to the memory hole. It was easier to pronounce the death sentence than to carry out the execution, because Turkey is neither China nor the US but, purportedly, on the road to Europe. And for Europeans, it was easier to prevent Turkey from implementing the sentence than to put pressure on it to solve the Kurdish question. While the execution of Öcalan would have made the already high hurdles facing Turkey's EU membership insurmountable for the foreseeable future, it is fairly unlikely that Turkey would face similar consequences for failing to change its policy toward the Kurds.

The goal of Öcalan's complaint is to induce the European Court of Human Rights in Strasbourg to put the Kurdish question back on the European agenda, for what is at stake here is not the fate of a single man but the future of a whole people. And this people is now in danger of slipping into oblivion in the wake of two other peoples of the Middle East, namely, the peoples of Palestine and Iraq. Given that constellation, Öcalan's comprehensive petition includes the vast aggregate of the Kurdish question, deals with its historical emergence, its cultural dimension, its political dynamic, and its democratic perspective, and leaves the legal arguments to the attorneys. The excerpt on "the Kurdish question and European law" that was published in German also leaves the legal questions of the litigation aside, instead addressing the general role of law as a specific institution of European culture and its role in finding a solution to the Kurdish question.[2]

The politicization of the Kurdish question on a European level was Öcalan's central goal after he was forced to leave Syria on October 8, 1998. It was for this reason that he moved to Rome and not to the mountains. He had ceased to see an exclusive focus on the Turkish-Kurdish contest as a realistic way out of the dead end of war. And despite his personal negative experience as a result of this choice, in the long run it nevertheless offers the only perspective for the self-determination and autonomy of the Kurdish people. All the disappointments and treacheries during his continental odyssey notwithstanding, this is still his credo and the red thread running through his petition even today.

Beyond what is already known, we don't learn many noteworthy details about his erratic flight from Italy to the Netherlands (where he wasn't even allowed to land), then to Moscow, St. Petersburg, Athens, and Kenya. His conclusion that all of this was part of a joint plot involving almost all of Europe's governments, but most of all, the US, Russia, and Greece, corresponds to the assessment of most observers at the time. Even though Italy, where a court in Rome later recognized his right to political asylum, put enormous pressure on him to leave the country at the time, it has not faced the same rebuke as the obvious masterminds of the plot. After some initial confusion in the NATO capitals, the goal of this plot was his liquidation; Öcalan, as the focal point and motor of the Kurdish demands, had to be eliminated. This was not so much about the person but about preventing the symbol of a struggle from developing a public presence in European society. Apparently, one of the tools used in all this was a pistol that the Greek ambassador in Kenya provided to Öcalan—not to enable him to defend himself but in the hope that he would commit suicide.

None of this even remotely conforms to European standards of the rule of law, which would have required granting the leader of the PKK the status of a political refugee in any country that acted in accord with the Geneva Convention on Refugees. There was some brief consideration of having him tried before an international court, but in the end extraditing him to Turkey seemed preferable—and this is exactly what the preconcerted denial of asylum amounted to. For one thing, it was believed that this would prevent the feared solidarity of European Kurds. For another, this served to circumvent the embarrassment of a tribunal at which the conduct of war and the human rights violations on the part of the Turkish military, as well as the support it received from its NATO allies, would certainly have been examined in excruciating detail. And, finally, the reality of the Turkish judiciary was too well-known for anyone to have had any illusions about the outcome of a trial. Öcalan was delivered for trial to a state constitutional court whose proceedings had already been condemned many times by the European Court of Human Rights as incompatible with European standards.

The abduction unequivocally contradicted European law, and there have been criticisms and admonitions about the detention conditions from the Commission of the European Council, which have, alas, not led to any change in Öcalan's solitary confinement on İmralı. With the death penalty, matters are different. Its prohibition is included in the Code of the European Convention on Human Rights, but Turkey has also refused to ratify the Supplementary Protocol in which all other states of the European Council have agreed to its ban. What is no longer acceptable at the level of European rule of the law is, in this case, still legally possible— the death penalty is not part of the catalog of human rights violations! If the decision of the state constitutional court were to be thrown out, this could only be justified by the irregularities of the kidnapping and of the following court procedure.

Öcalan should be believed when he says that the revision of his verdict is neither his main concern nor the central goal of his complaint. It is *his* way of returning to Europe, even if the continent doesn't want him. Having been forced to understand that the military struggle will not lead to a solution and that his political proposals are getting bogged down by the strategic interests of the NATO clan, this is his last remaining tool in his struggle for the Kurdish people.

But what encourages him to hope for a solution in court to a question that is blocked by politics and to use the law as a lever against this political resistance? It is true that Turkey hasn't had a particularly positive experience at the Strasbourg court and was ruled against in almost every human rights complaint brought to it by Turkish citizens. In most cases, it has paid the compensation that was demanded, but, so far, it has not taken the appropriate steps to remedy its legal, police, and military systems. Therefore, any realistic expectation with regard to the Strasbourg proceedings can only be about Turkish observance of its decision and not much else.

But, even so, Öcalan's reflections on the solution of the Turkish crisis, and its most critical point, the Kurdish question, are correct. The "sick man of the Bosporus" suffers from manifold afflictions, the most obvious being the economic crisis accompanied by a fantastic level of inflation. It is also generally admitted that the deformation of the political-military class by corruption and crime hardly offers any prospect for improvement. The refusal to grant the Kurdish people equality with Turks, in particular, with all its forms of oppression, destruction, expulsion, and underdevelopment, is both a source and a daily expression of the misery experienced in Turkey. "The system of oppression even prohibits the language and thus continuously produces secession and violence," writes Öcalan[3]—and the system reacts to this with yet more repression. Just a few hundred kilometers to the south, in Palestine, the forms of mutual violence and terror to which such a system of repression can lead are already a daily practice.

Öcalan doesn't draw the comparison between Turkey and Israel, but on a certain level it is obvious. Both states have modern democratic institutions and civil constitutional states, without, however, being able to put an end to the criminal excesses of their governments and their military. In Turkey, much more than in Israel, this is undoubtedly due to the still imperfect structure of the constitutional state, but, in both states, it is certainly also a primary consequence of the support and backing of powerful allies. Even a fully developed constitutional state represents no guarantee against the political deterioration of its institutions, but it is certainly the indispensable precondition for the democratic control and the peaceful development of the political system. Seen from that angle, the Kurdish question is also a problem of the unfolding and enforcement of the constitutional state, for which, despite all flaws, there is at present no other model than the one of Europe. This is the approach Öcalan is taking.

On this road to becoming a constitutional state, Turkey has had barely eighty years, just a fraction of the time that the European core states needed after the Enlightenment to construct, through several revolutions, its present constitutional system, which has found its common expression in the European Convention on Human Rights. As opposed to NATO, the EU has turned this standard into a precondition for membership in its so-called Copenhagen Criteria. Moreover, it too regards reforms in the direction of the rule of law as indispensable for the solution of the

Turkish crisis. This includes not just *minimal* demands, such as the end of torture, of disappearing people, and of expelling them and destroying their houses and property but also the acknowledgement of the identity and autonomy of the Kurds, as well as of their language and their political and civil organizations. Öcalan invests great hope in this for the democratization of the Kurdish society.[4] The constitutional state is crucial to the right of self-determination; without it, the crisis can't be solved, and the equal status of the different peoples within a single state will remain a project for the remote future. At the end of his reflections on European law and the Kurdish question, Öcalan hints at the long path Turkey still has to travel to get to this point, and he warns: "In order to safeguard the process of peace and democratization, we need an appropriate qualitative and quantitative strengthening of the armed forces of the PKK. This is necessary not just because of the opponents of peace in Turkey but also because of potential attacks by reactionary forces, including Kurdish ones, in the Middle East."[5] This warning highlights Europe's responsibility, which, in the form of NATO, it has never risen to, and which it now has to engage all the more seriously in the form of the EU and the European Court of Human Rights.

Afterword 2019
In the eighteen years that have passed since the lines above were written, the world and its order have profoundly changed. Events such as the banking and financial crisis in 2008, the wars in Libya and Syria beginning in 2011, the people fleeing to Europe to escape the wars and the misery in their countries, and the accession to office of Donald Trump in 2017 are expressions of a deep crisis of the Western capitalist system. The means and the violence that are being used to save it are increasingly detrimental to democratic achievements, including human rights, the welfare state, and the constitutional guarantees that the European states very much like to turn into yardsticks to measure the performance of states outside of their realm.

The European Court of Human Rights has admonished the Turkish state constitutional court for the unfair proceedings in Öcalan's case and has classified the death penalty as a violation of the prohibition of inhumane treatment addressed in article 3 of the European Convention on Human Rights. The Turkish verdict was the result of an unfair trial and was pronounced by a court whose independence and impartiality are questionable. But the European court did not regard the abduction of the PKK leader from Kenya to Turkey as an offense against the European Convention on Human Rights—a very problematic decision. With this, it also reduced the pressure on the Turkish government to relax Öcalan's isolation, which since the autumn 2016 has been total, with neither relatives nor legal representatives having any access to Öcalan.[6] The brief period of talks between the government and Öcalan ended in the spring of 2015, because Erdoğan saw his electoral goals threatened by this contact. When he didn't succeed in putting a brake on the mounting popularity of the Halkların Demokratik Partisi (HDP: People's Democratic Party) and blocking it from parliament in the elections, he fell back on his established violent approach and launched a pathological persecution of all critical opposition and a merciless war against the Kurds.

None of Turkey's NATO partners prevented Erdoğan from acting in this criminal way against his own population. In the Security Council, no one was ready to take the Turkish government and army to the International Criminal Court for war crimes. Quite obviously, the strategic role played by Turkey as a military base and outpost in the Middle East and as a protective shield against refugees from war zones is more important than all avowals of peace and human rights. Therefore, there was also no one prepared to take the steps necessary to prevent the Turkish advance into Syrian territory and the occupation of the canton of Afrin. Like the Kurds in Turkey, the Kurds in the neighboring countries are never safe from Turkish military attacks. Meanwhile, the UN, NATO, and their member states safeguard their own strategic interests and stand by watching. Even though the European Court had only recently repealed the listing of the PKK as a terrorist organization, which was in place from 2014 to 2017, the European Council put the PKK back on the list in 2018. In the Federal Republic of Germany, criminal trials against Kurdish activists are still justified by their alleged membership in or support of the PKK. These are simply additional examples of the European Council and the German judiciary conducting business in Mr. Erdoğan's favor, a disgusting collaboration devoid of any morality.

In 2001, I wrote: "The war has bought [Turkey] not a single step closer to the solution of the Kurdish question, but has dragged it ever deeper down into the quagmire of state terror, corruption, and torture. The war hasn't only devastated the country itself, but the same is true of its political system." Unfortunately, in 2019, the same diagnosis holds; the only difference is that the devastation has grown worse. The understanding that violence and war have repeatedly failed and that the claim of the Kurds to self-determination cannot be repressed by military means has apparently again become anathema to the Turkish government. The HDP and the PKK proposals for a political solution are answered with persecution and arrests in a war that is being extended beyond Turkey's borders.

But as bleak as the current situation in Turkey and Syria may be, with Erdoğan's war-mongering and the permanent threat of war and military attacks, we shouldn't overlook or underestimate the successes of the Kurdish movement in those years. Despite the manifold attacks, the HDP has become an important factor in Turkish politics, with substantial success at the ballot box and considerable influence among the Turkish population—a genuine threat to the dominance of the Adalet ve Kalkınma Partisi (AKP: Erdoğan's Justice and Development Party). Despite his isolation, the significance of Abdullah Öcalan for the Kurdish movement is more far-reaching and more important than ever before; he was the official dialogue and negotiation partner of the Turkish government. His charisma and radiance are particularly evident in the development of the democratic model of society in Rojava, Syria. Rojava has given all Kurds in Turkey, Syria, Iraq, and Iran, but also in Europe and overseas, a new perspective: emancipation and liberation from repression and violence are possible and can be won even in terrible times and under adverse circumstances.

We shouldn't be satisfied with the assumption that the Erdoğan regime will one day come to an end. Active resistance is necessary and possible *now*. And in this Öcalan continues to play an important role. His liberation from prison must, therefore, be one of the immediate goals. The Kurdish people are not alone in this struggle but can count on the solidarity of peoples all over the world, because all of this is about the struggle for freedom, democracy, and socialism.

The first part of this essay was published in 2002 in *Aşitî*, the bulletin of the International Initiative, and, in 2003, as a foreword to *Gilgameschs Erben*, the German edition of *Prison Writings: The Roots of Civilisation*. The afterword was written in January 2019 for this book.

Norman Paech is an emeritus professor at Hamburg University, a former member of the Bundestag, the German parliament, and an expert in international law. He was born on April 12, 1938, in Bremerhaven, Germany. Paech started his career at the federal Ministry of Economic Cooperation in Bonn. He continued as a researcher at the Federation of German Scientists research center in Hamburg. In 1975, he became a professor in political science at the University of Hamburg and subsequently taught public law at the University of Economics and Politics, Hamburg. For nine years, he was chairman of the Association of Democratic Lawyers. He was the chief editor of the legal-political quarterly *Democracy and Law* and is a member of the Scientific Advisory Board of ATTAC, IALANA, and IPPNW. During the years 2005–2009, he was a member of the German Bundestag and was the foreign affairs spokesman for *Die Linke*. Paech is the author of numerous articles and books, largely concerning international law. His most recent publications include: Norman Paech and Gerhard Stuby, *Völkerrecht und Machtpolitik in den Internationalen Beziehungen* (Hamburg: VSA, 2013); Annette Groth, Norman Paech, and Richard Falk, eds., *Palästina—Vertreibung, Krieg und Besatzung* (Cologne: Papy Rossa Verlag, 2017); Norman Paech and Karsten Nowrot, eds., *Krieg und Frieden im Völkerrecht* (Cologne: Papy Rossa Verlg, 2019).

Notes

1 Contrary to this expectation, the decision was made public only on March 12, 2003.
2 Abdullah Öcalan, *Die Kurdische Frage und das europäische Recht* (Cologne: Internationale Initiative, 2002).
3 Ibid., 21.
4 Ibid., 49f.
5 Ibid.
6 In January 2019, Öcalan was allowed a brief visit with his brother Mehmet.

THREE

A Grand and Comprehensive Dialogue

Ekkehard Sauermann

The following voluminous work is a historical document of great significance and efficacy: an excellent personality of our time who possesses qualities and capacities that qualify him for important social functions on a national and an international scale is making himself heard in this essay. In the process, Abdullah Öcalan reveals outstanding acuteness and depth of mind, which should secure him broad public appeal. But as a consequence of his political activities, he is at present totally isolated and facing the extreme threat of physical and psychological annihilation.

Many enlightened contemporaries admire historical personalities who stand up to the spirit of the time, who are persecuted, incarcerated, and eradicated as a result, and who thus enter the conflictual history of human civilization as role models. The particular attention to the statements made by such personalities is also a result of the fact that their ideas and work were prevented from reaching the public during their lifetime, often reaching humanity only long after their death. When reading such works, any pedantic, know-it-all attitude is out of the question. Patience and understanding while reading them are based on the knowledge about the extreme conditions under which these works came into existence. The motive for reading such an essay and devoting particular attention to it is therefore connected to a moral and ideological declaration of solidarity with the persecuted author. The present work of Abdullah Öcalan and the challenge and motivation to apply oneself to a study of it stand in this tradition.

The topical merit of this work in comparison to its countless pre-decessors is that it directly addresses us all as contemporaries, affected allies, and comrades in arms of Abdullah Öcalan and helps us in the search for answers to the pressing existential questions of our time. A political approach to this work entails the opportunity for effective ideological and practical solidarity with the author, who—originally sentenced to death and, despite changes in the Turkish legal situation, is not necessarily beyond that fate—is forced to fight for his mental and physical survival as the only prisoner on the island of İmralı, surrounded by military guards. His book is the result of that struggle and bears witness to the incredible mental and psychic strain and exertion of the author, who directs his gaze beyond his own individual existence to the life and the survival of the Kurdish people, the people of the Middle East, and finally of all of humanity. In the face of the extreme challenge of his own fate, Abdullah Öcalan finds the strength and the greatness to turn his attention, from an elevated vantage point, to the fate of the Kurdish people, as well as that of the whole global community.

The results of this unusual orientation toward these issues are chal-lenging, provocative, and, in part, also irritating and shocking, but con-structive and productive throughout. Many of the difficulties he has faced and overcome and the insights he has gained could be the lot of anyone who has preserved their independence in the face of the dominant massive manipulation of opinion and found creative solutions.

Beyond this horizon of experience, which the author shares with many contemporaries, he includes in his work the concentrated political and social experience that he accumulated on a national, regional, and international level. Faced with an extreme individual test of stamina, Öcalan is able to boil down this treasure of experience in struggles and in life—in the same way steel is tempered by intense heat and extreme cold. What is crucial here is not just the ideological and political results achieved by the author. The road he has chosen to take is also of great importance and has a certain independent significance. Abdullah Öcalan does not simply want to delineate a certain goal, he also wants to take his readers with him on his road and convey to them the experiences and insights won in his search for a constructive alternative. In this area in particular he wants to enter into a *dialogue*. This work represents a far-reaching attempt at a dialogue with his comrades in arms, the women and men of his Kurdish people, as well as of the other peoples, all of whom face the challenge to become agents of their own histories.

Abdullah Öcalan reveals his own earlier and present struggle to assert and prove himself as an acting subject for social development. From there, he establishes a bridge to all those who are objectively faced with the challenge of developing a similar process in order to preserve their dignity and defend the dignity of humankind. His dialogue is geared to this individual but, at the same time, is a communal dialogue.

Because other opportunities for public debate are barred to him, and he is meant to be shut off and totally isolated by a wall of silence, Öcalan has focused his search for dialogue on the present work. Because of their dialogic character, neither volume of this work is finished and mature. Both must be understood as workshop books. Öcalan involves the committed readers who do not simply want to consume the essay but also to engage with it in an active and critical fashion like partners in the workshop of his thoughts. As dialogic workshop books the essays have other peculiarities, such as the cyclic approach, which includes multiple repetitions and confirmations, as in a dialogic conversation. This might irritate readers who want to finish this work and do so as quickly as possible. But those who are ready to get involved in a demanding and creative dialogue with this unusual author will also profit from these byways and reviews, which, together, in the end, form a whole network of paths.

This is one of those works about which the great eighteenth-century natural scientist and philosopher Georg Christoph Lichtenberg once said: "The sound of the clash of a head with a book does not only affect the book but also the head of the reader."

The Historical Development, Current Situation, and Perspective of the Kurdish People

In this essay, with its open discussion of his own earlier policies, the author uses the opportunity to reach his comrades in arms in the Kurdish liberation movement and convey to them, within the framework of a historical contemplation, concrete thoughts about the programmatic, strategic, and tactical continuation of their struggle. This document is a legacy of the former chairman of the Partiya Karkerên Kurdistanê (PKK: Kurdistan Workers' Party), who has been radically and physically separated from his party but still feels most intimately connected to it. In this way, he tries to convey to the members and followers of the Kurdish liberation movement the wealth of his insights won in the face of such extreme conditions and challenges.

The author proceeds on the assumption that a profound approach to the Kurdish problematic is decisive, both for a correct grasp and for the practical mastery of this challenge. He thinks his previous attempts at an explanation and solution of this problem were incorrect and misleading because of their very approach. Öcalan claims that the phenomenon of Kurdishness is like a black hole, that flawed ideas and concepts have formed around Kurdish reality, and that it is, for example, imprudent to define the Kurdish phenomenon as a nation, or even as a colony or semi-colony. The author impressively describes the historical and current tragedy of the Kurdish people, which he says consists in the fact that it has consistently faced numerous, often simultaneous, invasions, catastrophes, and wars unparalleled by almost any other people in history. For that reason, there have been very few opportunities for cultural and political achievements over the course of the checkered history of the Kurds. The Kurdish people were instead forced to focus on protecting their physical existence from the endless invasion and looting. In that situation, no promising voice was able to gain a hearing or develop its creativity.

This dramatic description finds its contrast in Öcalan's repeated observation that it was, of all people, the Kurds who played a decisive role at the beginning of the history of civilization. Öcalan assumes that his people had a particularly deep influence on the culture of Mesopotamia and thus contributed to creating the culture of an epoch, which, according to him, had a much more comprehensive and deeper influence on the history of civilization than is the case for today's main powers, the US and the European Union.

Which topical and future paths to a solution does Öcalan develop for his people?

He begins with the observation that the Kurdish people (especially in Turkey) is again, as so often in history, in a situation that can only be described as "neither war nor peace." This permanent state of emergency has become the norm. The explosive situation created thereby, says Öcalan, urgently necessitates a solution.

Carefully considering the long and dramatic experiences of the Kurdish liberation movement, Öcalan draws the conclusion that any nationalist and separatist way out of the crisis must be rejected for both strategic and principled reasons. The author starts from the assumption that the role of nations and nation-states is declining and being replaced by a worldwide development in favor of federal structures. Against this backdrop, Öcalan sees a solution based on a democratic unity of the countries inhabited by the Kurdish people.

For him, this means recognizing the existing borders in the Middle East as a historical fact, accompanied by a struggle for basic rights and democracy within these countries. Öcalan not only tries to prove that such a road is in the vital interest of the Kurdish people but also suggests that the Kurds, with their dedicated commitment to such a peaceful and democratic development, could act as a bridge between the three great nations of the Middle East. Because of their geographical, historical, and social situation, the Kurds are particularly suited to establish themselves as a pioneering democratic force in this new phase of the history of the Middle East and to become the active subjects of a struggle that serves their own liberation and integrates the neighboring peoples into the process of a democratic solution. Given this understanding of history, Abdullah Öcalan draws a parallel between the key role that the Kurdish people has played in the original emergence of civilization and its potential future role in the development of a democratic civilization across the Middle East. In his opinion, the Kurdish people holds the golden key that the peoples of the region have been hoping for throughout their history.

The Role of the Kurdistan Workers' Party (PKK)
Öcalan proceeds on the assumption that the PKK is an organic part of the Kurdish people, that it shares with that people both its strengths and its weaknesses, and that these two aspects have constituted both an external and an internal problem throughout its process of development. The author explains that the previous lack of a political movement able to consistently advocate in the interests of the Kurds made the founding of the PKK a historical necessity. In his assessment, this gap also existed in the popular spiritual movements that followed the rebellious religious tradition. In Öcalan's opinion, the PKK must both fulfill its political function *and* create spiritual values. With regard to the latter, the author compares the Kurdish liberation movement with the historical movements in the Middle East that were led by the prophets. Not unlike Jesus and his apostles, the PKK is also surrounded by the poor and downtrodden who await a miracle, and it is this faith in the PKK that forms the basis of its power to lead one of the greatest struggles in history.

As Öcalan understands it, this commonality of the PKK with the movement of the apostles and prophets is the result of the general mystical atmosphere of the Near and Middle East. For that very reason, the modern Western organizational forms cannot serve as a model for this region. As such, the author characterizes the PKK as a synthesis of a semi-modern socialist organization and a typical Middle East identity. He suggests that both the strengths and the weaknesses of the PKK are the result of this synthesis.

Even though the author deals with a number of events and problems in the history of the PKK in the second volume of this work, he doesn't present a systematic history of the party. Rather, he highlights the previous enormous efforts and the dramatic setbacks that the liberation movement suffered. He says that at times a gang culture developed, and that there had been unjustified acts of war that cost the lives of many innocents and did great political and moral damage. He claims a key reason for this was that the PKK had neglected to lay a sufficiently strong theoretical foundation for the strategy of legitimate self-defense. Öcalan sees the decisive basis for overcoming these serious flaws in a process of renewal that places the new principles and strategic orientation toward a democratic civilization at its center.

Autobiographical Traits of the Work

One reason for the selective—and, in particular, very subjective—character of his treatment of PKK's history seems to be Öcalan's strongly autobiographical approach. In a certain sense, this two-volume book is essentially an autobiographical work, which is understandable, given that these volumes were written as a legal petition. Making the personal thinking and experiences of the author apparent is also important for any book designed to enlighten a broader public. But, most of all, Öcalan's self-representation is addressed to the Kurdish movement that he feels he is a part of and to which his personal legacy is dedicated—and he had to assume while writing it that it could mark the final word of his legacy, because he was still under the original death sentence when he authored these books.

Both the content of the work and the way that Öcalan presents himself represent a particularly pertinent challenge for the reader. It is crucial to understand the fact that Öcalan made the statements about himself in the context of an extreme struggle for psychological and physical survival. It is important that he didn't simply commit himself to the struggle for his own survival, as such, but also to the most extreme exertion of his will to live, as well as to creative thought and work under these extremely threatening conditions. A central motivation is his feelings of heightened responsibility toward the Kurdish people and the PKK, particularly in this tense situation. He therefore wants to act as efficiently as possible. The fact that Öcalan, in his treatment of the development of the PKK, devotes particular attention to his own positive role in its successes is certainly not least intended as a challenge to critics and opponents who want to use his absence from the scene to try to influence the orientation and effectiveness of the PKK.

In his accounting of the grave errors and flaws of the PKK, Öcalan talks about his own role but presents his achievements much more clearly and concretely than he does his failures. He often attempts self-criticism and generally supports the necessity of a self-critical approach, but the results remain fairly general and, in part, mystical, leaving the heroic role he attributes to himself largely undamaged. He always downplays his own responsibility for the tendency toward gang culture, which he sharply condemns, and directly and indirectly suggests that the fighters in question acted against his orders and intentions. But these statements remain relatively vague. But we must take into account that Öcalan, particularly in the context of such a petition, cannot accept legal responsibility for misdeeds committed by his organization.

Abdullah Öcalan's View of History

In a certain sense, these two volumes are an original, distinct, and unconventional contribution to the history of civilization. The author provides an exemplary treatment of the history of civilization in the Middle East and, from that perspective, of all of humanity. He analyzes the current situation and perspective of humanity with a particular emphasis on the Middle East, as well as the history, situation, and perspective of the Kurdish people.

Abdullah Öcalan turns the emergence of humanism and democracy, as well as the struggle for their implementation and preservation and their permanent endangerment, into the consistent criterion of his conception of history. This constitutes the cornerstone of his work. It contains a passionate avowal of humanism and democracy—and not just in an eye-catching and noncommittal sense, as is often the case with such declared beliefs. Abdullah Öcalan insistently identifies criteria and obligations for the development and realization of humanism and democracy, such as an appreciation for the role of woman and oppressed peoples.

Öcalan's fairly comprehensive view of history has a number of merits that distinguish his book in certain ways from thematically comparable works. The general virtue of the strong personal attachment to this problematic and his strongly humanist point of view, which is on principle irreconcilable with religious or political fundamentalism, become even more pronounced in the wealth of problems he deals with and in the strength of his picturesque language. His style of presentation challenges, conveys impulses, and forces the reader to think and to enter into a productive dialogue with the author. Regardless of whether readers of this work are political activists or interested laypeople, anyone who seriously tries to grapple with this work will emerge from the process a changed person, inspired, more thoughtful, and enriched—and, of course, challenged to register dissent.

The potential impact of the work is due to the fact that the author did not simply want to write a standard work of history about the Middle East and the Kurdish question. His primary aim is to discuss future, topical routes to a solution to the perilous conflicts in this region, part of a larger attempt to overcome the civilizational crisis of humanity. Such a far-flung and complex historical work is a courageous undertaking and would be even for a team of expert authors or an experienced historian who wants to cap his life work with a weighty publication. Quite certainly, the scientific approach and the methodology play a decisive role in the realization of such an enterprise. Öcalan's methodology is strongly influenced by his particular topic and concerns.

His point of departure is that the peoples of this region, including the Kurdish people, remain shackled to the past and are paralyzed when it comes to coping with the current extreme challenges, which condemns them to the role of a plaything of ambitious world powers. Even though his characterization of this situation is consistently realistic, it is at the same time so dramatic that the reader gets the impression that salvation depends on a miracle. This is the basis of the main thrust of Öcalan's book, namely, his fundamental thoughts about a way out of this situation and a historical opportunity for these peoples.

The author assumes that humanity is now in a stage of civilizational development primarily determined by the achievements of the scientific-technological revolution. At this stage, he sees a potential for the global community of peoples to solve all its affairs on the international, national, and regional levels in a civilized, meaning humanistic and democratic, way, on the basis of legal and social norms. Öcalan sees fundamental opportunities to solve the problems in the life of the Kurdish people in this framework and, moreover, the problems of the countries in which Kurds reside. As previously mentioned, the experience of the Kurdish liberation struggle led him to reject purely nationalist solutions. Thus, Öcalan rejects a separate path for his people. He does, however, assign it the special responsibility of daring to begin this process, of leading by good example, and of thereby being a beacon of hope.

Because such a path accords with the interests of the peoples of the region, as well as of the whole world community, Öcalan expects its prospects of success to increase in the long run. But the author is conscious that such a constructive path is confronted with strong destructive, that is, imperialist and comprador, forces, and that any success, even the most minimal progress, can only be achieved by a purposeful and persistent struggle against these inhumane forces on the basis of convincing, winning over, and mobilizing humanist and democratically oriented counterforces.

Even though using the democratic potential of European civilization to unfold the creative civilizational forces in the Middle East is very important to Öcalan, he also emphatically insists that the discharge and realization of this potential must be primarily the work of the peoples of this region themselves. Identifying the regional and national forces that are able to realize this work demands enormous intellectual and political exertion on Öcalan's part, because, in a certain way, he has already denied the possibility of an optimistic evaluation with his dramatic assessment of the present ineptitude of these forces. To begin to solve this apparently intractable problem, Öcalan develops a peculiar perspective that cannot be implemented without exaltation, drama, and mythologizing.

One of the features of this perspective is a radical recourse to the Neolithic Age and the primitive social conditions of this region, which, he argues, are still prevalent and continue to be manifest in the rural milieu. At this point, it's important to note that Öcalan once had some hope for real socialism but, disappointed with the latter's historical flaws and final demise, is now looking for alternate socialist projects.

Of course, Öcalan does not limit his historical reflection to the Neolithic stage of development. Still, he often opposes past and contemporary exploitative societies, particularly the ideological deformations they cause, with the germinal form of primitive society as a permanent potential counterweight in the memory and persistent power of the oppressed and exploited. Among other things, Öcalan bases this approach on his thesis that Neolithic forms of existence and consciousness are still present in the contemporary Middle East, particularly among the Kurdish people. In this, he sees a decisive basis for the ability of the old culture to survive and, therefore, for a successful resistance to alien influences on the part of the rural population of this region.

On the other hand, Öcalan bases his historical optimism about the future-oriented creative power of the peoples of the Middle East on the great hope he finds in the role played in times of social transformation by ideas and personalities rooted in resistance. From that angle, he devotes particular attention to the prophets of the Middle East. This includes remarkable studies of Jesus of Nazareth and the Prophet Mohammad. When describing things, Öcalan's language is particularly emphatic and poetic. For him, the PKK is part of the succession of resistance movements he discusses, and he is part of the succession of prophetic resistance fighters.

Since this approach enables Öcalan to continuously connect historical and topical relationships and to handle big historical intervals with large steps, it is no problem for him to locate himself as an individual agent within the succession of Socrates, Abraham, Noah, Zoroaster, Jesus, and Mohammad. The decisive point for him is that he is connected to these personalities by the fact that all of them have taken the lead of a future-oriented popular movement during a transformational historical period, attempting to forge a link between a glorious past and a glorious future. That, for Öcalan, respect for these historical personalities does not pose a particularly high inhibition threshold to such historical parallels is the result of his proud certainty that, in the course of his own history, he has escaped the ideological shackles of the past, which reduce the toiling people to mere objects without a history.

The author sees his description of history (which is oriented around two characteristic features, the decisive role in history of both progressive ideas and personalities close to the people) as a scientific undertaking that is different in principle from everything previously published on these topics, which in his assessment has been shaped by the point of view of the exploiting classes and a colonialist Eurocentrism. From this standpoint, Öcalan criticizes the Marxist view of history for its—supposed—disparagement of the role of ideology and progressive personalities.

Another point of criticism is the—again supposed—underestimation of the social order of primitive society, as well as of the emergence of the slaveholding society in Sumer. The author pays particular attention to these historical germinal forms, because he is also searching for already existent progressive germs in the Middle East, especially among the Kurdish people, germs that he expects could develop into a powerful movement for a democratic alternative.

In all of this, Öcalan's relation to Marxism is ambivalent: in his treatment of the history of civilization, the author uses the Marxist materialist approach to historical science by taking the dialectics of productive forces and the relations of production as his methodological basis, and thus traces the continuous succession of historical modes of production. That approach also allows him to characterize the antagonistic social conditions and to draw conclusions about the objectively conditioned class struggle of the oppressed and exploited. Öcalan also agrees with the Marxist view of history, in that he deduces the social superstructure from these materially determined conditions. For Marx, the succession of the materially conditioned modes of production is by no means an automatic and mechanical process. While Marx regards this succession as the primary continuity in history, Öcalan attributes a strong autonomous weight and autonomous laws to a specific continuity of the social superstructure, particularly of the state and ideology. This results in the schism in his sketch of civilizational history between the concrete and historical treatment of the various social developmental stages, on the one hand, and an abstract, suprahistorical treatment of the exploiter state and exploiter ideology, as well as the social, political, and, in particular, ideological countermovements (and the preeminent personalities representing them), on the other hand. Within this voluntarist framework, Öcalan has no difficulty putting the real socialist states on the same level as the Sumerian exploiter state and locating Marxism, though with qualifications, in the neighborhood of exploiting ideologies.

Öcalan's statements on Marxism are yet another testimony to the persuasiveness and effectiveness of the methodology of social analysis developed and applied by Marx (and his creative successors). This is precisely the basis for Öcalan's historical method and some of his historical premises. At the same time, these statements show the selective, reductionist, and simplistic nature of the Marxist ideas he and many sympathizers of the Marxist movement embrace. Öcalan has apparently not had the opportunity to acquire detailed knowledge of the numerous works by Marxist scientists in the realms of history, philosophy, and sociology that investigate the independent role of superstructural phenomena, particularly of ideology, and, most pointedly, the historical role of religion and of progressive personalities in this environment.

Given these circumstances, rather than pointing to the author's lack of competence in interpreting and applying Marxist doctrine, one should recognize his willingness to use those methodological aspects of Marxism that he recognizes as indispensable.

Programmatic Orientation at the Beginning of a New World Order

The programmatic and strategic-tactical orientation for the Kurdish liberation movement is touched upon in the first volume and takes up a lot of space in the second. This approach establishes its credibility by the far-reaching and complex nature of the book, particularly the way it places the Kurdish question in a broader historic and geopolitical context. In this way, a certain pragmatic point of view is countered and Öcalan's particular concern gains historical respectability and conceptual depth. In terms of content, this profile is shaped in a special way by the fact that Öcalan, when reminiscing on his historical excursion, draws the conclusion that at this point the goal of a democratic world civilization is on the agenda in the developmental history of humankind and must therefore be the determining factor in the objectives of the Kurdish liberation movement. This is the pivotal point of Abdullah Öcalan's programmatic thinking.

Under the current conditions certain criticisms come to mind. One of them relates to his evaluation of nationalism and real socialism. Even though it is one of the particular merits of his historical analyses that he works out both the contrasts and the interplay of light and shadow, his assessment of real socialism after its defeat is ambivalent and often crude and broad-brush. Among other things, this is politically and scientifically problematic because the current global imperial offensive requires an analysis of all counterforces that is as well-founded as possible. Just as in the case of many other strongly affected people, quite obviously bitter personal disappointment and a lack of historical distance with regard to this serious defeat also play a role. The author's statements about this complex of problems serve to show that a differentiating scientific analysis of this phenomenon and, especially, of the deeper causes of its historical defeat is still pending. Given the conditions under which he worked on his book, to demand from Öcalan a constructive contribution that further develops that analysis would be unrealistic, especially if one takes into account that a vast number of the scientific thinkers educated under socialism, who would seem predestined to tackle that task, haven't dared to confront the challenge.

Marx insisted that the socialist developmental stage was the lower phase of a new formation of society that is afflicted by the birthmarks of capitalism. Unlike the majority of his followers who were active under real socialism, any idealization of this socialist stage was completely alien to Marx. It is especially in this realm that the specialists responsible for this subject matter have largely failed, and not just during the time of real socialism but particularly since its defeat. During this extremely burdensome and trying situation, the majority of these specialists, who enjoyed a Marxist education, turned away from Marx instead of rectifying their previous failure by a deeper engagement with his scientific methodology. Because of this, sympathizers of the Marxist doctrine and movement were left swinging in the wind. And it is apparently exactly this basic feeling that has shaped Öcalan's work in important respects: the feeling that he has been deserted by just those forces and figures from the Marxist movement in whom he had a certain hope, casting him back onto an enforced reliance on his own personal forces. He has illustrated this particularly clearly with his statements about the betrayal he experienced in the plot against him at the hands of, of all possible people, former representatives of the Soviet Union.

While many of Öcalan's pioneers and progenitors have studied Marx's *Capital*, especially when incarcerated in severe conditions, and have gained conceptual and methodological approaches that allow for a deeper understanding of both history and the future, Öcalan, in the grip of his disappointment, is looking for an alternative to *Capital* and chooses other points of departure to get a grasp on the origin of things.

These critical remarks do not aim to devalue the historical statements made by Öcalan or the perspective they represent but, rather, at their partial relativization in the sense of the dialogue the author requested. Here, we can safely assume that the character of the present book as a workshop book will become particularly clear in the context of this topical and future-oriented problematic—all the more so as history itself is at the core of this workshop process.

The Verdict of the Court in the "Öcalan Case" and the Verdict of History

It took the European Court of Human Rights (ECtHR) almost two years to rule in the suit brought by Öcalan. Many assume that this was the result of the stubbornness of the Turkish representative, who, in the end, voted against the decision. The result of the vote: six to one. The verdict pronounced on March 12, 2003, includes two very important statements.

For one thing, the legality of the court decision by which Öcalan was sentenced to death on June 29, 1999, is called into question. Even though the death penalty was lifted in 2002, and from the Turkish perspective, this defused the explosive character of the "case," the ECtHR raised procedural objections. This was not, however, for any principled reason but was simply a matter of procedural considerations.

On the other hand, both the plot and the inhuman prison conditions are judged to be legal. The complaints by Öcalan's lawyers concerning the abduction of their client and his aggravated solitary detention were rejected. But in his statements, it is exactly these aspects that Öcalan pushed to the front and center: the international conspiracy that led to his kidnapping, mistreatment, and conviction.

This is exactly what allows us to draw the connection between the "Öcalan case" and the factors that have led to the large-scale plot that, since autumn 2001, has moved to the center stage of contemporary history as a worldwide uninterrupted "war on terror." Against this backdrop, Öcalan is cast as the prototype of a terrorist. The judges of ECtHR didn't feel they had any responsibility to investigate this slanderous accusation.

This labeling of Öcalan was apparently a premise of the proceedings. Actually, the decisive premise of the "war against terrorism" is that no court can simply decide if someone is a "terrorist" or how that person will be dealt with. This is presumed to be the exclusive competence of the US leadership and its accomplices. This is what creates *the possibility* for figures like Öcalan to be labeled terrorists, regardless of whether they fit the bill or not. That is why, for the US leadership and its Turkish allies, Öcalan's constructive decision to reject all forms of terrorism and his consistent focus on a peaceful and democratic solution is not a positive development to be built upon but an additional irritant to be ignored and obstructed. For these destructive forces, Öcalan's constructive demeanor, especially his writing, presents a decisive challenge.

The decision of the European Court does not only affect Öcalan's case. This court decision sets a precedent. The signal sent is: in the search, capture, and treatment of alleged terrorists—alleged, for whether or not they are actually terrorists is a matter for legal proceedings—there are no judicial constraints. The ECtHR claims to only have jurisdiction over certain elementary rules of court proceedings in a narrow sense, which, according to this decision, also applies to defendants accused of "terrorism." With its decision, the court has limited its sphere of action as a matter of principle, accepting a certain loss of face in the process. Its focus on procedural errors allowed it to mitigate this state of affairs a bit and to convey a certain appearance of independence.

This case of class justice serves to show how farsighted and profound Öcalan's characterization of the politico-legal nature of his own case actually is. Had he concentrated on the injustices in the conduct of his trial, he would have somewhat weakened the thrust of his argument. On the other hand, the approach actually pursued by Öcalan, namely, clarifying the historical and world political dimension of the politico-judicial crime and presenting his case as a clear example, is not at all undermined by the court decision but instead has a greater impact and increased mobilizing power as a result.

It is difficult to predict a historical process—particularly in a period of serious transformation like the current one, when history unfolds in time-lapse mode. It is even riskier and more uncertain to forecast the "judgment of history"—the conclusions and evaluations of future generations after careful investigation, examination, and consideration of the acting subjects of the historical process who will have either paved or blocked the way for them.

As far as "Öcalan's case" before the European Court goes, we are not only talking about an individual facing serious existential challenges who has come before the court hoping to put his powerful opponents in their place. The decisive factor is the historical circumstances under which this political figure must prove his assertions and win his rights. Characteristically, as is the case in such circumstances, it is not just Abdullah Öcalan who is being challenged to the utmost, but also the Kurdish people and its organizations, as well as the peoples of the Near and Middle East.

Abdullah Öcalan systematically pointed to regional and world political sources and warned of the impending danger. His description of his persecution, arrest, unjust incarceration, and the imposition of the death penalty revealed a plot carried out by the governments and secret services of the US, the UK, and Israel, supported by representatives of Turkey and Europe.

Öcalan's abduction and sentencing were a portent of the later dramatic breaches of law on a world political scale: since the official end of the Afghanistan campaign, the US leadership has been concentrating on the war on the Middle East that it proclaimed in September 2001. The planned comprehensive recolonialization of this region began with the war against Iraq and is to be extended from there to the rest of the region. This is a radical challenge to resistance in the region. It is in this context that Abdullah Öcalan's core propositions about the current and potential role of the peoples of the Middle East gain particular weight.

The fate of humanity very much depends on the degree to which the New World War Order promoted by the US leadership can be brought to a halt in the current struggle over war and peace. The Middle East is the theater in which this struggle is going to proceed particularly intensely and dramatically both now and in the near future. The military victory of the US and UK troops in Iraq has not put an end to this but has opened yet another strategic-tactical stage of fierce contestation on various levels and on a national, regional, and international scale. The political-economic forces in this region and worldwide have been pushed into violent motion and are regrouping, restructuring, and reconnecting in new ways. Here, powerful diverging interests are engaged in a "game" aimed at shaping the near and medium future in the here and now. In this struggle between war and peace, as well as between different conceptions for the future of the region, the Kurdish people occupy an important place. This objectively carries with it a major historical responsibility for the Kurdish liberation movement that goes far beyond what has been demanded from it up to now and what it has previously attempted.

Öcalan's prediction of a specific key role for the Kurdish people in the further development of the Middle East is already becoming a fact—even if in a contradictory way, with all of the characteristic contradictions that Öcalan has traced and described in the conflictual history of the Kurdish people coming to light in a controversial form: there has been a split in the Kurdish movement between those (particularly in Northern Iraq) who recognize the US and British invaders based on personal interests and the forces (particularly in Turkey and Iran) that consistently oppose all expansion and aggression. Within these forces, Öcalan's lasting and profound orientation toward an independent, truly democratic, and peaceful development in the region is effective and alive.

Only if it commits itself to developing in this direction will the Kurdish people be able to turn itself into the agent-subject of historical development. If not, it will be degraded into the object of alien interests—as subcontractor, vassal, comprador. The impending dramatic development in the Middle East will convey to the peoples of the region—and particularly to the Kurdish people—a lasting experience applicable to their own vital interests, as well as clarifying who their true allies and enemies are. With his book, Öcalan has supplied a fundamental basis for connecting these experiences with the rich experience of history and for drawing sustainable conclusions. His own life and struggle, rich with experience, provided the basis for this intellectual achievement and for his capacity to meaningfully connect his personal experience with that of his people and of humanity.

It is Abdullah Öcalan's legacy that the Kurdish people, true to the great examples in its history, should occupy a dignified and honorable place in the current and future struggle for a democratic world civilization. It is most of all this legacy as a fruit of his life of struggle that Öcalan contributes to the test bench of history. With this alone, he is more present in the current international political struggle for the future of the Middle East than the numerous politicians around the world who are currently very busy conducting their economic and political war and postwar dealings in this region where history is so charged.

This essay was originally published as the foreword to *Abdullah Öcalan, Gilgameschs Erben* (Bremen: Atlantik Verlag, 2003), the German edition of *Prison Writings: The Roots of Civilisation* (London: Pluto Press, 2007) [Turkish: *Sümer Rahip Devletinden Demokratik Uygarlığa* (Cologne: Mezopotamien Verlag, 2001)] and has been edited for this book.

Professor Ekkehard Sauermann was born in Dresden, Germany, in 1929. After having worked as a teacher and school headmaster in Saxony and Brandenburg beginning in 1945, he taught and was a researcher at the Humboldt University Berlin and Martin Luther University Halle/Wittenburg from 1953 to 1990 (retirement). He was an educational scientist, sociologist, and revolutionary theorist. His interdisciplinary specialty addresses how key figures and social movements cope with extreme social change—especially radical upheavals. Ekkehard Sauermann passed away on November 15, 2010.

FOUR

Preface to *The Road Map*

Immanuel Wallerstein

The Road Map offers "a solution to the Kurdish question" in Turkey. But it raises issues that are far more general and widespread than the specific geohistorical questions it discusses. There are, it seems to me, four separate, if deeply intertwined, contradictions within the operations of the modern world-system, which is a capitalist world-economy. They are:

(1) the search for sovereignty by the states;
(2) the thrust of all states to become nations;
(3) the demands that states be democratic;
(4) the ways that capitalism maintains its equilibrium.

Each of these contradictions requires a book-length exposition to be treated adequately. Here, I can only briefly outline the issues.

(1) Sovereignty: the formal structure of the interstate system that has been created as part of the modern world-system is that all the states are sovereign. Sovereignty in theory means that the states make their decisions autonomously, without interference either from other states or from institutional structures within the boundaries of the state.

Of course, as soon as one asserts these theoretical characteristics, it is obvious that there is not a single state that meets these criteria of sovereignty. It turns out that the claim of a state to be sovereign is just that—a claim, an aspiration, one that some states meet better than others but none meet totally.

Furthermore, notice that it is a claim in two directions—outward beyond the boundaries of a state and inward toward groups within the state. The less a state is able to defend itself outward the more emphasis it places on defending itself against inward erosion of its claim to sovereignty. Republican Turkey falls into this latter category, although, of course, not only republican Turkey. This is the situation of the vast majority of states in the modern world-system.

(2) A nation-state: the basic mechanism by which states seek to defend their sovereignty against groups or institutions within its boundaries is what we have come to call Jacobinism. One can define Jacobinism very simply. It is two things. First, it is the demand that all "citizens" of a state recognize their membership in a single "nation"—however, this nation is defined. Second, it is the demand that loyalty to this "nation" take priority over all other loyalties of the citizen—loyalties to class, to gender, to a religious group, to an "ethnicity," to kinship groups, in short, to any group other than the "nation" as defined by the state.

While the pressure to create this national loyalty (which can then get the label of patriotism) seems to strengthen the state in its outward assertion of sovereignty, it obviously creates significant internal strains. All kinds of groups resist being subordinated to the demand for national loyalty. And sometimes, even often, the resistance becomes violent.

In the last few decades, Jacobinism has lost its sheen, and in many countries there are demands that the state define itself as "plurinational"—something that can take many different institutional forms. The problem here is to define the institutional forms and the "limits" of plurinationality. Merely asserting that a state is plurinational does not solve the problem.

(3) Democracy: one of the great legacies of the French Revolution was to legitimize worldwide the concept that "sovereignty" belongs neither to a ruler nor to a legislature but to the "people." The problem is that this concept, while rhetorically legitimate, terrifies those with power, prestige, and privilege. They seek to dilute the claim in every way possible.

As of the late twentieth century, there remained hardly any state that did not claim it was "democratic." Usually, the claim was based on the existence of national elections and a multiparty system. It is not difficult to show that holding such elections every several years and conferring representative power, even alternately, on parties that have only limited differences in actual programs scarcely exhausts the idea of popular sovereignty. Personally, I do not believe that there is any state today that meets my definition of democracy, although some are surely worse than others.

The struggle for democratization has become much more active and acute in the last half-century, with more and more groups insisting on increased real participation in decision-making. This is very positive, but a task just begun, far from being even half finished.

(4) Capitalism: our modern world-system is a capitalist system, based on the drive for the endless accumulation of capital. In terms of this criterion, it has been a quite successful system for the last five hundred years. There has been constant growth in capital and continued concentration and centralization of the accumulators.

Like all systems of any variety, its processes fluctuate with some regularity—the cyclical rhythms of a system. The system survives because there are in-built mechanisms that force these fluctuations back to equilibrium, a moving equilibrium. Slowly but relentlessly, the processes move toward asymptotes. The secular trends reach points where the fluctuations move too far from equilibrium, and the system can no longer maintain the relatively stable environment in which it had normally operated.

When this happens, the system comes into terminal crisis. It bifurcates and becomes "chaotic." The struggle is no longer over the survival of the system but over which alternative prong of the bifurcation wins out and is the basis of a replacement system. We are in that period of systemic transition right now. We face another twenty to forty years of struggle before the collective "decision" will have been made. It is intrinsically impossible to predict the outcome, but it is very possible by our individual and group action to affect it. One possible outcome is a new system that replicates the worst features of the capitalist system—a system that is hierarchical, exploitative, and polarizing—with a noncapitalist system that is perhaps even worse. The other possible outcome is a system that is relatively democratic and relatively egalitarian, a kind of system the world has never known but that is quite feasible.

Conclusion: we cannot assess the utility of political action within the Kurdish community in Turkey unless we place our analysis within the framework of these four contradictions: the continuing drive of the Turkish state to reinforce its sovereignty; the thrust of many in Turkey to employ and reassert the Jacobin option; the thrust of many to achieve greater democratization; and the ways in which all these kinds of political action will affect the worldwide struggle about what kind of system will replace the now doomed capitalist world-system.

This essay was originally published as the preface of Abdullah Öcalan, *Prison Writings, Volume 3: The Road Map to Negotiations* (Cologne: International Initiative, 2012).

Professor Immanuel Wallerstein is best known for having developed world-systems analysis, a macrohistorical approach to understanding capitalism. He served as distinguished professor of sociology at Binghamton University (State University of New York) from 1976 until his retirement in 1999, and as head of the Fernand Braudel Center for the Study of Economies, Historical Systems, and Civilizations until 2005. During the 1990s, he chaired the Gulbenkian Commission on the Restructuring of the Social Sciences. The object of the commission was to indicate a direction for social scientific inquiry for the next fifty years. In 2000, he joined the Yale sociology department as senior research scholar. Professor Wallerstein died on August 31, 2019, at the age of eighty-eight.

FIVE

Prologue to Abdullah Öcalan's
The Road Map to Negotiations

Arnaldo Otegi

It is my honor to receive, while in the Logroño prison serving a sentence related to my political activism, the proposal that I write a prologue for the Spanish edition of comrade Abdullah Öcalan's work *The Road Map to Negotiations*, originally made public in January of 2011 at the European Court of Human Rights. Since July 27, 2011, comrade Apo has not received any visits, even from his lawyers, and, as such, nobody except for the Turkish government knows his current state.

First, I wish to send revolutionary greetings to all of his comrades in struggle and to the Kurdish people on the behalf of the Abertzale left, a reminder of something that you all know very well, that your people, and your struggle will always have fraternal solidarity of our people. As a reminder of these profound links, I call to mind both the solidarity message sent in 1966 to the Committee in Solidarity with the Kurdish Revolution and the Basque participation in the Fifteenth Congress of the Association of Kurdish Students in Europe, held in Budapest, in 1972, alongside members of the Palestinian Al Fatah and the PDF, which ended with a call for a worldwide front of oppressed peoples, as well as for a show of solidarity with the Kurdish, Palestinian, and Basque struggles.

The road map that is presented here has its roots in the contact and open-ended dialogue between the Turkish government and the very same Öcalan, as well as other representatives of the Partiya Karkerên Kurdistanê (PKK: Kurdistan Workers' Party), in the years 2009 to 2011. A secret process of which we know something, as in its wake, when we found ourselves in an ongoing process of open-ended negotiation with the Zapatero government, we were contacted by some of Kurdish political organizations with whom we have fraternal ties, seeking clarity about the development of our own process.

This process of open-ended dialogue with the Turkish government was derailed, and, reading about it, I can't fail but to see a reflection of a similar development in the Spanish government's attitude. Until the Kurdish movement and Öcalan presented proposals, the Turkish government seems not to have had any plan in mind, adopting the approach of the Spanish representative to our negotiations, arriving with blank paper and nothing to offer. At the peace process at Loyola, it always felt that the Abertzale left presented constructive proposals for the debate, as was also the case in the dialogue that we maintained in Geneva, where at least the international facilitators played a constructive role. Similarly, the approach of the Turkish government is to treat the goodwill of the Kurdish movement as a weakness, hoping to signal that the PKK's confidence building actions, such as the sending of guerrilla peace delegations, represent little more than surrender. This was also the consistent approach of the Spanish government, which perceived signs of engagement and steps to construct dialogue as signs of the weakness of the Abertzale left.

This is a mode of dialogue and negotiation where one party seeks the defeat the other and not a shared victory. Finally, the maintenance and even increase of the repressive policies in times of détente and dialogue, coupled with illegal acts, massive arrests, expansion ad infinitum of the concept of terrorist organization and activity—all of this is familiar to the Abertzale left. This is how the Turkish and Spanish governments are both currently operating in response to the legitimate aspirations of the Basque and Kurdish people. In both cases the battle is political, with the objective of blocking the legitimate desires of the Kurdish and Basque peoples. Neither now nor previously is the underlying problem for these governments violence. The problem is a refusal to accept democratic scenarios where the sincere aspirations of peoples (whatever they may be) are respected. This is the great difference between the attitude shown by the Spanish state to the Basque and Catalan nations and the Turkish state to the Kurdish nation compared to that of the Canadian or British governments to the aspirations of the Québécois and the Scottish. In short, the difference lies in the democratic failings of the Spanish and Turkish regimes, both direct heirs of dictatorial states that never fundamentally broke with their pasts. It is the lack of democratic culture that leads these two governments to opt for repression and the denial of legitimate aspirations. The problem is not Basque or Kurdish; the problem is not Catalonian. The problem is Spanish, and the problem is Turkish.

As for the road map that Öcalan presents, I can do little more than state my total respect and support. It is a road map presented by a movement that clearly represents the will of the majority of Kurdish people, who understand that in the historical context it is what best meets the needs of the Kurdish people. International solidarity between peoples in struggle for their liberation is never based on telling others what they should do but, rather, in supporting to the greatest degree possible what these people legitimately decide. That is and has always been the historical and political response of the Abertzale left to the Palestinian, Sahrawi, Irish, and Kurdish struggles.

Furthermore, I understand that this proposal is based on two fundamental premises, which also underlie a shared political philosophy; the recognition of peoples as subjects who are able to make decisions and the need to establish democratic frameworks and develop scenarios whereby these subjects can decide how they wish to organize internally, as well as the nature of the relationships they hope to have with other peoples.

Starting from this premise, Öcalan makes a proposal that best considers the historical, statist, and regional context of Kurdistan, which is inevitably distinct from the historical, statist, and regional context of the Basque people. The solution to the Basque conflict is faced with a similar scenario, encompassing premises that make it possible to shape a democratic framework in which all political projects are achievable, including the project of Basque independence and territorial unity to which the Abertzale left aspires. The political conflict and its solution must create that framework. And that is where Basque society, the combined Abertzale and democratic forces, must direct their efforts, toward the historical commitment that the political, unionist, and social Abertzale and the democratic forces of this country must establish. This must be the goal of all "Abertzales" and all true democrats. An agreement on the road map will lead to the recognition of Euskal Herria as a people and nation, with the full right to decide its future. A right that means we can freely decide the internal relations between the diverse decision-making frameworks that we Basques currently have at our avail, as well as our external relations with the Spanish and French states and with Europe. A democratic scenario. A scenario that will allow us to reconstruct our people.

The strategic shift the Abertzale left, with Zutik Euskal Herria as the driving force, had and has the sole objective of bringing about the unity of forces necessary to achieve these objectives. There is now no reason or excuse for various democratic forces and the "Abertzales" not to agree on a commitment to action that will lead us to that scenario—something made increasingly necessary by the profound quadruple crisis that the Spanish state currently faces (financial, economic, territorial, and institutional). That is our task. We have a historic opportunity to move forward, and we can't let it pass us by. I appeal to all "Abertzale" forces and all democrats to move forward in the common commitment to address and resolve the consequences of the armed conflict (e.g., prisoners and escapees, demilitarization, and recognition of and reparation to all victims) and to recognize Euskal Herria as a nation with the right to decide its own future.

I am convinced, as such, of the path forward for the Kurdish people in their struggle for a democratic and peaceful scenario. The assassinations of the three Kurdish militants in Paris, to whom I pay homage, indicates how nervous those who seek to cling to the past have become, those sectors that live and enrich themselves on conflict. We also see them in the Spanish state. It is the agenda of "pseudocrats," those who live on and for conflict. It is possible that they may continue to try to return us to the past, but that is futile. They will not succeed.

In closing, I would like to send my unwavering support to the "Abertzale" left of Euskal Herria and to our Kurdish brothers and sisters in their struggle for their land and freedom. I am convinced that together, with comrade Öcalan, sooner rather than later, we will walk down those open avenues that President Allende talked about, those avenues "through which pass free man (and woman)." A fraternal hug of solidarity from the comrade in the nearby cell.

Gora Euskal
Herria Askatua

This essay was originally published as the prologue to *Abdullah Öcalan, Hoja de ruta, Hacia la paz en el Kurdistan* (Navarra: Txalaparta, 2013). [Turkish: *Türkiye'de demokratikleşme sorunları, Kürdistan'da çözüm modelleri (Yol haritası)* (Neuss: Mezopotamien Verlag, 2011)].

Arnaldo Otegi leads the Basque left-wing pro-independence coalition Euskal Herria Bildu. He played a pivotal role in the Basque peace process and is among the architects of the new strategy based on a unilateral commitment to peaceful and democratic means and respect for the will of the Basque people. This strategy completely transformed the conflict. Imprisoned for years for peace building initiatives, dozens of international personalities supported the campaign for his release.

SIX

From World System to Democratic Civilization

Barry K. Gills

I wish to begin by saying to you that I feel I am corresponding with a friend and a comrade, one in whose work I have found a new source of great insight and inspiration.

My dear friend Andre Gunder Frank passed away fourteen years ago. I know that he, like myself, would have been eager to meet you and discuss ideas. He, like myself, would have been deeply moved and profoundly happy to learn that you have read our work on the world system and the five thousand years of its historical rhythms, cycles, and crises. I will try to convey to you, in his absence, a further expansion on some aspects of his and our joint analyses of the world system—in a spirit of dialogue.

I know you share our rejection of Eurocentric understandings of development and world history, and that you likewise adopt an alternative "humanocentric" perspective. I know that you undertake historical analysis and theorization with the aim of contributing to a profound new type of human liberation. Your work on democratic modernity, the democratic nation, and democratic civilization goes far beyond what we have been able to articulate, but I am confident that, like me, Gunder Frank would have been most keen to welcome these concepts and discuss and debate them in detail.

Our shared post-Eurocentric perspective involves the recognition that the "rise of the West" to global dominance occurred very "late" in world system history, and that its hegemony is only temporary. Like us, you seek a new transformative praxis to construct a radically just and democratic world. But your work has gone much farther than ours in the

45

profound depth and inspiration with which you explain the new forms of radical social, political, economic, and ecological practices that constitute the new society of human freedom and ecological harmony.

Much of Frank's work, which you may not be familiar with, analyzes the "global crisis of capital accumulation" in a historical and contemporary perspective. His thinking developed in parallel to and dialogue with others, including his friend Samir Amin (whom he met in Paris in 1968), Giovanni Arrighi (who first introduced the "world system" approach to Frank), and Immanuel Wallerstein, who, in the 1970s, with Frank, developed the analysis known as "world-systems theory." In many ways, this was an organic process leading from critiques of colonialism and post-independence realities, producing, in Frank's case, the emergence of dependency theory and its call for a radical break with national capitalist development through a socialist revolution.

Frank predicted in 1974 that the Third World's response to the global crisis would be predicated upon increasing exports to world markets, and this transition to export-led growth would be organized under national authoritarian regimes (including in East Asia and Latin America), while inevitably leading to the amassing of gigantic unsustainable debts—i.e., the debt crisis—and "vastly increased foreign dependence."

Frank analyzed the tendencies of globalization, including the replacement of productive investment by financial speculation and the consequent increase in imbalances between regions and countries of the world economic system. He argued that increasing marketization and privatization as responses to the crisis would only further exacerbate underlying poverty, inequality, and marginalization, leading to tremendous pressures on democratic political culture and to the inexorable rise of both progressive and reactionary social movements to fill the void left by the national state's incapacity and unwillingness to deliver radical change. The work by Frank on crisis, combined with our later joint work on world system theory, leads to a post-national(ist) perspective on (world) development patterns. I think you share some of this perspective.

I know that you have read our joint work *The World System: Five Hundred Years or Five Thousand?*[1] This work outlines the long cycles of world system development going back not centuries but millennia. It includes key concepts, including: the origins of the world system five thousand years ago; the centrality of capital accumulation in the world system; the five hundred-year-long A/B phase cycles of the world system;

the hegemony/rivalry pattern in the world system; the center-periphery/ hinterland structure of the world system; the "economy/polity contradiction" in the world system; and the cycles of "world system crises." I cannot elaborate on all these concepts here, but I hope that we can meet in person someday and discuss them in full detail.

Our work led us to make a radical break not only with Wallerstein's conception of the European origins of the world-system (and of "capitalism") but also with Marxist historiographical conventions, such as "modes of production" and the "transitions" between them. In our world system perspective, which I think in many ways you now share, we see that "too many big patterns in world history appear to transcend or persist despite all apparent alterations in the mode of production." In my own recent work, I have been developing an analysis of the historical relations between capital and *oikos* and their "ontological incommensurability" in history. In this perspective, capital and oikos cannot inhabit the same social and territorial space simultaneously. This is because the existence and reproduction of capital requires the destruction of oikos, in order to create the social relations of exploitation of humans, non-humans, and the natural resources of the land that thus produce surplus value for capital (a line of analysis first seen in the *Communist Manifesto* and later further developed by Rosa Luxemburg). In a profound historical sense then, our task is to recreate oikos in a postcapitalist society. Your writings and the Rojava revolution have done remarkable work to realize this in actual practice.

In Frank's penultimate work, *ReOrient: Global Economy in the Asian Age* and in the posthumously published *ReOrienting the 19th Century*,[2] he once again challenges received theory about the "rise of the West" and the dominant role played by the market and "free" trade, as opposed to the actual predominance of coercion and imperialism. In the final analysis, our perspective insists that it is the world system as a whole that is the inescapable framework of both analysis and practice, and that global development will never be uniform across the world. Shifts in (temporary) competitive advantage (not always achieved by noncoercive "market" means) and the presence or absence of "hegemonic power" are historically persistent patterns that still predominate in the long-term development of the world system. In the face of national authoritarianism, imperialist interventionism, and state terror in the Middle East, you and the courageous people of Rojava have built a new paradigm, embodying radical democracy, women's freedom, autonomous self-organization, and the aspiration to construct a new type of ecosocialist economy.

In these times of accelerating climate change and deepening crises, the product of centuries of imperialism and the past few decades of hyper neoliberalism and ecological destruction, your struggle for freedom and peace has become our struggle, and your example a beacon for untold millions who will yet follow. Thank you, my brother. Thank you.

Barry Gills is a professor of Development Studies in the Faculty of Social Sciences, University of Helsinki, Finland. He cofounded the World-Historical Systems Theory Group in the International Studies Association in 1989 with David Wilkinson. This group included the late professor Andre Gunder Frank, with whom professor Gills coauthored a new five thousand year world system analysis. Professor Gills is founding editor and editor in chief of *Globalizations* journal and a fellow of the World Academy of Art and Science. He is the 2019 recipient of the International Studies Association's James N. Rosenau Award for services to the field of globalization research.

Notes
1   Andre Gunder Frank and Barry K. Gills, eds., *The World System: Five Hundred Years or Five Thousand?* (London: Routledge, 1993).
2   Andre Gunder Frank, *ReOrient: Global Economy in the Asian Age* (Berkeley: University of California Press, 1998); Andre Gunder Frank, *ReOrienting the 19th Century: Global Economy in the Continuing Asian Age* (London: Routledge, 2013).

SEVEN

"A Prisoner Who Is Becoming Mythical"

Antonio Negri

It is extraordinary to read this book by Abdullah Öcalan [*Manifesto for a Democratic Civilization: Civilization, Volume 1: The Age of Masked Gods and Disguised Kings*], a man in jail but still capable of developing a thought that destroys all closure, a political leader who—under impossible conditions—continues to produce and renew an ethical and civil teaching for his people. An Antonio Gramsci for his own country. An example for everyone.

In this book, Öcalan discusses the origins of civilization and the dualism (class and civilization) that has characterized our civil life since the beginning of history: on the one hand, the state and, on the other, the community. What, in anthropological and ethnological terms, has been uncovered by him of the history of Indo-Aryan languages and the social structures of the Fertile Crescent and subsequently of the development of civilized society is really a great metaphor, a paradigm that anticipates the figures of capitalist society. In these pages—he tells us—"I first investigated how the ground was prepared for the rise of 'capitalist modernity' and I showed how false is the claim of capitalism to present itself as a definitive final system"—otherwise said, how false the claim is that capitalism represents the "end of history." This imperial fairy tale, circulated after the end of the Cold War, represented the capitalist hope of a stable and permanent status quo, in which the hegemony of the capitalist elites was definitive and their accumulation of wealth finally guaranteed. Öcalan mocks this hope and shows how it is not only false in itself but harmful to every regime of truth, to every honest possibility of telling the truth.

The latter consists in being part of the transformation of history and the struggles that determine it; only in this way can truth be grasped in its relativity and affirmed in its absoluteness. But that's not enough. Here we also study—the main thesis of this volume—"the struggle (which can be traced back at least five thousand years) between civilization-state and democratic civilization, the latter consisting of pre-state agricultural and village communities. All ideological, military, political, and economic relations, all conflicts and struggles, take place under these two main systems of civilization." Now, "the system of statist society, built on the basis of the intertwined formation of classes, cities, and states, has multiplied up to the financial phase, the last phase of capitalism, which is based mainly on the exploitation and oppression of farming communities and villages and, later, of urban workers. The continued existence of the statist civilization for five thousand years in spite of the democratic civilization is essentially possible due to its ideological hegemony. Systems based on coercion and tyranny can only succeed if they have ideological hegemony. Therefore, the main conflict takes place not only at the level of class division but also at the level of civilization."

From these assumptions derives the programmatic conversion that Öcalan has impressed on the Kurdish national liberation movement since the 1990s, turning it into a project of "democratic autonomy." Öcalan states that the three evils of contemporary civilization are nation-states, capitalism, and patriarchy, which together constitute what he calls "capitalist modernity." The aim of "democratic autonomy," instead, is to recreate a political and moral society that has been destroyed by capitalist modernity. What happened in Rojava, in Kurdish Syria, gives us an idea of what decolonized democratic autonomy can be and a measure of the power of that idea.

Let us observe this premise well: it is a declaration of theoretical war against—it is still Öcalan who speaks—"the primitive nationalism that aspires to a nation-state." Let us observe the revolutionary power of this affirmation, both in the world of ideas and the sphere of politics. Let's look at it in an era in which left and right tend to be confused in sovereign, nationalist, and reactionary ideologies. But Öcalan insists that his rejection of nationalist sovereignty is also specifically directed against any traditional left-wing movement that adheres to these concepts and therefore "to the stupid ideologies on which the Western capitalist system is based." Öcalan's position reminds us of the struggles that the autonomous movements in the second half of the last century supported against those "Third Worldist" positions that (especially in the anti-colonial movements) in the name of national unity forgot all connotations of class, thus delivering themselves up to being neutralized and tampered with by the capitalist command! This theoretical war is therefore developing with great consistency, identifying in the Kurdish people—this "nation that is not a nation"—a true example of an engine of struggle against "capitalist modernity," that is, against capital and every sovereign conception of the nation. The great majority (of these people), who aspire to a life in freedom, will find their own vanguards to realize this desire. This majority has both the strength to leave the medieval way of life behind and to flee from the nation-state ideal offered by the system and considered a power by capitalist modernity—a system that has not provided any other people with the possibility of living in freedom. Given the historical, geographical, and hereditary peculiarities of Kurdistan and the Kurds, *democratic confederalism* is the most suitable political form. This form of administration also offers the best chance of achieving the ideals of equality and freedom. It is on this model of community, in the political form of the "democratic confederation," that Kurdistan and the Middle East can be rebuilt.

It is not enough to admire the formidable "last-ditch effort" of the perception of a *Geist* of the performative history of a community, of a democratic confederation, that this man, undisputed leader of a community of free people scattered across the world, has been able to imprint on a struggle for national liberation, transforming it into a completely new and powerful figure of proletarian internationalism. Other leaders of national liberation processes and decolonization projects, such as Aimé Césaire and Leopold Senghor, had refused to accept the *doxa* that self-determination requires a sovereign state. But these authors and leaders have not kept their promise. The strength of Öcalan and his people in moving toward the "democratic confederation" has been successful to date.

Öcalan defends the right to utopia and testifies that every revolutionary can only do so. Let us not be moved, however, by this enlightened option. Öcalan's utopia—as is soon discovered—is extremely concrete; it is embodied in the struggles and the order of the zones liberated by the Kurdish communist militias! A real utopia, the one that Öcalan supports, a precious gem that strongly opposes the rebirth, so common today, of national fascisms. The utopia of the democratic confederation of peoples embodies a real process that will win every battle.

Öcalan is a prisoner who is becoming mythical; as Mandela was in the twentieth century, so he is in the twenty-first. He expresses a series of concepts that in the twenty-first century are increasingly becoming the building blocks for the political construction of a new world.

This essay, written in February 2019, was first published as a foreword to *Abdullah Öcalan, Zivilisation und Wahrheit* (Münster: Unrast, 2nd edition, 2019), the German edition of *Civilisation* [Turkish: *Demokratik Uygarlık Manifestosu, birinci kitap: Uygarlık. Maskeli Tanrılar ve Örtük Krallar Çağı* (İstanbul: Aram, 2009)].

Antonio Negri (1933) is an Italian Marxist sociologist and political philosopher, best known for his coauthorship of *Empire* (London: Harvard University Press, 2000), with Michael Hardt, and his work on Spinoza. Born in Padua, he became a political philosophy professor in his hometown university. Negri founded the Potere Operaio (Workers' Power) group in 1969 and was a leading member of Autonomia Operaia. As one of the most popular theorists of autonomism, he has published hugely influential books urging "revolutionary consciousness." He taught at the Paris VIII (Vincennes) and the Collège international de philosophie, along with Jacques Derrida, Michel Foucault, and Gilles Deleuze. Among his books, besides *Empire*, are *Multitude: War and Democracy in the Age of the Empire* (New York: Penguin Books, 2004) and *Commonwealth* (Cambridge, MA: Belknap Press, 2009)—both also coauthored with Michael Hardt. Negri has also published the first two volumes of his autobiography.

SECTION II
The Roots of Civilization

EIGHT

Abdullah Öcalan

Peter Lamborn Wilson

Recently, I had the rare and uncanny experience of picking up a book by someone whom I don't know personally and discovering that the author thought exactly like me on a certain subject. The subject was Sumerian mythology. Not many people have ever bothered to think about Sumerian mythology, and until now I imagined my thoughts about it were unique. As for the author, it's not surprising I've never met him, because since 1999 he's been locked up in solitary confinement on a prison island in the Sea of Marmara, in Turkey. His name is Abdullah Öcalan (the "c" is pronounced as a "j"), and he cofounded the Kurdish Partiya Karkerên Kurdistanê (PKK: Kurdistan Workers' Party) in the 1970s, when he adhered to a revolutionary Marxist Third World nationalist political philosophy, which I never shared. (I have been an anarchist activist since 1984, and a philosophical anarchist since I was a child.) I visited Iranian Kurdistan in the 1970s, but was only interested in meeting Sufis. (They used to stick knives through their cheeks, handle scorpions, eat light bulbs—and they were superb musicians.) I've always sympathized with the Kurds, who are the largest "nation" in the world without a state of its own—but I never took an interest in the PKK, which I suspected of Stalinism.

Recently, however, I learned some fascinating facts from articles written by anarchist comrades whom I know and trust. The story I learned from these sources amazed me. In prison, Öcalan had plenty of time to read, and in the course of time came to renounce Marxism. He was converted to a new way of thinking by the works of the late Murray Bookchin and the example of the Zapatistas. Although he does not use the word "anarchist," in effect he has become, let's say, an antiauthoritarian proponent of radical direct democracy, or "democratic confederalism," as he calls it. He has compiled three volumes of *Prison Writings* that somehow "escaped" from confinement and have been published (including in English translation). These works in turn have inspired the PKK—in the wake of the general uprising against the Syrian government—to launch a revolution in Rojava ("western" or Syrian Kurdistan) on the principles of "stateless democracy." In effect, if not in so many words, this is an anarchist revolution, like the Zapatistas, and, so far, a successful one. As such, it parallels the anarchist revolution during the Spanish Civil War and deserves the solidarity of every antiauthoritarian in the world. In a world devoid of revolutionary hope, Rojava offers that hope. In the future, if there is a future, we will all be judged on the question of whether or not we gave it our support.

The idea of anarcho-federalism (i.e., confederalism) was first proposed, I believe, by Pierre-Joseph Proudhon (in his masterpiece, *The Federative Principle*, which exists in English translation);[1] subsequently the system has been advocated by all "social" anarchists from Murray Bookchin to Subcomandante Marcos. In brief: society will organize from the bottom up in autonomous groups, which will send revocable delegates (not "representatives") to regional conferences, where executive decisions about common goals, production, and "self-defense" can be implemented. Freedom will reside first with the individual, then with the "democratic" collectives; the conferences will be bound by the will of the people. The idea that a revolution must succeed or fail on the basis of women's freedom was first proposed (I think) by the "utopian socialist" Charles Fourier. This principle was ignored by all historical revolutions—until Rojava. By the terms of their "social contract," every organized group must consist of at least 40 percent women—and Rojava is already famous for all-women militias. According to Öcalan, enslavement of women by patriarchy constitutes the very basis of "civilization" and must, before all other injustices, be resolved.

However, before delving into Öcalan's ideas about the origins of civilization and alienation in Sumerian mythology, one more vital point must be made about the current situation (January 2016) of the Rojavan revolution. It is surrounded by a sea of potential and actual enemies. The Syrian government, the "Free Syrian" forces (mostly Sunni Islamists), the Turks, Iran, the Arabs, and the Americans (who classify the PKK as "terrorists") are all arrayed against Rojava—but its worst and most active enemy is ISIS, the Islamic Caliphate, which is exactly analogous to Spanish fascism—only worse. If Rojava represents the principle of *life*, the Caliphate represents *death*. It is as simple as that. It's astonishing that any situation in this "complex modern" world can be so clear. ISIS is evil. Rojava is good. ISIS must be destroyed. Rojava must be saved.

•

A cuneiform tablet called the Sumerian King List states that "kingship first descended from heaven in the city of Eridu," in the south of Sumer. Mesopotamians believed Eridu to be the oldest city in the world (in the sense of "civilization") and modern archeology confirms the myth. Eridu was founded about 5000 BCE and disappeared under the sand around the time of Christ.

Eridu's god Ea, or Enki, (a kind of Neptune and Hermes combined) had a ziggurat where fish were sacrificed. He owned the me, the fifty-one principles of Civilization. The first king, named "Staghorn," probably ruled as Enki's high priest. After some centuries came the flood, and kingship had to descend from heaven again, this time in Uruk and Ur. Gilgamesh now appears on the list. The flood actually occurred; Sir Leonard Wooley saw the thick layer of silt at Ur between two inhabited strata.

Bishop James Ussher once calculated that based on the Bible the world was created on October 19, 4004 BCE at 9:00 in the morning. This makes no Darwinian sense, but provides a possible date for the founding of the Sumerian state, which certainly created a new world. Abraham came from Ur of the Chaldees; Genesis owes much to the Enuma Elish (the Mesopotamian creation myth). Our only text is late Babylonian and obviously based on a lost Sumerian original. Marduk the war god of Babylon has apparently been pasted over a series of earlier figures beginning with Enki.

Before the creation of the world as we know it a family of deities held sway. Chief among them at the time, Tiamat (a typical avatar of the universal Neolithic earth and sea goddess), described by the text as a dragon or serpent, rules a brood of monsters and dallies with her "consort" (shaman) Kingu, an effeminate Tammuz/Adonis prototype. The youngest gods are dissatisfied with her reign; they are "noisy," and Tiamat (the text claims) wants to destroy them, because their noise disturbs her slothful slumber. In truth the young gods are simply fed up with doing all the shitwork themselves, because there are no "humans" yet. The gods want progress.

They elect Marduk their king and declare war on Tiamat. A gruesome battle ensues. Marduk triumphs. He kills Tiamat and slices her body lengthwise in two. He separates the halves with a mighty ripping heave. One half becomes the sky above, the other earth below. Then he kills Kingu and chops his body up into gobs and gobbets. The gods mix the bloody mess with mud and mold little figurines. Thus, humans are created as robots of the gods. The poem ends with a triumphalist paean to Marduk, new king of heaven.

Clearly the Neolithic Age is over. City god, war god, metal god versus country goddess, lazy goddess, garden goddess. The creation of the world equals the creation of civilization, separation, hierarchy, masters and slaves, above and below. Ziggurat and pyramid symbolized the new shape of life.

Combining Enuma Elish and the King List we get an explosive secret document about the origin of civilization not as gradual evolution toward an inevitable future but as a violent coup, a conspiratorial overthrow of primordial rough egalitarian Stone Age society by a crew of black magic cult cannibals. (Human sacrifice first appears in the archaeological record at Ur III. Similar grisly phenomena are also found in the first Egyptian dynasties.)

Another vital text describes the goddess Inanna of Uruk stealing the fifty-one me or "principles of civilization" from Enki of Eridu, their original inventor and owner. The Mesopotamian texts are open, clear, easy to understand, unlike the Egyptian texts which are more opaque and "esoteric." Reading Sumerian mythology as a boastful explanation of the "invention" of hegemonic power renders the mythemes quite transparent. The Neolithic polity of gynandric rough equality, goddess worship, relative peace and quiet, surplus food, village life, etc. changes into a state of patriarchal violence and inequity, outright slavery, war gods, war, upheaval, surplus for the few and hunger for the many, and so on. And all this was depicted as progress—and still is.

About 3100 BCE, writing was invented at Uruk. Apparently, you can witness the moment in the strata: one layer no writing, next layer writing. Of course, writing has a prehistory (like the state). From ancient times a system of accounting had grown up based on little clay counters in the shapes of commodities (hides, jars of oil, bars of metal, etc.). Also, glyptic seals had been invented with images used as heralds to designate the seals' owners. Counters and seals were pressed into slabs of wet clay and the records were held in temple archives—probably records of debts owed to the temple. (In the Neolithic Age the temples no doubt served as redistribution centers. In the Bronze Age they began to function as banks.)

As I picture it, the invention of real writing took place within a single brilliant family of temple archivists over three or four generations, say a century. The counters were discarded and a reed stylus was used to impress signs on clay, based on the shapes of the old counters, and with further pictograms imitated from the seals. Numbering was easily compacted from rows of counters to number signs. The real breakthrough came with the flash that certain pictographs could be used for their sound divorced from their meaning and recombined to "spell" other words (especially abstractions). Integrating the two systems proved cumbersome, but maybe the sly scribes considered this an advantage. Writing needed to be difficult, because it was a mystery revealed by gods and a monopoly of the new class of scribes. Aristocrats rarely learned to read and write—a matter for mere bureaucrats—but writing provided the key to state expansion by separating sound from meaning, speaker from hearer, and sight from other senses. Writing as separation both mirrors and reinforces separation as "written," as fate. Action at a distance (including distance of time) constitutes the magic of the state, the nervous system of control. Writing both is and represents the new "creation" ideology. It wipes out the oral tradition of the Stone Age and erases the collective memory of a time before hierarchy. In the text we have always been slaves.

By combining image and word in single memes or hieroglyphs the scribes of Uruk (and a few years later the predynastic scribes of Egypt) created a magical system. According to a late syncretistic Greco-Egyptian myth, when Hermes-Thoth invents writing he boasts to his father Zeus that humans now never need forget anything ever again. Zeus replies, "On the contrary my son, now they'll forget everything." Zeus discerned the occult purpose of the text, the forgetfulness of the oral/aural, the false memory of the text, indeed the lost text. He sensed a void where others saw only a plenum of information. But this void is the telos of writing.

Writing begins as a method of controlling debt owed to the temple, debt as yet another form of absence. When full-blown economic texts appear a few strata later we find ourselves already immersed in a complex economic world based on debt, interest, compound interest, debt peonage, as well as outright slavery, rents, leases, private and public forms of property, long-distance trade, craft monopolies, police, and even a "money-lenders' bazaar." Not money as we understand it yet but commodity currencies (usually barley and silver), often loaned for as much as 33⅓ percent per year. The jubilee or period of forgiveness of debts (as known in the Bible) already existed in Sumer, which would have otherwise collapsed under the load of debt.

Sooner or later, the bank (i.e., the temple) would solve this problem by obtaining the monopoly on money. By lending at interest ten or more times its actual assets, the modern bank simultaneously creates debt and the money to pay debt. Fiat, "let it be." Even in Sumer the indebtedness of the king (the state) to the temple (the bank) had already begun.

The problem with commodity currencies is that no one can have a monopoly on cows or wheat. Their materiality limits them. A cow might calve and barley might grow but not at rates demanded by usury. Silver doesn't grow at all.

So the next brilliant move, by King Croesus of Lydia (Asia Minor, seventh century BCE) was the invention of the coin, a refinement of money just as the Greek alphabet (also seventh century BCE) was a refinement of writing. Originally a temple token or souvenir signifying one's "due portion" of the communal sacrifice, a lump of metal impressed with a royal or temple seal (often a sacrificial animal, such as the bull), the coin begins its career with mana, something supernatural, something more (or less) than the weight of the metal. Stage two: coins showing two faces, one with image, the other with writing. You can never see both at once, suggesting the metaphysical slipperiness of the object, but together they constitute a hieroglyph, a word/image expressed in metal as a single meme of value.

Coins might "really" be worth only their weight in metal, but the temple says they're worth more, and the king is ready to enforce the decree. the object and its value are separated; the value floats free, the object circulates. Money works the way it works because of an absence not a presence. In fact, money largely consists of absent wealth—debt—your debt to king and temple. Moreover, free of its anchor in the messy materiality of commodity currencies, money can now compound unto eternity, far beyond mere cows and jars of beer, beyond all worldly things, even unto heaven. "Money begets money," Ben Franklin gloated. But money is dead. Coins are inanimate objects. Then money must be the sexuality of the dead.

The whole of Greco-Egyptian-Sumerian economics compacts itself neatly into the hieroglyphic text of the Yankee dollar bill, the most popular publication in the history of *history*. The owl of Athena, one of the earliest coin images, perches microscopically on the face of the bill in the upper left corner of the upper right shield (you'll need a magnifying glass), and the Pyramid of Cheops is topped with the all-seeing eye of Horus, or the panopticonical eye of ideology. The Washington family coat of arms (stars and stripes) combined with imperial eagle and fasces of arrows, etc.; a portrait of Washington as Masonic Grand Master; and even an admission that the bill is nothing but tender for debt, public and private. Since 1971, the bill is not even "backed" by gold, and thus has become pure textuality.

Hieroglyph as magic focus of desire deflects psyche from object to representation. It "enchains" imagination and defines consciousness. In this sense, money constitutes the great triumph of writing, its proof of magic power. Image wields power over desire but no control. Control is added when the image is semanticized (or "alienated") by logos. The emblem (picture plus caption) gives desire or emotion an ideological frame and thus directs its force. Hieroglyph equals picture plus word, or picture as word (*rebus*), hence hieroglyph's power and control over both conscious and unconscious—in other words, its magic.

•

Most of the above analysis of "Sumerian economics" was written in 2002. It represents the gist of the result of a project I undertook circa 1984 to try to understand the truth behind the illusion of history as the triumphalism of the state. I read the histories of religion, of money, of science, of art and culture, archaeology, anthropology, political theory, and especially of hermeticism, which provided me with the most important keys to understanding. My conclusion was that civilization itself had been a mistake, a violent derailing of human society from its natural "organic" evolution as a process of "mutual aid." The origin of the state was a coup d'état, carried out in opposition to the "customs in common" that had prevented its emergence for half a million years.

The most important writers for my thesis, aside from the Sumerian mythographers who had "blown the secret" so openly, included the anthropologists Marshall Sahlins (*Stone Age Economics*) and Pierre Clastres (*Society against the State* and *The Archeology of Violence*). I used Nietzsche and Charles Fourier, and to a certain degree anarchists like Kropotkin (*Mutual Aid*), Proudhon (*Property Is Theft*), and Gustav Landauer (*On Socialism*).[2]

However, I found that the classical anarchists were still intoxicated by the idea of technological progress, so I needed to also read the new anti-civilizationists, such as Fredy Perlman and John Zerzan. Later I discovered that many of my ideas had been independently arrived at by David Graeber in his *Debt: The First 5000 Years*,[3] although he made much less use of mythology and "magic" as heuristic devices.

In volume 1 of Abdullah Öcalan's *Prison Writings: The Roots of Civilisation*,[4] I noted at once that, unlike Graeber, he was reading Sumerian myth in the same hermeneutic manner I had attempted. He saw the Mesopotamian Neolithic Age as I did, as a culture shaped by the feminine principle of life. It was betrayed in a sense by its own success. The development of irrigation agriculture and bronze-based metallurgy created so much wealth and abundance that the temptation to appropriate it for the benefit of a ruling elite grew too powerful to resist. The overthrow of the goddess not only symbolized the disaster of the state, it was literally the historical mode of its realization as the beginning of "history" as we know it.

The essence of the state in Öcalan's analysis was "slavery": debt-peonage and outright chattel bondage in a system ruled by priest-kings on behalf of a war-mongering pantheon of male deities. The essential spirituality of Neolithic paganism was monopolized, betrayed, and transformed by the new hegemons as an ideology of social control. Henceforth, religion was to serve the power of oppression. "Civilization," with the high culture so prized by its historians, has consisted of six thousand years of misery for most humans, culminating in capitalism and the apotheosis of the 1 percent. We are all Sumerians.

On some points I differ (hesitantly and respectfully) with Öcalan's perspective. He values the Neolithic Age very highly but pays little attention to the Paleolithic Age; as a result, he scants the significance of the development of agriculture and domestication as problematic technologies destined to unbalance the "old customs" of nonauthoritarian tribal society integral to a hunting-gathering economy. It's true that the state did not "emerge" during the Neolithic Age. It's also true that we contemporary humans cannot hope realistically to "go back" to a Paleolithic economy— although we might just manage some kind of neo-luddite late Neolithic scenario!—so it makes sense for anarchists to think (in Paul Goodman's phrase) like "Neolithic conservatives."[5]

Öcalan has a powerful critique of technology in the grip of capitalism—but like many "progressives" (including anarchists and Marxists) he still values science and technology as potentially positive forces. In the leftist perspective, technology is "neutral"—it can be good or bad, dialectically, according to its economic base. What the historical left has largely failed to consider, oddly enough, is the sociology of science/technology. Once an invention is socialized—released into the social sphere—it begins to work on that sphere and shape it. We create technology, but technology also creates us.

This should not be difficult to understand. The "communications technology" that Öcalan sees as tending to instigate "democracy" also has a dark side. The technology has proven as useful to ISIS and other oppressors as to the "Arab Spring," the Iranian "Greens," and other progressive forces. But above all, it possesses an inherent "built-in" tendency to destroy genuine sociality by inculcating mediation as alienation—by degrading physical presence and hyper-valuing the image. An understanding of magic from the perspective of a Giordano Bruno (or a modern spin doctor) would help us to grasp the potential of the image to shape the social subconscious. The image is itself a technology, or heavily technologized. And the image of technology is perhaps "more real" than the machinery itself.

Incidentally, Öcalan is far from insensitive to the spiritual aspect of the struggle against civilization as oppression. If organized state-sanctioned exoteric religions are part of the problem, he sees esoteric heresy as part of the solution. Ever since the overthrow of Stone Age egalitarianism by ideological hegemony, underground sects and secret societies have provided a tradition of resistance; Öcalan specifically mentions Sufis like Rumi, Ibn Arabi, and Hallaj, and heretics such as the Kurdish Alevis and the Yezidis. My own experience of Kurdish culture is based on meetings with Qadiri Sufis and the "Shiite extremist" heretics called Ahl-i Haqq (People of the Truth). The Rojava Social Contract makes no mention of Islam (although it does once refer to "God"), but it specifically provides protection for religious minorities such as the Yezidis and Syriac Christians. Öcalan mocks both fundamentalism and Marxist flattening of religion into a mere "opium of the people." For him, it can once again include worship of the goddess and a spirituality of ecological holism lost for six thousand years but not irrecoverable.

•

It seems somehow appropriate that Öcalan has been locked up in a Turkish prison for sixteen years. Of course, I'd like to see him free, but I feel it's logical that he is persecuted in an insane and evil world, like, say, Jesus or the martyrs of anarchism or any other champion of the poor. Where else would you expect to find a world-class political genius than... prison?

I don't use the word "genius" lightly. Almost alone among actual leaders of actual revolutions in today's sad world, Öcalan offers a way out of the ideological traps of both left and right—a way out not merely intellectual and theoretical (although it certainly is that) but also practical. He has inspired, from his lonely rock, a vast armed and self-organized populace to embrace a genuinely nonauthoritarian political strategy of resistance to oppression, as well as positive work on the liberation of human society. In this essay I have not even touched on his deep and impressive analysis of history, economics, the affairs of the Middle East, proposals for practical utopianism, or discussion of specifically Kurdish culture and politics. Since I am a historian of religions and "comparative mysticism," as well as an anarchist, I wanted to emphasize Öcalan's unique contributions in those fields.

Öcalan dreams of a "renaissance" for the Middle East that would base itself on the positive aspects of Neolithic, and even Sumerian, civilization, as well as on a scientia freed of its slavery to hegemonic oppression and capitalist catastrophe.

I've often asked: What would science be like today if the state had never emerged? Öcalan has attempted an answer—not just for science but for human society as a whole.

For years now, I've admitted that I find it impossible to be an optimist. The forces at work for an "end of the world"—overpopulation, technopathocracy, poisoning of the elements, the triumph of greed and the "ugly spirit," and so on—seem too powerful to evoke an optimistic response. The best I've been able to muster is what I call anti-pessimism, the refusal to give up acting as if an uprising were possible. If only for "existentialist" reasons, one clings to the notion of gratuitous acts of resistance.

The Zapatistas brought a moment of hope, but their call for world-wide movements like theirs fell on deaf ears. Occupy Wall Street cheered me up for about a month. Otherwise... not much.

But I have to admit that the Rojava revolution has raised my hopes again, and reading Öcalan has renewed my faith in the anarchist cause. Of course, the American liberal/left media remain largely clueless that something different is happening in Syria. Consciousness needs to be raised here. I offer the following reading list as a starter course. *What is to be done?* I don't know—but at least we can read a few books!

Abdullah Öcalan. *Prison Writings: The Roots of Civilisation.* Translated by Klaus Happel. London: Pluto Press, 2007. This, the first volume of his prison writings, is Öcalan's longest and most theoretically rich work; it begins with the stunningly brilliant analysis of Sumerian civilization that immediately convinced me of his genius.

Abdullah Öcalan. *Prison Writings II: The PKK and the Kurdish Question in the 21st Century.* Translated and edited by Klaus Happel. Preliminary notes by Cemîl Bayik. London: Transmedia Publishing, 2011. This second volume deals more specifically with Öcalan's personal history and includes the deeply moving story of his own political, intellectual, and spiritual becoming. He is humble and admits his mistakes—but points out that millions of people believe in him, and that he feels responsible to them. It outlines the conspiracy (which included the CIA) that landed him in prison.

Abdullah Öcalan. *Prison Writings, Volume 3: The Road Map to Negotiations.* Cologne: International Initiative, 2012. The Turkish government invited Öcalan to outline his plan for a just peace between Turkey and the Kurds. This book is the result. Written in 2009, it represents Öcalan's most recent thinking on what he calls "democracy" and is, therefore, highly relevant to the experiment in Rojava. The Turkish government made no response. It sat on the text for eighteen months, then refused Öcalan all visitation rights and arrested all of his lawyers. He's still in prison today.

Abdullah Öcalan. *War and Peace in Kurdistan.* Cologne: International Initiative, 2017 [2009].

Abdullah Öcalan. *Democratic Confederalism.* Cologne: International Initiative, 2017 [2011]. I would also recommend the version of Democratic Confederalism in Renée In der Maur and Jonas Staal, ed. *New World Academy Reader #5: Stateless Democracy.* Utrecht, NL: BAK—Basis voor Actuele Kunst, 2015.

This essay was originally published in Dilar Dirik, David Levi Strauss, Michael Taussig, and Peter Lamborn Wilson, eds. *To Dare Imagining: Rojava Revolution* (Brooklyn, NY: Autonomedia, 2016).

Peter Lamborn Wilson is author, editor, or translator of more than fifty books, some translated into fifteen or sixteen languages (including Turkish). Recent titles include *Spiritual Journeys of an Anarchist* (San Francisco/Brooklyn, NY: Ardent Press/Autonomedia, 2014), *Spiritual Destinations of an Anarchist* (San Francisco/Brooklyn, NY: Ardent Press/Autonomedia, 2014), and *Heresies: Anarchist Memoirs, Anarchist Art* (Brooklyn, NY: Autonomedia, 2016). In the 1970s, Wilson visited Iranian Kurdistan several times to hang out with Qadiri Sufis and Ahl-i Haqq (People of the Truth).

Notes

1   Pierre-Joseph Proudhon, "The Federative Principle" (1863), in *Property is Theft! A Pierre-Joseph Proudhon Reader*, ed. Iain McKay (Oakland: AK Press, 2011), accessed September 30, 2019, https://theanarchistlibrary.org/library/pierre-joseph-proudhon-the-principle-of-federation.

2   Marshall Sahlins, *Stone Age Economics* (Chicago: Aldine-Atherton, 1972); Pierre Clastres, *Society against the State* (Brooklyn, NY: Zone Books, 1989); Pierre Clastres, *The Archeology of Violence* (Los Angeles: Semiotexte/Foreign Agents, 2010 [1980]); Peter Kropotkin, *Mutual Aid: A Factor in Evolution* (Scotts Valley, CA: CreateSpace Independent Publishing Platform, 2014); Proudhon, *Property Is Theft!*

3   David Graeber, *Debt: The First 5,000 Years* (Brooklyn, NY: Melville House, 2012).

4   Abdullah Öcalan, *Prison Writings: The Roots of Civilisation* (London: Transmedia Publishing, 2007).

5   Paul Goodman, "Notes of a Neolithic Conservative," *New York Review of Books*, March 26, 1970, accessed July 16, 2019, https://www.nybooks.com/articles/1970/03/26/notes-of-a-neolithic-conservative.

NINE

Öcalan's Manifesto and the Challenge of Transcending Centricity

Donald H. Matthews and Thomas Jeffrey Miley

Introduction

Respect for Abdullah Öcalan, the imprisoned leader of the Kurdish freedom movement, "chained to the rock of İmralı," a symbol of resistance, of fortitude and resilience, a responsible leader, a prophet, a man with a powerful political vision. A vision that has inspired the revolutionaries in Rojava, Syria, and which fuels the Kurdish resistance to Erdoğan's tyranny in the southeast of Turkey (and beyond).

The heroic defense of Kobane caught the world's attention—the movement's will to struggle, its ability to mobilize the people for collective self-defense, to sacrifice and to die for a cause, and not just for any cause, for a good cause: the project of "democratic confederalism," a project that represents the only alternative to the negative dialectic of tyranny and chaos currently tearing the Middle East apart, or, in Öcalan's terms, the only alternative to "hierarchical and dominated civilization."

The project of "democratic confederalism" in construction in Rojava is an experiment in radical direct democracy, based on citizens' assemblies, defended by citizens' militias.

It is a radical democratic project that emphasizes gender emancipation by implementing a model of copresidency and a quota system that enforces gender equality in all forms of political representation, by organizing women's assemblies and women's academies, and by mobilizing women in their own militia for self-defense.

It is a radical democratic project that redefines "self-determination" as direct democracy against the state, that renounces as divisive and utopian the equation of the struggle for national freedom with the goal of an independent nation-state, and that seeks to overcome the danger of majority tyranny by institutionalizing a "revolutionary-consociational" regime. A consociational regime whose "social contract" guarantees multiethnic, multilingual, and multi-religious accommodation, again, as with women, by implementing quotas for political representation (concretely, for Arabs and for Assyrian Christians), by direct assemblies of different constituent groups, and by mobilizing these groups in their own militias of self-defense.

And it is a radical democratic project that stresses the importance of "social ecology" and environmental sustainability, in a place where the soil bleeds oil, and imperial and sub-imperial vultures circle in the sky.

In sum, an alternative to the dialectic of tyranny and chaos, an alternative to the machinations of imperial and subimperial divide and conquer, a project that combines radical democracy, self-defense, gender emancipation, multicultural and multi-religious accommodation, and social ecology. A real road map for peace.

A road map sketched by an imprisoned leader with a prophetic message, a man who, especially since his abduction, has, even in the harshest of conditions, been eloquent and prolific in elaborating his model of "democratic confederalism"—initially as part of his defense in his trial. Paradoxically, prison has proven a space of intellectual freedom for Mr. Öcalan—like it was for Trotsky, for Gramsci, for Malcolm X, and even for Mandela before him. While behind bars, he has spent much of his time reading (though with very limited access to books), writing, and reflecting upon his predicament, that of his people, and that of the modern world.

The first of his five-volume *Manifesto for a Democratic Civilization* has recently been translated into English by Havin Guneser. In this volume, subtitled *The Age of Masked Gods and Disguised Kings*, Öcalan sets out to uncover the deep historical roots of the tremendous problems plaguing "capitalist modernity" and to recover the even deeper historical sources of the democratic alternative he proposes.[1]

Especially considering the conditions in which the volume was composed—the inhumane, indeed torturous, isolation, not to mention limited access to books—the result is an intellectual and existential accomplishment of a high order.

Against Hierarchy

In volume one of the *Manifesto*, Öcalan mounts an assault on hierarchy in all its forms. He counters hegemonic, near ubiquitous, pseudoscientific, social Darwinist accounts that reify and essentialize competitive egoism and the penchant for hierarchy, accounts that would locate these social pathologies near the very core of human nature, as the products of natural selection, as "hard-wired" in our brains, even encoded in our genes. Öcalan insists, to the contrary, that the roots of hierarchy do not run so deep. He locates these roots not near the core of human nature, but a mere five thousand years in the past, emerging with the "birth of civilization" in the Neolithic Age. And he goes on to sketch a compelling account of a dialectic between domination and resistance, between hierarchy and freedom, that was then triggered and that continues to this day.

Like Foucault before him, whom he hails (with Nietzsche) as a "philosopher of freedom," Öcalan stresses the "extraordinary effort" involved in the interpellation of individuals by dogmas and myths to justify quiescence and subordination to hierarchy and domination. "Socialization can only be achieved through a continuous effort," and, indeed, it is impossible for any individual to "escape being constructed according to the dictates of society." Even so, Öcalan contends, such efforts can never be entirely successful. The impulse to "freedom," the urge to resist "classed and hierarchic," "oppressive and exploitative societies" can be suppressed but never extinguished. Individuals "will not readily accept societies that construct slavery," despite the constant "endeavors not only to transform [them] as they pass through the oppressive and educational social institutions but also to eliminate them." The point is all the more powerful and persuasive coming from a man who has spent close to two decades in solitary confinement.

Öcalan's approach is nothing if not ambitious. It corresponds to his awareness of and sensitivity to the critique of the modernist faith in the trinity of science, technology, and progress, combined with his sober assessment that our imprisonment within the confines of "capitalist modernity" ultimately has less to do with the power of its "money" or its "weapons" than it does with its capacity to constrict the horizons of our consciousness.

Öcalan identifies the cult of power and hierarchy and the worship of the state as deeply ingrained traditions conditioning our mentalities and constricting our ideological reflexes, even capable of co-opting movements of resistance, as exemplified perhaps most dramatically by the experience of state socialism. If the cult of power corrupts, the exercise of power corrupts even more. Indeed, Öcalan contends, "one of the most striking examples of the corruptive force of power can be found in the experience of real socialism." Such are the difficulties faced by those who would resist the dynamics of hierarchy. They are up against "a culture of domination" that is deeply entrenched, having been prepared by "hundreds of brutal emperors and various other dominating forces." Indeed, Öcalan concludes, "therein lies the true importance of the quote attributed to Mikhail Bakunin, 'If you took the most ardent revolutionary, vested him in absolute power, within a year he would be worse than the Czar himself.'"

Öcalan has abandoned the illusion of any linear notion of "progress." For him, finding the way "forward" requires a return to the deep past. Only by returning to the deep past, only by providing "a proper historical interpretation of our problems," expansive in scope, with "reference to origin," can we hope to "illuminate our future." Only after these origins have been revealed and comprehended will we be prepared to transcend the culture of hatred and death, "to make the transition into a life where love reigns" supreme.

Yet, references to Braudel notwithstanding, Öcalan's recourse to the deep past, his provision of a "proper historical interpretation of our problems," is not undertaken with the pretense of a professional historian in pursuit of the elusive goal of "scientific objectivity." This is why his admission that his account is "amateurish and unpolished" should not be read solely as a disclaimer and gesture of humility. For Öcalan is a proponent of the "mythological method," a method he insists "should be given back" its prestige.

He contrasts the method of myths to those of both "monotheistic religious dogma" and the "science" that succeeded it. Despite the differences among these consecutive successor "regimes of truth," Öcalan insists they are nevertheless similar, at least insofar as they both "alleg[e] to bow" before "absolute laws." Not so with myth.

Öcalan's own "historical interpretation" is thus best interpreted as providing a "noble myth" of sorts, an account of humanity's fall and of its potential for redemption in this world that is at the same time a manifesto reflexively in favor of myth and against dogma of either the religious or the secular-scientific kind.

Öcalan laments the conversion of science into "a new religion," one that takes "the form of positivism," with its "objective laws" representing "nothing but the modern equivalent of the 'Word of God' of antiquity." Science, united with power and capital, comprising "the new sacred alliance of modernity." Science has been fetishized, idolatrized, rendered a new dogma, turned into an "ism." Those who espouse this new dogma of "scientism" he deems guilty of hubris. In perpetuating the pretense that "science alone can render truth about the world and reality," they would belittle, dismiss, deny all that "cannot be apprehended by the scientific method."

Öcalan emphasizes the ideological function of this all-pervasive modern "ism." He insists that "the world of science has become the power that constructs, legitimizes, and protects the system's methods and contents." Not only the system of "capitalist modernity" but the system of state socialism too. Though, in the end, it would sow the seeds for the demise of that false alternative.

Indeed, according to Öcalan, "the objective scientific method played a determining role in the failure of scientific socialism." This because faith in science is closely associated with rule by experts. "One of the biggest errors of the Marxian method" was to perpetuate such elitist convictions. In so doing, it actively inhibited "the mental revolution" required for the democratic construction of a new society, a genuine alternative of collective emancipation.

Even worse, Öcalan alleges the "rationalism" and "positivism" implicated in the new dogma of science have positively "paved the way for the 'fascist flock.'" They have done so by inculcating "robotic and mechanical human being[s]," as well as "simulative perceptions of life," thereby propelling us toward the destruction of "the environment and the history of society."

Dogmatism, either religious or scientific, is an enemy of emancipation. It leads to reification, to presenting unjust, hierarchical, and oppressive social arrangements not as social constructs but as "unchangeable," as "sacred," as "divine[ly] establish[ed]," as reflecting unchangeable laws.

A Focus on Patriarchy

One of the most compelling parts of Öcalan's account is the close attention he pays to the issue of patriarchy, and the links he makes between the oppression of women in particular and oppression in general. Öcalan has elsewhere equated patriarchy with "[w]oman's slavery" and diagnosed this as "the most profound and disguised social area where all types of slavery, oppression and colonization are realized."[2] In volume 1 of the *Manifesto*, he elaborates on this point. Ironically, he invokes Nietzsche to this end—referring to the German philosopher's talk "about how society is made to adopt wife-like features and is enslaved by modernity." More substantially, he relies on feminist scholar Maria Mies in sketching a perceptive analysis of the links between patriarchy and hierarchy and in tracing their mutual origins.

According to Öcalan, women suffer from the oppressive status of *housewifization*—this time dubbed "the most advanced form of slavery." But to make matters worse, in capitalist modernity, such slavery of women has been compounded, perhaps even fueled, by "the housewifization of man—after his castration through citizenship."[3] Capitalist modernity, distinguished for its relentless pursuit of the subjection of all in the "public sphere"—a subjection of all crafted in the image and likeness of the subjection of some, of half, of women, in the "private sphere," the home.

A democratic alternative, Öcalan insists, requires the replacement of the current family system, "based on the deep-rooted slavery of women," and the creation of an entirely "new family system, based on deep-rooted freedom and the equality of woman." Such a creation would promise in turn to "help abolish the male-based hierarchic and statist order."[4]

With respect to the origins of housewifization, "the most ancient form of enslavement," Öcalan contends that "it has been institutionalized as a result of woman's defeat by the strongman and his attendants," a defeat that "required a long and comprehensive war," indeed a struggle so "intense and fierce" that "it has been erased from our memories, together with the consequences thereof." The result, according to Öcalan: "Woman cannot remember what was lost, where it was lost and how it was lost. She considers a submissive womanhood as her natural state. This is why no other enslavement has been legitimized through internalization as much as woman's enslavement."[5] A case of collective amnesia, associated with the trauma of subjugation, compounded by the patriarchal biases built into the "his"-torical record, resulting in reification, essentialism, and naturalized quiescence by woman, even naturalized identification with her subordinate status in society.

The deep-rooted and insidious patriarchal biases plaguing the "his"-torical record help justify Öcalan's heterodox—indeed, mythical—interpretation about gender equality in the "Neolithic" Age—a period crucial to Öcalan's broader metanarrative about the emergence of hierarchy.

According to Öcalan, before humanity's "fall," that is, before its fateful descent into oppression and inequality, there had been a "moment of creation," a "quantum moment" and "chaotic interval" whose epicenter was located in the Fertile Crescent—where what Gordon Childe termed "the Neolithic Revolution" occurred. This period signaled the end of the "monotonous life of hunting, gathering and defense" of "clan communities, hundreds of thousands years old." With the transition to "settled life and farming," clan society gave way to "broader structures," including the birth of "ethnic ties." It was an era of momentous upheaval and creative fertility, in which "thousands of mental revolutions" took place. Most prominent among these, the introduction and invention of "numerous nutriments, means of transport, weaving, grinding, architecture," as well as complex symbolic forms of "religious and artistic" expression.[6]

The "symbol of the Neolithic society" was the mother-goddess Inanna. Worship of her rose symmetrically to the decline of the totem, "the identity of the old clan society," which decreased in significance.[7] The cult of Inanna in turn reflected the prominent role of women in this period. Indeed, according to Öcalan, "During the Neolithic, the driving force had been the mother-woman."[8] Thus the attribution of sacredness to her.

The residues of this "quantum moment" remain ingrained as sediments that survive in the human psyche and are capable of being revived, of coming once again to structure social relations, and not only in terms of gender relations. Indeed, a whole host of "treasured moral values ... more precious" than those of capitalist modernity—values such as "respect, affection, neighborly relations, and solidarity"—are products of and remnants from this period.[9] These values thus have a deep historical basis, and they underpin the unextinguishable will to resist oppressive, hierarchical social forms. They have been congealed and transmitted in collective memories that have never been fully suppressed. As is, for example, evidenced in "the narratives of the Holy Books," where the memory of those times is sublimated "into the idea of *paradise*."[10] A paradise never fully lost; a paradise that can be recovered.

The descent into hierarchy, patriarchy, and class inequality would come, in Öcalan's account, with the rise of the Sumerians, whose main legends recount "the rivalry between the crafty male god Enki and the leading female goddess Inanna," a cosmic rivalry among the gods that Öcalan interprets as reflecting and projecting transformations in material and social relations among humans—specifically, "the transition from the Neolithic village society that had *not* allowed exploitation, to that of the urban society—newly constructed by the priests—which *was* open to exploitation."[11]

Öcalan thus again employs a materialist hermeneutic of religious belief. Whereas the prominence of Inanna in the religious expressions of the Fertile Crescent during the Neolithic Age stands as evidence and reflection of "the social strength of the creative and leading power of the Neolithic—namely, woman," the rivalry with and rise of worship for the crafty male God Enki signaled the rise in prominence of a new social class, "the priestly class," now sublimated and "exalted in the new religion."[12]

Religion, Monotheism, and Hierarchy

The Sumerian "priestly class" plays a particularly nefarious role in Öcalan's account. Not only does it represent and act as a protagonist for the birth of class divisions, it is also to blame for the subordination of women and for the transition from mythical to dogmatic belief systems. According to Öcalan, the priest's main task—a thoroughly secular one— "was to administer the requirements of the growing urban society."[13] But, at the same time, it usurped access to the world of the gods, since "anyone wanting to hear the word of god had to listen to the high priest." The combination of these two roles rendered the priestly class "the group bearing the biggest responsibility for the formation of both the civilization of modernity and of civilization in general."[14]

With the consolidation of priestly power, the rivalry between the crafty male god Elki and the mother-goddess Inanna was decided in favor of the former. "Over time, less and less figurines of the woman-goddess were made," and by the "onset of the Babylon period, the woman-goddess had been destroyed" altogether, another signal of the increasing oppression of woman, now subjugated as "an official public and private prostitute as well as a slave."[15]

The Sumerian priests were the first to disguise their power and legitimate their usurpations and expropriations by dawning the masks of the gods whose worship they ritualized and regulated. But the kings would soon learn this most useful trick from the priests.[16]

These masked men managed to cast a spell on the exploited, on the workers, who, as if hypnotized, came to increasingly accept a new subservient role legitimated by the dictates of "newly manufactured gods."[17]

Öcalan's interest in the relatively deep past is never divorced from his concerns about the present. Indeed, he insists that a proper analysis and understanding of the process of descent into hierarchy achieved by Sumerian society promises to "enhance our understanding of our own society." This because such analysis can help us to identify and "pull off the masks that cover," to see past dominant mystifying and legitimating tropes, to see "the true faces, the real profits and the actual status of the different role-players" in contemporary society.[18]

Öcalan contends that the spell of submission to hierarchy first cast by the Sumerian priestly class has yet to be broken. Indeed, those who have "claimed to rebel for their tribe, nation, or religion" have in reality only usurped the "crown of power."[19] The class division first wrought by the Sumerian priests has remained "a fundamental characteristic of civilization" ever since. Provocatively, he insists, "in the few cases where [power systems] were overthrown by their subjects and proletariat, the new administration has usually been far worse than the previous oppressive and exploitative regime."[20] Along with and as a tool for the emergence of hierarchy is the emergence of the state, consecrated by the worship of its rulers, who dawn the mask of gods. The state, which Öcalan defines as "the unity of power relations through which the general coercion and exploitation of classed society is enabled."[21] The state, with the development of capitalist modernity, tends to fuse with the nation in "the mask-less new god—the nation-state."[22] The cult of hierarchy remains alive and well in the contemporary cult of the nation-state, which, Öcalan concludes, is "the god that has removed its mask" and that "is being sanctified … in all modern societies."[23]

To break from the spell of hierarchy thus requires a break with the state, as well as a disciplined strategy of resistance to the hypnotic powers of the modern priestly classes. A first step in this direction is to decode and understand the source of such hypnotic powers—and here is where the category of dogmatism comes into play.

The Sumerian priestly class sought to legitimate emergent inequality, the formation of social classes, and division of society into exploiters and exploited, by overseeing and encouraging the demise of the "mythological method" and its replacement with "dogmatic religious perception."

According to Öcalan, "the relationship between the newly formed classes of the exploited and the exploiters demanded indisputable dogmas" capable of "disguis[ing] and legitimiz[ing] the exploitation and power of hierarchical and class interests." The emergent despots, the dominators, the exploiters hid behind the mask of gods, not just any gods, ones "endowed with 'indisputable' characteristics" and revealed in sacred texts containing allegedly "infallible words."[24] The transition from the "mythical method" to "dogma" is thus related to the invention of the written word—and the priestly class's power was based in its role as interpreter of the indisputable, infallible words of gods contained in sacred texts. The consolidation of the priestly class's role as conduit and interpreter of the word and the will of the gods meant the cultivation of a new "slave-like submission" and a "fatalistic perception" on the part of the exploited. "A shepherd-herd dialectic was" thus "established."[25]

Öcalan diagnoses dogmatism as a disease first propagated by the Sumerian priestly class, and still at the core of the ideological legitimation of hierarchy. Unlike orthodox atheist critiques of religion, Öcalan's critique is not framed as an exercise of "demystification" but instead focuses on the usurpations of the priestly class and on their propagation of dogmas.

Öcalan makes it clear that he is no enemy of the mystical, the sacred, or the divine per se. Instead, his problem is with those who don the mask of gods and claim to be conduits of the Divine when justifying exploitation and tyranny. Indeed, among the reasons he gives for his admiration of Neolithic society in comparison with contemporary capitalist modernity, Öcalan mentions an alleged harmony between Neolithic society and nature, as reflected in their view of nature "as filled with sacredness and divinity," in their belief that nature is "as alive as they were themselves." According to Öcalan, in Neolithic society "divinity had nothing to do with coercion, exploitation and tyranny."[26]

It was the Sumerian priests who introduced this connection—with their penchant for dogmatism and their novel attribution of "punishment and sin to the notion of *god*," for the purpose of developing "the sense of obedience." These innovations allowed the notion of god slowly to fuse with and turn into the state. This is the key to the "reform brought about by the Sumerian priests."

Punishment and sin linked to the promise of an afterlife—a connection allegedly first made in Sumer, later in Egypt, then inherited by the

Abrahamic tradition. More than a connection, a "paradigm of heaven, hell, and life to come." Öcalan contends that this connection, this paradigm, provided a crucial and "strong legitimization device, needed to convince the slaves, who certainly did not have an easy life."

A "strong legitimation device" capable of conjuring submission and quiescence in this life by promising reward in the next. A utopian projection, "a promise of paradise," "talk about millennia of happiness," all of which, Öcalan adds, reminds him "of the longing for an oasis." And, thus, he surmises, a reflection of "[i]ts opposite," "an infertile life." Echoes of Bob Marley's refrain—"But if you know what life is worth, you would look for yours on earth." But Öcalan goes further, concluding in a decidedly secular vein, "the quest for paradise is nothing but a promise of a future in a new world," "a harbor inevitably constructed by those who have lost hope."[27] A contentious point, no doubt, since belief in paradise can just as easily conjure the courage to struggle and the willingness to die for a cause as quiescence and submission to the status quo. The historical record is full of examples.

Examples of which Öcalan is well aware. Indeed, he makes explicit mention of the many "wars waged in the name of Islam, Christianity, and Judaism," though he interprets these as "in essence struggles for dominance over Middle Eastern civilization," with religion serving as but a pretext, a means of mobilizing support, "masking the real reason behind bloody wars." The instrumental efficacy of religious convictions would become all the more transparent when they were later directly appropriated by the state and "declared official state ideologies." Conversely, within and against the hegemonic religious and national projects institutionalized in given states, the mobilization of "dissident sectarian" sentiments and loyalties have reflected and channeled "class conflict" and have "signified the rebellious attitude of the marginal societies excluded from civilized societies." As with wars of religion fought between states, Öcalan insists, sectarian struggles within states are also best interpreted as all too often but "a pretext" masking "real" reasons, indeed, "a type of nationalism."[28]

Here Öcalan displays the profound and continuing influence of materialist thought upon his hermeneutic—even seeming to flirt with a characteristic left-atheist double dismissal of religious consciousness as simultaneously pacifying and dangerously divisive. A historical materialist influence and impulse, to be precise, that he marshals relatively consistently in his interpretation of Islam, both past and present. In speaking about the birth of Islam, he denies the sovereignty of supranatural in favor of mundane causal forces, contending that the birth "was not a 'miracle in the desert' but the product of strong material and historical circumstances."[29] Likewise, in speaking about the spread of "radical, or political, Islam" in the present, he emphasizes the "need to understand [the] structural aspect of it."[30]

Consonant with his advocacy of the mythological method, Öcalan limits his critique of religion to the critique of *religious dogmatism*. He rejects a "spirit-matter dichotomy," and even denies that the "richness of life ... can be explained through the dogma of an external creator." Even so, he is openly adamant that "[i]t is meaningless to claim that there is nothing besides a physical life."[31] Perhaps most crucially, he considers the religious impulse akin to the artistic impulse, or even the impulse to cultivate knowledge—all important "metaphysical feature[s]" he alleges to be "indispensable" for "endur[ing] war, death, lust, passion, beauty, etc."[32]

For Öcalan, religious convictions are closely connected with collective memory. This helps explain their persistence. The sacred religious books continue to be revered not due to the appeal of the dogmas and doctrines about an "abstract god" or even associated "rituals," but, instead, because "humans can feel the meaning and traces of their own life and story in these books." They are books that contain and congeal "the memory of living society," which humanity "will not abandon so easily."[33]

Öcalan's take on religion has evolved over the past decade. In *The Roots of Civilisation*, Öcalan was already emphasizing the link between dogmatism and official religions dedicated to the legitimation and perpetuation of hierarchy.[34] Nevertheless, in that work, he was relatively friendly to monotheism, contending that the monotheistic religions "emerged at a period of profound crisis in social development," and, indeed, that they triggered "a revolution in the mental and ethical character of humankind."[35] In comparison with the "polytheistic" and "totemic" conceptualizations that had preceded it, Öcalan then contended, monotheism had "represented a higher form of logical reasoning," potentially appealing "to the whole of humankind," relating to "a more complex stage in the history of human intellect."[36] Moreover, in his discussions of the history of Christianity and Islam, he explicitly distinguished between an original revolutionary and emancipatory impulse from below, later co-opted by rulers and converted into an instrument of hierarchy and control.

However, in volume one of the *Manifesto for a Democratic Civilization*, Öcalan seems to have reconsidered. He now laments the demise of the mythological method and its substitution by "religious dogmatism" serving to justify hierarchy, which he now associates directly with monotheism. Moreover, he now appears much more sympathetic to polytheism and to notions of immanent divinity. He even goes so far as to claim that "polytheism occurr[ed] during an era of tribal equality," and that the "decrease in number and the ranking of gods according to supremacy is closely related to the administrative protocol."[37] A questionable generalization, at best, given the polytheism that characterized and served to legitimate Greek patriarchal and slaveholding city-states, not to mention the Roman Empire.

In fact, monotheism has been both a force for enslavement and emancipation. The same is true for polytheism. See Greece and Rome in the moves toward democracy and domination. The grand narrative of monotheism versus polytheism binaries falls apart under intense historical scrutiny.

In nominally monotheistic traditions, a close look at those from the oppressed classes reveals a consciousness that appreciates a polyphony of divine presences, whether they be found in the Kabbalah or among the Sufi, Quaker, or other mystics of Judaism, Islam, and Christianity. The march toward a spiritless monotheism has been led by societal elites since Akhenaton, Josiah, and Zoroaster, who made intellectual and ritual acceptance of monotheism a primary weapon against the "superstitious" peasant classes still in contact with the myriad expression of the One, yet without the need to curtail the expression of others.

However, even in the strongest self-proclaimed monotheistic societies, the peasants and some fortunate few from other classes find themselves confronted by spirit(s) that are beyond the doctrinal proscriptions of monotheistic religious dogma. Freedom is free even from its monotheistic master. Nat Turner, Frederick Douglass, Harriet Tubman, Martin Luther King, Jr., Malcolm X, Sojourner Truth, John Brown, and many more experienced a spiritual presence that urged them on toward freedom.

This point against grand narratives that would pose a monotheism versus polytheism binary is crucial and worthy of closer attention. Indeed, one of us (Don) spent much of last summer researching the origins of monotheism and its importance for the West. This was not intentional, but since we kept finding different views regarding its origins and place in history, we had to pursue it more deeply. It is the Holy Grail of Western religious ideology. Scholars expressed deep differences in opinion but carefully refrained from directing their critical comments toward any of their scholarly comrades.

Hypothesis 1: monotheism originated with the Pharaoh Akhenaton (1300s BCE) when he claimed that deities other than the sun (Aton) did not exist. He changed his name from Amenhotep to signify this change. This led him to destroy images of other deities (Amon among them) and to close down the temples of those who proclaimed allegiance to other gods. He was, however, more of a lover than a fighter, and his kingdom experienced military defeat. A serious no-no if you want your god to be held in high esteem. He died mysteriously, and many scholars believe he was assassinated by the priests of the temples he had closed. His worship of Aton never seemed to gain popular appeal.

Hypothesis 2: other Egyptologists believe that Egyptians exhibited a belief in monotheism by their theological understanding that a single and mysterious high god, composed of male and female elements, began creation through a dialectical process that led to a Trinitarian or "Triadic" structure that is found expressed in various forms throughout Egyptian history. Others call this a henotheistic structure, henotheism being defined as god at the apex of creation that is immanently related to the lesser deities. It is not "polytheism," which would mean many gods that operate independently.

As you can begin to see, this whole business of "monotheism" has become increasingly complex for scholars to accurately define. Yet the development of a "true" monotheism is seen as an important development in human consciousness. It desacralizes the world to an extent that the possibility of human invention is increased. But this has extreme political importance, because it is used to distinguish "godly" societies from lesser "pagan, ungodly" societies. The development of monotheism is a dividing point between the wise and the foolish, the wicked and the good, the civilized and the uncivilized.

Hypothesis 3: monotheism springs from the teaching of Zoroaster/Zarathustra, 600–500 BCE. The Jewish exiles in Babylon recognized this and incorporated it into their post-exilic religious understanding as a form of lost knowledge that was recovered during the time of Josiah immediately before the exile of the Jewish state. In this version, Josiah discovered the Deuteronomic texts that insisted that God is One God, and since the Jews had been worshipping other false gods they were going to be punished by being taken into exile. Jewish scribes never assign credit to either the Egyptians or the Persians for their monotheistic belief.

However, there is no historical evidence that shows that the people of Israel and Judah ever practiced a monotheistic devotion to YHWH as the only God. The historical evidence shows that the Jewish peasants worshipped other gods throughout their rise to power in Palestine.

Even so, monotheism became a marker that distinguished the Jewish religion from others. This belief was passed down to Christians and Muslims, who, when they gained power, made this the litmus test on steroids. Those who failed this test were persecuted. And since the three major expressions of monotheism had different understandings of what that looked like, they also persecuted each other for their "unorthodox beliefs."

On a sociological and theological level this belief in monotheism holds no water, since Jews, Christians, and Muslims not only differ with each other in how they conceptualize and practice "monotheism," but there have been and are competing expressions of monotheistic belief within their own traditions.

Against Orientalism?
Öcalan elaborates what could be called a "Fertile Crescent–centric" metanarrative about the arc of human history, including a story about the rise and trajectory of "civilization." It is a metanarrative that is ultimately overly dependent on Eurocentric historiography, one that at times even reproduces certain rather crude and dubious tropes about Aryans versus Semites. Indeed, like so much of the Eurocentric historiography on which his account relies, Öcalan's treatment of ethnicity often displays a tendency to anachronism, essentialism, and reification, and too often ignores liminal spaces and downplays the prevalence of hybridity.

So too does Öcalan's metanarrative reproduce certain characteristic exclusions. Most tellingly, for Öcalan, the story of human history begins with an exit from Africa. In his account, even Egypt is rendered derivative, its Africanness basically denied. This is especially problematic given Öcalan's expressed ambition to provide a metanarrative capable of underpinning and fueling resistance to capitalist modernity in favor of an alternative "democratic modernity." As Cedric Robinson has rightly emphasized, "the obliteration of the African past from European consciousness was the culmination of a process a thousand years long and one at the root of European historical identity."[38]

Alas, Öcalan is not infallible, but his narrative is nonetheless powerful. Quiescence, consent, and support for the injustices of neoliberal capitalism, not to mention support for the war crimes and spiraling violence committed in the ongoing Orwellian global war on "terror"—such attitudes are underpinned and perpetuated by the propagation of dominant myths. Effective resistance means that such myths need more than just deconstruction. Belief in viable and desirable alternatives to the present order need to be encouraged and elaborated as well.

In this vein, Öcalan's sweeping historical vision of the dialectical struggle between domination and resistance as the motor of history is not to be underestimated. Indeed, his "dialectical naturalist" (Bookchin) effort to denaturalize hierarchies, to identify their origins, and to uncover even deeper egalitarian and libertarian alternatives is most commendable, especially given the conditions of duress in which it has been composed.

But knowledge is always social, and Öcalan's manifesto is, of course, not the first or the last word. He certainly points in at least some of the right directions: both forward and backward (if not upward, even though the verdict is by now unanimous that Nietzsche is dead, while the jury is still out on the God of Abraham).

This is an edited version of the 2016 review of Abdullah Öcalan, *Manifesto for a Democratic Civilization: Civilization, Volume 1: The Age of Masked Gods and Disguised Kings* (Porsgrunn, NO: New Compass Press, 2015) [Turkish: *Demokratik Uygarlık Manifestosu, birinci kitap: Uygarlık. Maskeli Tanrılar ve Örtük Krallar Çağı* (İstanbul: Aram, 2009)]. The unabridged version was published on the website of the Peace in Kurdistan campaign (https://peaceinkurdistancampaign.com).

Donald H. Matthews is an ordained Methodist minister who received his PhD from the Divinity School at the University of Chicago. He has written numerous books, articles, and papers and has taught at several universities and seminaries, including the University of California Santa Cruz, St. Louis University, Colgate-Rochester-Crozier Divinity School, and the University of Puget Sound. He directed the Black Studies Program at the University of Missouri, Kansas City, and the Master of Divinity Program at Naropa University.

Thomas Jeffrey Miley is a lecturer of political sociology at the University of Cambridge. His research interests include nationalism, religion and politics, and empirical democratic theory. He has published widely on the dynamics of nationalist conflict and accommodation in Spain and, increasingly, in Turkey. His current research project is on comparative struggles for self-determination in the twenty-first century. He has participated in several delegations to Turkey and different parts of Kurdistan, including to Rojava, and is a member of the executive board of the EU Turkey Civic Commission (EUTCC).

Notes

1 Abdullah Öcalan, *Manifesto for a Democratic Civilization, Volume 1: Civilization: The Age of Masked Gods and Disguised Kings* (Porsgrunn, NO: New Compass Press, 2015); 2nd revised edition will be published by PM Press in 2021.
2 Abdullah Öcalan, *Democratic Confederalism* (Cologne: International Initiative, 2011).
3 Öcalan, *Manifesto for a Democratic Civilization, Volume 1*, 91.
4 Ibid., 94.
5 Ibid., 163.
6 Ibid., 122–24.
7 Ibid., 122.
8 Ibid., 139.
9 Ibid., 123.
10 Ibid., 124.
11 Ibid., 139.
12 Ibid., 140.
13 Ibid., 142.
14 Ibid., 140–1.
15 Ibid., 146.
16 Ibid., 149.
17 Ibid., 159.
18 Ibid., 154.
19 Ibid., 157.
20 Ibid., 160.
21 Ibid., 158.
22 Ibid., 54.
23 Ibid., 81.
24 Ibid., 43.
25 Ibid., 44.
26 Ibid., 194.
27 Ibid., 274.
28 Ibid., 169.
29 Ibid., 269.
30 Ibid., 272.
31 Ibid., 62, 76–77.
32 Ibid., 76–77.
33 Ibid., 117.
34 Abdullah Öcalan, *Prison Writings: The Roots of Civilisation*, trans. Klaus Happel (London: Pluto Press, 2007).
35 Ibid., 56.

36 Ibid., 62.
37 Öcalan, *Manifesto for a Democratic Civilization, Volume 1*, 168.
38 Cedric J. Robinson, *Black Marxism: The Making of the Black Radical Tradition* (Chapel Hill: University of North Carolina Press, 1983).

TEN

Historiography, Gender, and Resistance

Muriel González Athenas

In the following remarks, I will concentrate on Abdullah Öcalan's defense briefs found in his book *Beyond State, Power, and Violence*, which was completed in 2004. I will particularly focus on the subchapter on the liberation from social sexism.[1] This passage of the book, embedded in social analyses that make proposals for social liberation, addresses women and their enslavement. The outline of a social liberation from capitalism, statism, exploitation, and war is comprehensively conceptualized, and it is not only directed against certain social structures and policies but seeks a fundamentally different society, with a completely new human being imaginable: a new or different human being, who, in his or her human relations, will behave differently than what we have known up to now. The conversation I want to have with this book is concerned with the epistemological approaches taken to relations between the sexes.

Power through Gender Relations—an Ordering Category

From the outset, it is clear that the naturalization or biologizing of gender roles is seen critically. We read: "All scientific, moral, and political approaches to this topic used to insinuate from the outset that what is happening to the woman is simply natural."[2] In many places in the book, Öcalan makes clear what exactly he means when he talks about what "is happening" to the woman, namely, enslavement. In this subchapter, he is quite explicit: "It has to be brought to consciousness that no tribe, no class, and no nation has ever been subjected to a slavery as systematic as the slavery of the woman."[3] The inequality of the sexes, the argument goes,

is presupposed as a natural episteme (disposition in the realms of thinking, perceiving, and speaking) by various social institutions, including
religion. The concept "women are like this and men like this" and, concomitantly, their hierarchical evaluation is attributed to almost every line
of thinking. I would add that it is very difficult to think differently about
this perspective or presupposition, as it has not been historized or prop-
erly situated.[4] Positing a relationship of inequality without ever calling
it into question or even allowing it to become visible as a construct pries
this way of thinking away from historicity and, therefore, from recognizing its development into what it has become. If we don't know that it is a
construct, because nobody dares to say so, then we have no choice but to
regard it as a part of nature. Going a step further, it seems necessary to
me to also call into question biology or the sciences of life if they postulate
bipolar biological sexes. Here, I am taking up the ideas of Harraway, Butler,
Voß, and very many others, who, always in connection with a critical contemplation of the role of science, regard biological sex as a whole as a construct: biological, social, and moral. Our modern sciences play a big role in
the biologistic narrative of the sexes. On this issue, I don't think Öcalan's
book goes far enough and frequently falls back into the naturalization
of the conceptual split into two sexes. I will address this further later on.

Let's come back to the biologizing of the social roles. This biologizing simultaneously hierarchizes, or, at least, that is its goal. It is thus not
surprising that it is not just those who profit from or are privileged by
such an understanding and such a social structure (that is, masculinity)
but also the supposedly weaker parties who reproduce it. This is the only
way the gender relationship can function as a modern ordering system.
If the oppressed were always held in their role by violence alone, neither
Europe and its states nor for that matter the entire global capitalist system
would work. This is the functionality of power. Power is productive for all
who participate in such a system. It does not only produce the privileged
but also those around them. It is the mechanics of power that makes it
so difficult to break it down. And human beings crave power. The many
regulative and—politically expressed—hierarchical social structures by
which different mutually dependent axioms work are not hierarchical
in a pyramidal way.[5] Instead, they must be thought of as circular and as
the matrix of our actions. Categories such as gender, ethnicity, class, age,
sexual orientation, physical integrity, religion, etc. are social constructs
that are presupposed and are thus perceived as quasi-natural or biological.[6]

And all individuals strive to fulfill these biologisms. Depending on the political constellation, women too possess power and exploit it in their relationships with others. We only need to call to mind female politicians or the racist policies of the white women's movements at the beginning of the twentieth century and in the 1970s and 1980s, as well as so-called third-wave feminism.[7] The Black women's movement, the Chicana movement in the US, the autonomous women's and lesbian movements in the Federal Republic of Germany, as well as, more recently, the queer women of color movement in Germany, all criticize the Eurocentrism in feminist positions that ignore the positionings and identities of racialized women or play them off against each other, as in the case of the tightening of the German law governing sexual offenses as a trade-off for the tightening of the asylum law.[8] Such examples are often found in the history of the women's movements, for example, in the white suffragette movement in the US, which fought for the women's suffrage at the expense of the demands of the abolitionists. This meant the vote for women but only for the white women. It was with good reason that Sojourner Truth asked at a women's rights convention in Akron, Ohio, in 1851: "And ain't I a woman?"[9]

There were similar antagonistic developments in the German women's movement, specifically, between liberal and proletarian demands. The colonial women's movement in Germany is another wonderful example of this that I want to touch upon. When analyzing social power relations and their mechanics, it is helpful to track their development and genesis, that is, to historize them. Their historical origin can tell us something about the way discourses are enabled and about their role in social conflicts. It is not just the various feminisms that must be criticized as insufficient or analytically false, as Öcalan does in various places. Our task is, in fact, an exacting analysis of the functioning of power.[10]

German Colonialism and Gender Relations

Since the beginning of the eighteenth century, both anthropology, which was then emerging, and philosophy have tried to capture the world by metrical-statistical procedures. Colonial voyages and predatory raids also generated massive collections of numbers that were ordered according to the recommended schemas of measurement and description.

At the same time, a mass of stolen objects, bones, and skulls were steadily transported to European archives and museums, and there are even merchants who shipped human beings to Europe and its ethnological expositions. Here, they were, among other things, examined and measured by anthropologists. All these numbers are, like today's algorithms, quantified and qualified, and the results are presented to a large public in professional journals, expositions, conferences, popular science books, museums, etc., and thus inscribed into an everyday discourse.

The epistemological interest of the classification of "races" is to secure the superiority of Europe, in many different ways and with the help of various scientific disciplines. In the German Empire, this form of science was closely connected to colonial policy. This measuring madness reached a hideous climax after the Herero Wars, when skulls of hanged and shot Herero were shipped en masse to Germany. Herero women held in prison camps were forced to separate the flesh from the skulls with glass shards. The genocide of the Herero and Nama was carried out during and after the suppression of uprisings of these peoples against the German colonial power in German-Southwest Africa from 1904 to 1908.

The category of gender/sex is constitutive for this measuring and classification procedure. The supposedly objective numbers are won on the basis of racializing and genderizing presuppositions. They represent measuring procedures that purport to be aspects of scientific data acquisition. Since they are subject to racializing presuppositions, the results produce "races" as a starting point. Actually, it is the classification into different "races" and sexes that generates them, filling the category of "race" with content (in a notably open and almost pliant way). But this discourse would never have been successful had there not been a widespread socialized interest in it. In was only the supposed knowledge about the colonies, their inhabitants, and geopolitical-geographical innovations that allowed the scientific discourse around "races" to fall on a fertile soil. But this specifically occidental form of "world appropriation" began with the Enlightenment and did not require a lot of "rehearsing" before being used to racialize humanity in the nineteenth century.

The latter was preceded by the categorization and normalization of gender. An asymmetrical and biological ordering of the sexes had already begun by the end of the fifteenth century, reaching the climax of its implementation in the witch trials, the Inquisition, and the Reformation of the sixteenth and seventeenth centuries. All of this means, for example, that the sexual division of labor had already been established and that ideologies such as that of Adam Smith (the breadwinner model—the husband is the principal earner in the family) did not require any justification.

At the same time, the scientification of society set in during the course of the so-called Enlightenment, making it relatively easy for the various scientific disciplines to establish a certain biologistic gender and racializing ordering as the basis of all research. Starkly simplified, the Enlightenment meant the replacement of God by the sciences. Now, the hierarchization of the population was no longer fixed by a divine order but, instead, by the order of a so-called nature, which was "confirmed" by the sciences. At the end, there is, so to speak, a genderization down to the last bone. The biologistic charging of the female body took place in the 1750s, engineered by physicians, anatomists, etc. The gender construct was broken down to its minutiae and invaded every body part.[11]

I must once more return to Öcalan's book to stress that my analysis of the development of European societies during the Enlightenment is less positive than his.[12] It shifted thinking but did not necessarily improve the situation for society at the level of rights. We must not forget that the terrible witch trials and the activities of the Inquisition all over Europe took place during the Enlightenment not in the Middle Ages. The final result of the Enlightenment was the French Revolution, whose political declaration of human rights does not even know of women; Olympe de Gouges found herself forced to write a *Declaration of the Rights of the Woman and the Female Citizen* in 1791.[13] It is probably also a result of modern historiography that the course of humanity's history is always portrayed positively. The emphasis is always on progress, modernity (whatever this is supposed to mean), and development.

But these characteristics of the categories of gender and "race" are modern, not medieval or ancient, which, as is always the case, has to do with the interests at play and the distribution of power. The commonality is the collective attribution of properties that justify subordination, discrimination, and hierarchy. But that is the extent of the commonality.

In the case of racism, whole closed groups are created that are then forced in their entirety into asymmetries. With the gender relationship, it is more individualized and dependent on both issues surrounding intimate relationships and categories like class. Therefore, women can also easily enjoy privileges that they can express vis-à-vis racialized human beings.

For example, later in the nineteenth century, the age of the economic and political rise of the European bourgeoisie, bourgeois gender ordering and colonial ordering were inseparably connected. This was also true for the German colonies. The reordering of gender relations in the nineteenth century propagated a dualist, heterosexist picture of the bourgeois family, based on the idea of the family as the "germ cell" of the nation. The characters of the sexes thusly constructed were considered natural and universal. Discussions about the relations of the sexes or their respective role attributions were used by the bourgeoisie to demarcate itself from other social classes and, particularly, from other nationalities. Examples for this are the juxtaposition of the "German housewife" and the "coquettish Frenchwoman," the "backward, uncivilized Chinese woman" and the "licentious and wild factory women" or, alternately, the "industrious, honest, and virtuous factory woman." Thus, distinctions in the gender relations served to distinguish the German colonialists from those alleged to be "uncivilized." This argument also served to legitimate colonial rule—the "civilizing" mission continued to play a decisive role in the nineteenth century. Moreover, the colonies were described as "virgin" territories waiting to be discovered, conquered, and, of course, civilized by the white man. In this way, the populations of the colonized areas were additionally connotated as female. They were then attributed so-called feminine characteristics, such as passivity, irrationality, and naturalness. With this, a transfer of one's own gender ordering to the colonial relationship and the latter's continued influence were fixed. The colonialists were confirmed in their masculinity (and their gender roles as a whole), as well as in their colonial and imperial superiority. Therefore, the women in the colonies were always turned into objects of white desire in travel reports, media, letters, and public political discourses, as well as in science. African women and men were associated with licentious sexuality. White males regarded sexual "conquest" or "civilizing" as their prerogative.

In the German colonies, what was regarded as masculine or feminine was never simply a matter of a person's sex but also of the social status, nationality, and "race" attributed to individuals. It was precisely this interweaving of the categories that brought ambiguity to the colonial gender order, which had to be constantly discussed and renegotiated. This did not only happen in the colonies but in the empire as well. Thus, there were very few marriages or informal relationships between German women and colonized males. Such relationships were frowned upon and seen as totally disrupting the colonial gender order. Such "mixed marriages" blurred desired borders, and it was these borders between black and white that colonial rule rested upon. The children of such relationships couldn't be categorized within this binary logic of color. Moreover, there was a "fear" that German men who lived in a mixed family of this sort would forget their own national culture, which, in turn, would fundamentally call into question white German claims to power.

A widespread recipe for countering this potential so-called "loss" was to settle more German women in the colonies, so that white males would no longer feel obliged to marry colonized women. As such, white women of a nubile age were recruited for emigration to the colonies to marry white men and produce white children. Some currents of the German women's movements participated in these enlistment campaigns and policies, not least the Women's League of the German Colonial Society (1907).[14] These women were also expected to establish German culture and bourgeois norms such as discipline, cleanliness, and order in colonial societies.

Recent research has classed the nationalist and imperialist minded women and their associations as part of the then rising new political right. According to researchers, the crisis of the traditional party system and the structural changes in German society around 1900 opened more space and allowed more influence for these positions and the agitation policy of these associations. This was one of the lines that contributed to the nationalist slant of the Empire's political culture at a time when liberal democratic and socialist demands for individual freedom, equality, and political participation could also clearly be heard.

At the same time, the colonies created an imaginary world that allowed both men and women to project their dreams into the "wild, natural world of Africa." More individual freedom and a new self-understanding inspired colonial fantasies. In this way, colonial discourse offered a connection between internal equality and external discrimination. The dominating principle of this new discourse was racial ideology, which differentiated between the domestic constitutive people, on the one hand, and the colonial peoples, on the other hand.

All of this was based on the German gender order in the Empire. Ideas about marriage, sexuality, household, and child-rearing were to be primarily conveyed by German emigrant women. For many German women, emigrating to the colonies and founding a household over which they presided, gaining dominion over colonized women and men in the process, meant a rise in social position. We know from many colonial reports, literary documents, and letters that German women contributed to the construction of race and gender in the colonies. Not only did they control the colonized household personnel, they were able to assign them roles at will.[15] On the basis of a racist-biologistic conception of the human being—"inept" and "lazy" domestic servants—certain kinds of work were assigned to women and men. But this genderized division of labor, at least in part, bumped up against previous and different gender orderings. Thus, colonized men sometimes refused to engage in certain kinds of work that they regarded as feminine or as the task of women. Even so, they were forced by their "mistresses" to do such work, including sweeping, cleaning, and laundering. In this way, the power base was continuously restored, and, at the same time, colonized men were "feminized" in order to subordinate them to the racializing colonial order. But the fact that this order had to be, time and again, produced and cemented in all social areas (politics, administration, household, etc.) through a permanent colonization process also shows that it was neither natural nor self-evident—as does the fact that the colonized repeatedly resisted and subverted, rejected, ignored, transformed, etc. this order in their everyday survival strategies.[16] But the colonial gender order, parts of which are still in effect today, was a very powerful one, which established itself not just in the colonies but also in the Empire. Women of color are still eroticized and exoticized, while men of color are still frequently presented as a threat to white women, much as individuals of color as such are presented as a threat to the Occident. Even today, the exoticizing and sexualization of a group serves the elevation of one's own status in the context of a European civilizational discourse or a right-wing populist nationalism.

Of course, history, even if it has been spun here very briefly around two common threads (scientification and colonialism), is not linear, chronological, and consistent. German colonial history is also discontinuous, angular, full of contradictions, as well as being a little bit refractory. There were certainly criticisms of both the dominant gender order and of imperial colonial policy toward the end of the nineteenth century.

The example just given aims at making resistance thinkable through a different kind of historiography, of recognizing power axes, and of developing the ability to fight or change them in our political practice.

Strategies in the Political Struggle

One can interpret the struggles described above as grappling for power or as the rise toward power. Sometimes, the strategy is "We would rather have a small piece of the cake than none at all," even though the cake is poisoned, but generally these political positions don't contradict each other. A woman can be a feminist but certainly also a racist or not have any consciousness of racism, because she isn't affected by it—but perhaps also because she closes her eyes and her heart to it as a survival strategy. Different categories of power can also have different effects within an individual's biography, for example, the effects of impoverishment, of getting older, of war, of exile, of a change in gender, etc. The categories cut right through us, draw us in, but remain permeable. This is not to deny that there are categories that are not permeable, or, rather, that some, in their interplay, don't leave space for permeability. Racism and gender are categories that have been biologized or, to put it another way, naturalized so vehemently and for so long that they are difficult to break through once they have both deprivileged you. A woman of color or a Black woman has no *passing* in these categories, but class can allow her to acquire a different social position, as we see in the case of Michelle Obama. Nonetheless, being both Black and a woman, she was repeatedly a focus for the media in a way that no male political figure would ever experience.

These categories, on which, in my opinion, the axioms and power axes of our society are built, are flexible and adjustable, depending on the specific political and economic elite, which inevitably involves the whole of society in its projects. Thus, in the 1960s, there was a small but economically and socially powerful elite in the US around institutions such as the Ford Foundation or the Rockefeller Foundation that held the view that the planet was overpopulated—not just overpopulated in the sense that the previous capitalist population policy, which was about quantity and not the quality of life, ought to be criticized and rethought. For them, there were and are simply too many poor people in the world. Since this lobby had and still has a huge influence, starting in the 1960s, scientists have been developing birth control programs for countries in the Global South, such as India and China, that is, for regions with huge populations. Among them are some of the countries with the largest populations in the world, making them home to very many poor people. At the same time, these were also countries that were willing to accept forced population policies, such as the one-child policy, legalized abortion, and forced sterilization, in exchange for economic aid. Combined with a preference for boys, this led to a defeminization of the population that is now taking its revenge on capitalism. Today, the tables have turned, and there are millions fewer women than there are men. And, again, the women have to pay the price, with an increase in kidnappings, forced marriages, etc. Abortion is again prohibited and sometimes punished in a draconian manner. How could it be otherwise? The female body is a plaything of the powerful. It is the particular task of occidental feminists to attack the policies and institutions that articulate and enforce such imperial strategies.

Is Gender Nature or Culture?

One pitfall I see in the argument in Öcalan's subchapter on the liberation from social sexism is the renaturalization of gender itself. What exactly is nature, and who determines what nature is? If we assume that the sciences are subjected to certain interests, as well as to the social power axes, how can we start with the scientific definition of nature? The determination of what qualifies as nature is in constant flux, and with it the determination of gender and sex. There has been a lot of research and much has been said about this, and in the process sex as a biological inevitable has been deconstructed. Let us talk of many sexes, or let us leave gender as a physical construction aside. Let us instead speak of the instances of action that produce gender (doing, or performing, gender). The reason for this step is that gender and gender relations must be understood as products of historical processes. Heide Wunder has shown that, with the institution of the married and working couple that shares responsibility for family and production in the household and on the farm or in workshop, early modern gender relations knew neither a separation into female and male spheres (interior/exterior) nor a separation of the work achievements into production and reproduction.[17] In this model, which Wunder developed based on her investigation of bourgeois, crafts, and peasant households, femininity was not defined by negation and dependency on the masculine but through work and economic activity.[18] These ideas about gender were derived from early modern economic knowledge and precapitalist knowledge about local production regimes. Wunder described this as the "familiarization of work and life," because, according to her, eleventh- and twelfth-century peasant and commercial production shifted from the large households of the masters to smaller households and family associations, and a division of labor established itself between the wage labor of professional and unskilled workers.[19] Both processes, she says, had repercussions on relations between the sexes: "The male/female division of labor in the shop or on the farm and in the family didn't strictly follow the allocation of domestic work to the wife and commercial production destined for the market to the husband. . . . The problem was solved differently, namely, by the division of labor within the sexes: hard physical work was often done by the (unmarried) maids or female day workers, while the wife took on the work of a more organizational character and of cooking."[20] That is, the division of labor was structured by the practical activity and empirical knowledge that translated gender relations into everyday life. Conversely, knowledge about gender was not completely submerged in the routines of economic activity.

As such, corporative society provided women with different opportunities than does the capitalist-bourgeois class society of advanced modernity: "Multipolarity opens up different scopes of action, and it remains to clarify in detail what was negotiated in each case about the use of gender stereotypes and gender orders so that it could be of such great importance for institutions and individuals."[21] Recent research has shown that these ideas were valid not just for married couples and could indeed be legitimately applied to an enlarged circle of family members. Moreover, these ideas didn't draw on the later ideal of the romantic relationship of a couple in love but were conceptualized as a contract-like working community.[22] Seen against this background, the bipolar, complementary gender model that has been the defining one until the present day and has shaped controversial public debates is by no means universal.[23] As Karin Hausen explained in her analysis of various bourgeois encyclopedias, it only emerged around 1800, as the result and expression of the social transformation from the "whole house" to the bourgeois family, which constituted a qualitative and quantitative displacement. About the nineteenth century, Hausen stresses that between the gender-specific division of labor, on the one hand, and the market-oriented economic development, on the other hand, the generation of the socially desired gender order had to be permanently reproduced anew in the sense of *doing gender*.[24]

I now want to talk about another example in history that undermines previous assumptions about gender relations: the evaluation of work and the sexual division of labor. The division of labor has long been understood as an ahistorical structural principle of society that has always been there or has existed at least since the Middle Ages. The division of labor has been linked to the gender relations. In the next section, I clarify why this is, in fact, a very modern approach.

The Social Division of Labor in Modernity

My thesis here is that it is historiography that prevents us from seeing gender relations in work, with the goal of securing capitalist dynamics, and which establishes a caesura between "the past" and "modernity."

Older historical research on the economy and crafts points to caesuras that distinguish the so-called modern system of economic thinking from previous, evaluating modernity as a positive development. But that was not actually the nature of these caesuras. Guild organizations, protests against new technologies, journeymen's uprisings, professionalization processes, women in the crafts and in the markets are now read as an extension of the scope of action, as economic strategies, and also as pointing in the direction of solidarity and collectivity. The conception of work implied here must be more closely examined if we are to accurately locate it socially and then evaluate it. The definition of work itself, its division into various categories and the way it is evaluated are among the crucial differentiation mechanisms within societies. Labor and the division of labor are key categories for understanding social, political, and, therefore, dominant hierarchical gender relations. But they cannot be evaluated separately from socially normative divisions of labor, such as intra-craft hierarchies (master craftswomen, widows, apprentice girls, etc.). In many histories of gender, the professionalization process at the beginning of early modernity is regarded as evidence of increased hierarchy in the division of labor and increase in the perception of "work" as a positive value. "Professionalization denotes the cultural profiling and increased independence of professional positions that are distinguished by privileged powers with regard to opportunities for access, qualification, and control, and which, therefore, enjoyed pronounced social prestige."[25] But whether and to what extent these divisions of labor meant increased hierarchy of the sexes must always remain an open question. Were there areas of work that were regarded as feminine or masculine? Was a different, that is, gender-related evaluation of work deduced from that? To pursue these questions, it was necessary to work out, in a network-like fashion, the social location, framework, and evaluation of the work done by women. The status of the individual craftswomen in the respective guilds determined her work areas and how her work was evaluated. This status is what gave "work" its value. That is, the value of the work was not determined by the way it was done or by the price it demanded but by the status of the person who did it. The way a commodity was produced determined its value and its price. In this, the materials used, the expenditure, and the price established in regional and transregional markets also played a role. It was, however, the individual product that was remunerated.

One of the locations that structured the division of labor was cohabitation in the family. Older research into the family and the household assumed that family economies were similar in the countryside and in the city. This idea has long shaped research on women and work. Perspectives that saw extended families living and working in a single household as the dominant economic principle could not do justice to the differing spaces in gender relations. Even the idea of a house as the spatial corollary of the family, as a social unit, cannot be transferred to the housing conditions of the time in question, just as the cross-generational housing and economic association cannot be transferred to the conditions of today. It is, however, safe to say that familial networks were important for economic activities as a whole.

The way of life that was established in the Middle Ages, which located housekeeping and economic activity within marriage, is the mode of life of the working couple.[26] In urban craft codes, this form was presupposed as the basic structure for joint economic activity. The working couple had established itself in the guild crafts by the Middle Ages. The concept was thus not merely an instrument of domination theoretically produced via discourses about marriage but was the actual practice of craftspeople. In the crafts' environment, marriage was not thought of as a bond based on love and passion. The house and the household were only possible through the liaison of the two spouses who were both fundamental to producing and acting in the urban economy.[27] The work of both was necessary to sustain a household or a workshop. The crucial issue here is that nubility became the precondition for social acceptance and, as a consequence, for being admitted into the craft.

But back to the economic caesuras that historiography has construed. Allegedly backward craftspeople have time and again been cited as examples of an "obsolete" economic mentality. In this framework, modernity and its economic mechanics are juxtaposed with this mentality as—allegedly—the final and highest stage of progress. But conflicts surrounding the crafts did not necessarily have anything to do with backwardness or opposition to modernization. This is nothing more than a contemporary interpretation—an interpretation of craftspeople as a class that is trying to sustain jobs, and for whom guaranteeing equal conditions to all was a goal that was closer to home. With regard to gender, it must be said that for the execution of a craft the question of gender played a subordinate role, with other categories being more important. A network of different mechanisms of inclusion and exclusion that includes social status and partially defines it determines who has access to the craft. Thus, in a big city like Cologne, until 1796, women were permitted to work in all crafts, could become journeywomen and master craftswomen, and were allowed to run their own workshops and train journeymen and women. Moreover, the concept of the working couple needs to be extended to include non-spouses: mother-daughter, father-daughter, father-son, mother-son, and master craftswoman-journeyman (with no obligation to marry).[28]

The discussion of the division of labor and gender could introduce greater diversity into the existing linear history written by white males— or, rather, undermine it and create the space for many other histories. These other histories could be tools for the development of resistance. But we must always remember: history has long been the narrative of the victors. The historiography of modernity emerged in order to recount this narrative. And to give this narrative content, the modern sciences emerged. We cannot know how a society without power works, because we have never experienced it, but step by step we can become conscious.

This essay was written for this book.

Muriel Gonzales Athenas has been politically active in the feminist movement, groups, and networks since the 1980s. More recently, she has been part of antifascist and migrant organizations, whose interconnection has always been a focus of her work. Since New Year's Eve 2015, she has been increasingly involved with publications, events, and actions with an intersectional view of racism and sexism. Of particular importance to her are collective organizing and feminist and antiracist solidarity. She has a doctorate in history on the subject of work and gender (2010). She is currently working at the Ruhr University, Bochum. Her academic work addresses gender history, the history of cultural industries, feminist epistemology and methodology, and the history of women's movements, as well as conceptions of space, postcolonial studies, and decolonial perspectives and practices. She is a member of the team of specialists working on the Zeitzeuginnen der Arcus-Stiftung project and the Queergesund Studienteams at TH Dortmund, with Professor Gabriele Dennert. She is currently working on a postdoctoral thesis on "Decentring Europe" via map analysis.

Notes

1 Page numbers refer to the German edition: Abdullah Öcalan, *Jenseits von Staat, Macht und Gewalt* (Neuss: Mezopotamien Verlag, 2010). For the relevant subchapter, see 189–97; English edition, Abdullah Öcalan, *Beyond State, Power, and Violence* (Oakland: by PM Press, forthcoming 2020).

2 Öcalan, *Jenseits von Staat*, 189.

3 Ibid.

4 Sandra Harding, *Feministische Wissenschaftstheorie: zum Verhältnis von Wissenschaft und sozialem Geschlecht* (Hamburg: Argument Verlag, 1990).

5 Michel Foucault, *The History of Sexuality 1: The Will to Knowledge* (London: Penguin, 1998).

6 Donna Harraway, *Simians, Cyborgs and Women: The Reinvention of Nature* (London: Free Association Books, 1991).

7 Chandra Talpade Mohanty, "Under Western Eyes: Feminist Scholarship and Colonial Discourses," *Feminist Review* no. 30 (Autumn 1988): 61–88.

8 Melanie Brazzell, ed., *Was macht uns wirklich sicher? Ein Toolkit zu intersektionaler transformativer Gerechtigkeit jenseits von Gefängnis und Polizei* (Münster: Edition Assemblage, 2018), 13–23.

9 Feminismus Seminar, ed., *Feminismus in historischer Perspektive* (Bielefeld: transcript, 2014), 51–115.

10 For example, see Öcalan, *Jenseits von Staat*, 192.

11 See Heinz Jürgen Voß, *Making Sex Revisited: Dekonstruktion des Geschlechts aus biologisch-medizinischer Perspektive* (Bielefeld: transcript, 2010).

12 For example, see Öcalan, *Jenseits von Staat*, 134.

13 Olympe de Gouges, *Declaration of the Rights of the Woman* (London: Octopus Books, 2018 [1791]).

14 Katharina Walgenbach, *"Die weiße Frau als Trägerin deutscher Kultur": Koloniale Diskurse über Geschlecht, "Rasse" und Klasse im Kaiserreich* (Frankfurt: Campus, 2005), 83.

15 Marianne Bechhaus-Gerst and Mechthild Leutner, eds., *Frauen in den deutschen Kolonien* (Berlin: Ch. Links Verlag, 2009).

16 Dörte Lerp, *Imperiale Grenzräume: Bevölkerungspolitiken in Deutsch-Südwestafrika und den östlichen Provinzen Preußens 1884–1914* (Frankfurt: Campus, 2016).

17 Heide Wunder, "Jede Arbeit ist ihres Lohnes wert": Zur geschlechterspezifischen Teilung und Bewertung von Arbeit in der Frühen Neuzeit, in *Geschlechterhierarchie und Arbeitsteilung: Zur Geschichte ungleicher Erwerbschancen von Männern und Frauen*, ed. Karin Hausen (Göttingen: Vandenhoeck & Ruprecht, 1993), 19–39 (24).

18 On the concept of the working couple, see Heide Wunder, "Überlegungen zum Wandel der Geschlechterbeziehungen im 15. und 16. Jahrhundert aus sozialgeschichtlicher Sicht," in *Wandel der Geschlechterbeziehungen zu Beginn der Neuzeit*, ed. Heide Wunder and Christina Vanja (Frankfurt: Campus, 1991), 12–26 (20–26); Heide Wunder, *"Er ist die Sonn', sie ist der Mond": Frauen in der Frühen Neuzeit* (Munich: C.H. Beck, 1992), 96–109.

19 Wunder, *"Er ist die Sonn', sie ist der Mond,"* 96.

20 Ibid., 102f.

21 Heide Wunder, "Normen und Institutionen der Geschlechterordnung am Beginn der Frühen Neuzeit," *Geschlechterperspektiven. Forschungen zur Frühen Neuzeit*, ed. Heide Wunder and Gisel Engel (Königstein: Ulrike Helmer Verlag, 1998), 57–78 (64).

22 See Muriel González Athenas, *Kölner Zunfthandwerkerinnen 1650–1750: Arbeit und Geschlecht* (Kassel: Kassel University Press, 2014).

23 For current pseudoscientific polemical works, see, inter alia, Axel Meyer, *Adams Apfel und Evas Erbe: Wie die Gene unser Leben bestimmen und warum Frauen anders sind als Männer* (Munich: C. Bertelsmann Verlag, 2015); Ulrich Kutschera, *Das Gender-Paradoxon: Mann und Frau als evolierte Menschentypen* (Berlin: LIT Verlag, 2016).

24 Hausen, *Geschlechterhierarchie und Arbeitsteilung*, 42.

25 Nina Degele, "Arbeit konstruiert Geschlecht: Reflexionen zu einem Schlüsselthema der Geschlechterforschung," *Freiburger Studien zur Frauenforschung* 11, no. 16 (2005): 13–40 (20); quoted in González Athenas, *Kölner Zunfthandwerkerinnen*, 18.

26 See Wunder, *"Er ist die Sonn', sie ist der Mond."*

27 Ibid., 58ff.

28 See González Athenas, *Kölner Zunfthandwerkerinnen*.

SECTION III
Weaving and Linking

ELEVEN

Reading Öcalan as a South Asian Woman

Radha D'Souza

As I write this foreword,[1] I cannot help feeling how much more exciting my engagement with Öcalan's book could be if I could sit face to face with him and discuss, over cups of chai, as is common in the Eastern social settings, the issues he raises in this volume. Hopefully Öcalan will be released from prison, and it will be possible to hear him speak to the book directly. Öcalan wrote this book as a "defense statement" in a submission to the European Court of Human Rights in 2008. That a court appearance was the only opportunity available to Öcalan to communicate his thoughts to the wider world is testimony to the state of affairs in the world we live in, a world where "democracy" imprisons freedoms, where the thoughts of one man become a "security threat" to states with stockpiles of the most lethal weapons the world has ever produced. Yet, in a strange way, amid the dystopic visions and cognitive dissonance that envelops us today, it is reassuring that the age-old adage "the pen is mightier than the sword" still rings true.

I cannot read Öcalan's book except as a South Asian woman. The book is permeated with words, concepts, historical references, events, modes of reasoning, allegories, analogies, and much else that connects to the wellsprings of shared intercultural meanings. The Middle East sits between the Occident and the Orient, both geographically and culturally. South Asia and the Middle East have close historical, cultural, intellectual, and political ties that go back to the first river valley civilizations on the Euphrates and Tigris (Mesopotamia), the Nile (Egypt), and the Indus (India). Nothing demonstrates the closeness of our civilizations better than the Urdu language. Born from communications between Arabs, Persians, Turks, and Indians, Urdu is the embodiment of the coming together of the civilizations of the Middle East, Persia, and India. Before the European colonization of our lands, our people, and our minds, the great philosophical and political debates and cultural exchanges of ancient times occurred between intellectuals from the Middle East, Persia, and South Asia. The confluence of Greek and Indian thought occurred on the banks of the Tigris under the Abbasid caliphate in the eighth and ninth centuries CE. The coming together of Western and Eastern thought resulted in the flowering of philosophy, poetry, science, and music in the centers of Baghdad, Kufa, and Sinjar. These sites are engulfed by destruction and unsurpassed human tragedy today. The emotive meanings of those place names handed down to South Asian children through stories and folktales—the antics of Nasruddin Hodja, for example, or Rumi's story of the parrot and the merchant on a trip to Hindustan, infuse subconscious elements into our understandings of contemporary geopolitical events in the region. For many young Europeans and North Americans, Kufa and Sinjar may be just place names that they hear from sound bites on TV news channels. These place names have historical resonances for South Asians. As I read the book, I wondered whether Euro-American readers and readers in the Middle East and Asia today would take away very different understandings from Öcalan's book.

Today, the intellectual exchanges that enriched our pasts in the Middle East and in South Asia are consigned to the dustbin of history, remembered, if at all, by exclusive circles of academic experts hidden in the concrete basements of distant universities. Öcalan is forced to write, as I am, about our histories and cultures, our pain and our suffering as nations and peoples, through the conceptual vocabularies of Bookchin and Braudel, Foucault and Hegel, Marx and Weber, even to speak to people of the Middle East or South Asia. Who would understand it if I referred to Shah Waliullah's (1703–1762) work on rise and decline of empires or his theories of state? Yet many educated people in India, Turkey, and the Middle East will know Shah Waliullah's European contemporaries Baron Montesquieu or Giambattista Vico or Edward Gibbon, who also wrote about rise and decline of empires and theories of the modern state. How many people in the Middle East know about Indian freedom struggles or vice versa? Yet even school children in both regions will know about the French, Russian, and American Revolutions. Those who control our minds rule over us. Those who rule over us control what we know, how we know, and how much we know. Öcalan's concern in this book is the "mentality" that enslaves us, willingly even, to the destructive power of capitalism. It is the "mentality" that makes us complicit in the destruction of society. His concern is to find ways to reestablish "the mental structures" that are needed to bring social life to the center stage of our deliberations.

The book is divided into six sections. Öcalan begins in chapter 1 by interrogating the "self." I find this extraordinary, because it is a tradition that has deep roots in the East. In Eastern traditions one begins an important undertaking with introspection: Who am I, and why am I doing this? It is this introspection that orients an author toward the arguments that follow. Öcalan locates himself in the longue-durée of the history of the Middle East and its tryst with capitalism. He ends, in chapter 6, with an attempt to "overcome the subject-object dichotomy without denying it." His efforts at transcendence is also extraordinary to a South Asian. The underlying philosophical orientation that seeks to "overcome subject-object dualism" is a non-dualist approach. Non-dualism is the dominant philosophical orientation in Eastern thought, whereas dualism is the dominant philosophical orientation in Western thought going as far back as Plato. The thread that runs through the book is the antagonistic and adversarial relations between states and communities. Öcalan's solution is, however, non-adversarial and non-dualist. Surely the non-dualism in Öcalan has deeper roots than appear on the surface.

Öcalan concludes with a call to put "[t]he World Democratic Confederacy, and regional democratic confederacies for Asia, Africa, Europe and Australia" on the agenda for political change. I am astounded by this call. One hundred years ago, the Ghadar movement, one of the earliest and most revolutionary anti-colonial movements in South Asia made exactly the same call. Ubaidullah Sindhi, a revolutionary freedom fighter, Ghadar Party leader, and scholar, drafted a constitution for the future *azad* Hindustan in 1922. In that draft constitution he called for a confederal form of government. Sindhi's draft constitution for azad Hindustan opposed a single unitary nation-state, instead calling for the multiple nationalities (*qawms*) of India to form democratic and egalitarian governments that would come together under a confederation of qawms affiliated to Hindustan as their homeland (*watan*). The constitution further called for a confederation of Asiatic and African republics opposed to capitalism and imperialism. I found the resonances in Ghadar movement's thinking a hundred years ago and Öcalan's today quite striking.

In four short chapters, Öcalan condenses histories of human civilizations from primitive communitarian stateless societies to Sumerian, Babylonian, Egyptian, Indian, Chinese, Phoenician, Median, Persian, Greek, Roman, Islamic, Christian, and modern civilizations. What is common to these civilizations as opposed to the primitive communitarian societies is the rise of the state as a repressive apparatus that centralizes power and appropriates wealth. Öcalan sees the institution of the state as the millstone around people's necks that is grinding down their capacity to live as human beings.

States have always oppressed people, but the capitalist state has the most advanced techniques of repression. The capitalist state destroys the very conditions needed for the existence of society. Science and technology have aided and abetted the extraordinary concentration of power over the lives of people and the destiny of humanity. People have always rebelled against state oppression. The histories of their rebellions hold the secrets of constructive knowledge to rebuild society and the possibilities of different modes of being in the world. Therefore, "[r]esistance, rebellion, and constructing the new must become our way of life." The philosopher-poet traditions in the East, wrongly labeled "mystic" by the West, have repeated over and over again for centuries that resistance and rebellion and constructing the new must always remain the spirit of humanity. As Jalaluddin Rumi, the Persian philosopher-poet, writes in his well-known text *Mathnawi* (also written as *Mathnavi* or *Masanavi*):

> Do thou arise and blow on the terrible trumpet, that thousands of the dead may spring up from the earth.
> Since thou art the upright-rising Israfil (Seraphiel) of the time, make a resurrection ere the Resurrection.
> O beloved if one say, "Where is the Resurrection?" show thyself, saying, "Behold, I am the Resurrection.
> Look, O questioner who are stricken with tribulation, (and see) that from this resurrection a hundred worlds have grown!" [IV: 1478–1481]

Rumi's call to "blow on the terrible trumpet" is an invitation to action and struggle, a gauntlet that must be picked up.

However, resistance and rebellion must always be directed toward consolidating communities and collective life. There is no point in seeking power when we know that it corrupts. There is no point is seeking to capture state power when we know it always becomes oppressive eventually. Yet we have a duty to struggle when the powers that be destroy the conditions necessary for life. Rebellion should accompany the equally important duty to rebuild the conditions of life. Rebuilding the conditions for human life is possible only in communitarian social orders. This has been the consistent message of the philosopher-poets of the East for many centuries. Öcalan's book brings back that sentiment. Öcalan's concern is that denial of social life "has rendered life meaningless and has led to the degeneration and decomposition of the society." Öcalan juxtaposes two parallel social orders that have always coexisted, which he calls "state civilization" versus "democratic civilization." It is possible for the two "civilizations" to coexist if they recognize and respect each other's identities. As a South Asian reading the book, Öcalan's engagement with power is infused with an approach that resonates with Sufi, Bhakti, Sikh, and Buddhist traditions. I am reminded of a verse by Hazrat Nizamuddin Auliya (d. 1325 CE):

> You are not my fellow traveler.
> Tread your own path.
> May you be affluent.
> And I downtrodden.

Öcalan, echoing Eastern philosopher-poet traditions, writes, "Military victories cannot bring freedom; they bring slavery." Rejection of worldly power and wealth calls for a different type of power (resilience) and wealth (human bonds) to realize the universal meanings of life and human destiny. The source of this latter type of power and wealth can only be found in human communities. Capitalism pollutes the wellsprings of this type of power and wealth, which has sustained communities throughout history.

Class and Community

For Marx, the point of departure for inquiries into capitalism was the emergence of commodity production as the general mode of social production. Commodity production spearheaded by European merchants and elites displaced rural populations, created an urban working class mired in poverty and the squalor of urbanization, state repression of the poor, and the disintegration of social order. A political exile from the

Prussian state, Marx turned to European social history for answers. From European history, Marx drew the conclusion that classes and class struggle were the primary drivers of history, and the state is, as Marx described it, "the executive committee of the bourgeoisie." For Öcalan, the point of departure is the displacement and disintegration of cohesive historically constituted communities, in particular rural communities, dispersed from their homelands, their identity, culture, and history by empires of West and East. Öcalan also turns to history for answers, but, for Öcalan, that history is the larger history of empires, colonialism, and imperialism. The history of the institution of the state is deeply entwined with the rise of empires. Communities preexisted states. Indeed, their labor and natural endowments have sustained states and empires in different civilizations throughout history.

Öcalan's starting point is what latter-day Marxists problematized as the "national question," a question that arose after Marx's lifetime in the course of the Russian Revolution. Confronted with external aggression by the Great Powers (Great Britain, France, Austria) and internal rebellions in the Russian colonies, the Russian Revolution's solution to the colonial question was very different from that of the Ottoman Empire, which was also confronted with external aggression by Great Britain, France, and Italy and rebellions in its colonies. The revolutionary Russian state offered its colonies a "new deal"—i.e., repudiation of unequal treaties with Czarist Russia and a new constitutional basis for renewed alliances of the colonies to the Russian state. In contrast, the Ottoman colonies, European and Middle Eastern, were dismembered from the Ottoman state and forcibly aligned to the Great Powers. In the end both suppressed rural communities and privileged urban industrialism.

The World Wars transformed the problem of colonialism into a problem of cultural identity and put the "national question" on the agenda of global politics. Throughout the post–World War II period, national oppression and conflicts have preoccupied the hyphenated nation-state. The Kurdish struggle is one of those, with a history going back to World War I. These conflicts are frequently manipulated by the big powers, empowered and enriched by big capital. National conflicts are typically fought around claims of independent statehood. Öcalan takes a new approach to the old "national question." Contemporary history shows, he argues, that competing claims for statehood have only brought destruction of the very same communities in whose names the struggles were waged. His point of departure is the post–World War II era when global capitalism "reached its peak" in the "fertile plains of Mesopotamia" that are home to one of the oldest river valley civilizations and to Öcalan.

In Europe, nationality and modern statehood were coterminous. Hence, the hyphenated nation-state. In the colonies, nationality and modern statehood were never coterminous. Instead, they were shaped by colonial wars and interimperialist rivalries. Modern political ideologies, including liberalism, Marxism, socialism, and anarchism, tend to conflate nationality with essentialist ethnocentrism or religious fundamentalism, on the one hand, and with statehood, on the other. Communities and society as the point of departure for understanding capitalism put Öcalan on a different track of inquiry. For Öcalan, the driver of history is the conflict between a repressive state, which concentrates political and economic power, and the struggles of communities to survive. This formulation takes the "national question" out of essentialist versus statist formulations and puts it on renewed historical footing. The conflict between communities and states is common to all civilizations. History cannot be reduced to class and class struggles, which are but one aspect of the struggle between state and communities. The genesis of capitalist exploitation and state power has deep roots in all human civilizations. Where there is a state, there are merchant financiers and property owners who keep the political class in power. In the East, the power of merchants and financiers was never legitimized. As Öcalan writes, "Throughout the history of civilization, and especially in the Middle East, these usurers and profiteers have always existed at the margins of society. . . . Not even the most despotic administrators dared to legitimize them." While it is important to recover lost cultural and philosophical resources from the intellectual histories of the Middle East, it is important to recognize that orientalism has distorted those traditions, and there is no going back to a nonexistent pristine past. For Öcalan, the struggle of diverse communities to survive has reached a crisis point in contemporary capitalism that destroys the very fabric of sociality. The conflict between powerful states and resilient communities that shapes and drives all other conflicts has acquired a renewed urgency at present.

If I were to assume that liberalism, socialism, Marxism, and anarchism are the only possible political theories and that Greco-Roman philosophical schools are the only schools of philosophy that we have as sources for our conceptual repertoire, then, undoubtedly, I would conclude from the above that Öcalan opposes liberalism, the ideology of capitalism, and comes close to a synthesis of Marxism and anarchism, the two consistently anti-liberal political ideologies that have challenged capitalism and modernity. Öcalan does not permit *me*, the South Asian woman, such rough and ready conclusions. For he writes quite explicitly in his critique of Western philosophy that "Eastern thought seems to have grasped this reality [the unity of body and mind] expressing it in the saying 'All can be found in the human being.'" The way Indians greet each other by saying "namaste" expresses in everyday life the reality that Öcalan alludes to. For, *namaste*—from the Sanskrit root words *"namaha"* + *"as té"*—means *I salute (namaha) that (as té)*, or more simply, *I salute that universe that is embodied in you.* By saluting each other we acknowledge the universe that exists within each one of us. These are deeply philosophical concepts that permeate our cultural vocabularies.

How can I miss Öcalan's references to the martyrdom of Husayn ibn Ali and Mansur Al-Hallaj? How can I brush aside the profound influence of thinkers like Shahab al-Din Suhrawardi on South Asian thought? These references to Eastern philosophy, history, and metaphors mean it is necessary to grasp the philosophical orientation that informs the book in order to appreciate Öcalan's political conclusions. In the sections that follow, I attempt, very briefly, to throw light on two concepts that inform Öcalan's analysis of modernity, state, and community. One is philosophical dualism/non-dualism and the other is the interrelated concepts of nation and state. The two concepts, one in philosophy and the other in political theory, I wish to argue, are, understood and addressed in markedly different ways in Western and Eastern intellectual traditions, used here in the broadest possible sense. I hope that making these latent ideas explicit will assist readers to appreciate Öcalan's arguments. Öcalan's book is about philosophical musings. As Öcalan writes, "without philosophy history cannot be written."

Dualism and Non-Dualism

Marx traces the emergence of all sorts of dualisms and binaries in analysis of society up to the emergence of capitalism. In *Grundrisse* Marx argues that in precapitalist societies communities were founded on the organic unity of nature and people. Capitalism forcibly tore apart organic communities by severing the ties of people to land and nature. Commodification transformed people's relations with nature into private property relations, and relations between people into labor (class) relations. The forcible rupture of nature from people by commodity production, argues Marx, introduces all sorts of dualisms into society, including the dualisms of nature/culture, of capital/labor, of state/citizen, of public/private, of economy/politics, of constitutional law/contract law, of economics/ethics, and so forth. Öcalan's starting point for critique is the "scientific method," which is founded on the subject/object dualism. The subject/object, the body/mind, material/spiritual, and mind/matter dualisms have deeper roots in Greco-Roman philosophical traditions long before the rise of capitalism. Indeed, the categories and concepts in Greco-Roman intellectual traditions provided the conceptual repertoire for capitalism and the legal and ideological resources for positivist science.

If we turn to philosophy instead of sociology or political economy, it is possible to see that the dominant mode of reasoning in Western philosophy is dualism. As early as Thales of Miletus (d. 547 BCE), we begin to see mind/matter dualism. The British philosopher Roy Bhaskar argued that one can go as far back as Plato and find certain problems that philosophy keeps returning to again and again in the West. Dualisms are sustained by antagonisms (thesis versus antithesis), which in turn produces more antagonisms. An endless cycle of thesis-antithesis conflicts follows as each synthesis generates a new conflictual thesis and antithesis. In this mode of dualist thinking, conflicts are perpetual and endless, indeed conflicts are the drivers of life itself. Philosophy of science straddles the dualisms but does not help to transcend them. Öcalan's critique of the scientific method is that it is founded on philosophical dualism. He writes, "The distinction between subject and object has roots that can be taken back all the way to Plato. Plato's famous theory of the duality of Forms (ideas) and their simple, observable reflections is the basis of all subsequently postulated dualisms." Philosophical dualism focuses on identifying differences, oppositions, confrontations, and acts as the source of conflicts. Western philosophy and positivist science argue that struggles and conflicts are necessary for motion, movement, evolution, progress, and history. In this tradition, facts, empirical phenomena, and the material world have primacy over ontology or cosmology. Positivist science, Öcalan writes, founded on "the subject-object dichotomy, is nothing but the legitimization of slavery."

In contrast, in the Eastern philosophical traditions, the dominant mode of reasoning is non-dualism. Concepts of unity in diversity, unity in duality, and the oneness of life-forms led Eastern philosophers to uncover the underlying unity that holds apparently opposing phenomena together. Conflicts and struggles are not to be denied, but the underlying unity of the world should also be acknowledged. Is it not a miracle that in spite of all our differences, conflicts, antagonisms, the world has continued for as long as it has? That the universe "acts in unity"? And that for all of capitalism's "scientific" efforts over five hundred years, we are unable to say we have "conquered" nature? If anything, we are only now finding out that nature "fights back" to reclaim itself, and more and more we are seeing that nature "fights back" with ecological vengeance. Eastern philosophers asked questions about the continuities in life, the miracle of cosmological unity that sustains so much diversity and difference. Human beings are unique because they have instincts, intelligence, and intuition to grasp empirical, rational, and ontological realities. The questions for philosophy in the East were about the eternal nature of Life with a capital "L," which continues in spite of the regularity of death and destruction, the cohesion of society and history that persists despite the diversity, difference, and discord in social life. As Öcalan writes, "it seems that the sole purpose of life is to find the mystery of the universe in the resolution of this dual antagonism, life and death."

Eastern philosophers sought answers for their questions in ontology and cosmology. They treated perception and empirical phenomenon as secondary to ontological truths about Life, which were, in their view, eternal truths. These philosophical ideas gave rise to "non-dualist" science, a science that recognized the contingency of human life on nature, the contingency of individual life on communitarian collective lives, and the inner lives of individuals—call it whatever: aesthetic, ethical, emotional, psychological, or spiritual. These ontological truths meant Eastern science saw its role not as an endless frontier open to human conquest but as an endowment, a gift from nature, God, whatever, which may be used to sustain life, which may be enriched, but it must always be held in trust for future generations. Individual lives are transient, whereas Life is eternal. Individuals were trustees of nature's endowment, and science must take account of the place of human beings in the universe when they investigate nature. As an endowment, nature's gift cannot be appropriated and owned as private property. The opening lines of the Rig Veda, "life lives on life," for example, set up a deep ecological principle, i.e., if we want Life to continue, we must make sure we conserve it. Since seventh century BCE, Jainism has advocated the methodology of "*anekantavada*," or the philosophy of many-sidedness. Anekantavada invites us to move away from dualist arguments like "A is right and B is wrong" or the reverse and ask instead: "If A is right and B is also right, what is the nature of reality that makes A see what A sees and B see what B sees." Mind and matter, economic and political, material and spiritual lives are not antithetical relations in Eastern intellectual traditions. Earning a living is a necessary condition for life, but at the same time earning an honest living requires deep spiritual commitment, just as spiritual life requires fulfilling biological needs (food, clothing, shelter, and such).

Non-dualist thought produced a very different type of political philosophy. Politics is ethical action. When discord, disunity, and divisions occur, when states and kings become tyrannical, when reproduction of the conditions for human life becomes impossible, then human beings must rebel, indeed it is their duty to rebel. The purpose of rebellion is to restore society and regenerate the conditions needed for human life to continue. The Sufi pirs, the Bhakti saints, and the Sikh gurus insisted on the unity of "this worldly" life constituted by communities (civil society) and states (political power) and "other worldly" life, which is concerned with the human purpose, human destiny, human conditions, and humanity's place in the universe. Politics as ethical actions must bring the two dimensions of life and Life, the empirical life and the cosmic life, together here and now in what we do and how we do it. The present is the site where the past and the future coexist.

The East never developed a theory of "divine rights" of kings as ideological justification for power. The first principle of Islam, "There is no God but Allah," insures against despotism of kings and subjects them to a higher law. Throughout history, popular rebellions have overthrown kings and reduced mighty states and empires to dust. Nor did the East develop laws of inheritance like primogeniture, which allows land to be inherited by the oldest male to the exclusion of other sons and daughters. The oldest male is undoubtedly the privileged patriarch, but he also has additional responsibilities that require him to hold land in trust for the extended family, take responsibility for the elderly, the sick, destitute relatives, and less able members of the community. Consequently, the institution of private property never acquired the kind of historical stability and continuity that it did in European societies. Depending on how we see these histories, we could argue that power and wealth created stable states and empires and landed aristocracies in the West. The political stability came at the cost of internal cohesion of communities. The East was colonized, subjugated, and frequently appeared chaotic. But communities remained resilient amid the political chaos. Their inner resilience continues to challenge powers of states and empires to this day.

Öcalan is worried that the spread of modernity may lead to disintegration of societies that have remained resilient so far. Modernity, he writes, "by denying the social life, has rendered life meaningless and has led to the degeneration and decomposition of the society." It is, therefore, important to overcome orientalist approaches to the culture and thought of the Middle East and instead recover from it philosophical and conceptual resources necessary to address the disintegration of society and community that disorganizes the conditions necessary for human life. Taken together, Öcalan's book seeks to transcend dualist approaches by moving away from adversarial conceptualizations of nature versus human beings, as in liberal science, or communities against states, as in anarchist thought, or politics versus economics, as in socialist thought. Instead, it seeks to synthesize different approaches to modernity by adopting nondualist approaches to diverse oppositional ideologies. These philosophical differences need to be borne in mind to avoid confusion in readers' thinking of Öcalan's evaluations with the reservations and qualifications of different modernist solutions offered by Western political theories to the problems of modernity.

Qawm and Watan
Öcalan is being satirical when he writes, "I am thankful for Hegel's insightful description of state as *God descending to earth* and Napoleon as *God's march on earth*. . . . I read the Hegelian philosophy and saw how the new god came down to earth as the nation-state and began its walk in the shape of Napoleon." Critique of the nation-state is a central thread in the book. Unfortunately, I have to rely on a translation of the book, an English translation at that, because of my ignorance of Turkish. With these limitations, I would like to alert readers to two words that are central to ideas constitutive of the European nation-state. Hegel more than any other European philosopher provides the hyphen in between the concepts of nation and state. The word "qawm" in Arabic, Turkish, Persian, and Urdu is often translated as "nation," and the word "watan" is translated as "homeland." The words "qawm" and "watan" do not have identical conceptual content in languages of the Middle East and South Asia as they do in English.

The hyphenation of nation and state in European modernity follows a particular understanding of nation and statehood. The *Oxford English Dictionary* defines "homeland" as "a person's or a people's native land." The OED defines "nation" as a "large body of people united by common descent, history, culture, or language, inhabiting a particular state or territory." A "state" is defined as a "sovereign state of which most of the citizens or subjects are united also by factors which define a nation, such as language or common descent." And the "nation-state" is a "sovereign state of which most of the citizens or subjects are united also by factors which define a nation, such as language or common descent." It is important to note that territoriality is common to all the four words in the English language. There is a historical sequencing in the definitions, with homeland being primal nativist identity with land, the nation-state the coalescence of family, civil society, citizenship, and statehood at the pinnacle of historical development. The idea of nation-state conjoins the concept of historically constituted communities and the historically evolved institution of the state occupying defined territories. In Europe, nations and states were coterminous and coevolved. This is not the conceptual content of the words "qawm" and "watan."

In the East, territoriality and historically constituted communities are not necessarily coterminous. It is possible to have "qawms," i.e., historically constituted communities, without territory. Equally, it is possible for several "qawms" to belong to the same "watan," i.e., for several historically constituted communities to have a shared homeland. These significant differences in meaning are lost in transliteration. Modernity brought with it real difficulties of translating concepts of "qawm" and "watan" into the modern political vocabulary of the hyphenated nation-state. Depending on the nature and type of anti-colonial nationalism in different parts of the Islamic world in Arabia, Maghreb, Turkey, Persia, and South Asia, the evolution of the word "qawm" to the modern day "*qawmiya*," translated as nationalism, and "watan" to "*wataniya*," translated as patriotism or citizenship, evolved along very different trajectories and acquired different modern meanings in different regions.[2] In South Asia, a diverse continent where many qawms have shared a common watan for a long period in history, the leaders of the radical anti-colonial Ghadar movement called for a radically different constitutional model for azad Hindustan (free India) after the end of British colonialism. Their vision for azad Hindustan was to establish a confederation of qawms with a shared watan. They called for "a federation of the republics of India," where each qawm of Hindustan would form a confederation, and Hindustan would be home to all those who lived there and made it their home. Unfortunately, the liberal, modernist meanings of nation and state prevailed and the struggles for control of nation-states and the bloody conflicts for partitions of the countries continue. The very fact that common words with shared meanings acquired diverse connotations in specific contexts of anti-colonial movements suggests the need for caution in the way ideas about nation, nation-state, and communities are understood in English and Eastern languages. Equally, it should alert us to the way we read Öcalan's juxtaposition of community and state in the book. If we understand community as qawm and state as the territorial authority, the arguments about reconciliation between state and community in the book become easier to grasp.

The conditions under which the book was written, as a "defense statement" in the European Court of Human Rights and smuggled out, means that it would be unfair to read the book as if it were the work of an erudite philosopher writing in the comfortable environment of a university. The value of this book lies in the fact that it comes from a person who has engaged in real struggles in the real world and has continued to do so under conditions of solitary confinement for over seventeen years. It is refreshing to see philosophy return to politics.

Postscript

In April 2016, I was invited by the EU Turkey Civic Commission (EUTCC) to join the İmralı delegation to meet with a member of the secretariat of the European Council's European Committee for the Prevention of Torture and Inhuman or Degrading Treatment or Punishment (CPT) in Strasbourg. Our purpose was simple. CPT officials had visited Abdullah Öcalan in January 2013. No one had access to Öcalan or had seen him, not even his lawyers, since April 2015. The solitary confinement and prohibition of family visits and access to lawyers breached the recommendations made by the CPT in 2013. Would the CPT undertake another visit to verify the conditions of Öcalan's detention and ascertain if the Turkish authorities had complied with the CPT's 2013 recommendations?

Sitting at the meeting room in Strasbourg, I was unable to resist juxtaposing the leaders of the two sides. The international İmralı delegation was led by the late Judge Essa Moosa, the inspirational South African judge and former lawyer of another famous political prisoner: Nelson Mandela. On the other side, the CPT had recently made a Ukrainian academic its chairperson, at a time when Ukraine was under the spotlight for widespread torture and abuse of political prisoners. The Ukrainian government boasted about the appointment of its national on its official website claiming, "The election... is... evidence of a high level of scientific development of international law in Ukraine in general," while at the same time denying the United Nations Subcommittee on Prevention of Torture permission to visit and investigate allegations of torture and abuse of political prisoners in Ukraine. I wondered what, if anything, the CPT's chairman had done about the UN subcommittee's visit to his own country. But meetings of the type I was in are not moments to contemplate the truth, and most certainly not for speaking one's mind. That much I knew very well, and I was relieved that we had Judge Moosa, a soft-spoken, gentle, dignified, and principled spokesperson to speak for all of us.

Toward the tail end of the meeting, more as a concluding reflection, I said to the CPT official: "I teach law in a university and my students often ask me why the stated purposes of the law are frequently not achieved. I would love to be able to tell my students that the law does offer justice and hope to many." The suave and composed demeanor of the CPT official fell away instantly. "Are you challenging me?" he asked, sounding stern. "Remember it is because of the Council of Europe, the European Convention on Human Rights, and the prohibition on death penalty in Turkey as a result that Öcalan is even alive today." Some conversations remain etched in our memories, and the CPT official's response to my interjection will remain with me for a long time. In ancient times, there were elaborate protocols that ordinary people had to follow when seeking audience with a sultan or a monarch. They knew they had to kowtow, swear allegiance, proclaim their loyalty loudly and clearly, and be subservient. Modern democracies promise equality of rulers and ruled, transparency and openness, even accountability of the rulers over the ruled. Yet those very things render opaque the existence, in reality, of protocols and practices when a person is in audience with those in power. Perhaps someone needs to write an activist handbook on *How to Conduct Yourself in the Presence of Officials When Campaigning for Your Rights!*

The fact remains that two and half years after the international İmralı delegation met with the CPT, and six and half years after the CPT's first recommendations on Öcalan's treatment in prison, he remains in solitary confinement without access to lawyers, family, or friends. In the mean-time, the situation in Turkey continues to deteriorate rapidly, and the number of political prisoners in Turkish prisons continues to swell, as it does around the world, in India, Sri Lanka, Philippines, Rwanda, Uganda, and countries far too many to list here. Mumia Abu-Jamal has been in prison since 1981 for his views on the Black nation in America, most of it spent in solitary confinement, and campaigners in the capital of the "Free World," the United States, continue to petition courts for his medical needs. We have yet to comprehend the global scope of suppression of political dissent and the sheer numbers of political prisoners around the world. If ever there was a moment in history when a sustained international campaign for the release of political prisoners was essential, that moment is now.

This essay was first published as the foreword to Abdullah Öcalan, *Manifesto for a Democratic Civilization, Volume 2: Capitalism: The Age of Unmasked Gods and Naked Kings* (Porsgrunn, NO: New Compass Press, 2017) [Turkish: *Demokratik Uygarlık Manifestosu, ikinci kitap: Kapitalist Uygarlık. Maskesiz Tanrılar ve Çıplak Krallar Çağı* (İstanbul: Aram, 2009)].

Radha D'Souza is a critical scholar, social justice activist, attorney, and writer, who has lived and worked in India, New Zealand, and the UK. Currently she teaches law at the University of Westminster. She has worked with democratic rights movements, trade unions, and anti-globalization movements. Radha has written and published extensively on a range of subjects and issues concerning social and global justice. Her recent book *What's Wrong with Rights? Social Movements, Law and Liberal Imaginations* (London: Pluto Press, 2018) maps, for the first time, the rights discourse and the transformations in transnational finance capitalism since the world wars and interrogates the connections between the two.

Notes

1   This essay was first written as the preface to Abdullah Öcalan, *Manifesto for a Democratic Civilization, Volume 2: Capitalism: The Age of Unmasked Gods and Naked Kings* (Porsgrunn, NO: New Compass Press, 2018); 2nd revised edition will be published by PM Press in 2020.

2   For an expanded discussion of this point, see E. van Donzel, B. Lewis, and Ch. Pellat, "Ḳawm and Ḳawmiyya," in *The Encyclopaedia of Islam*, vol. 4 (Leiden, NL: Brill, 1978), 780–94; P.J. Bearman, Th Bianquis, C.E. Bosworth, E. van Donzel, and P. Heinrichs, "Waṭan and Waṭaniyya," in *The Encyclopaedia of Islam*, vol. 11 (Leiden, NL: Brill, 2002), 174–77.

TWELVE

"There Can Be No Utopia or Reality That Is More Ambitious Than This": The Democratic Modernism of Svetozar Marković and Abdullah Öcalan

Andrej Grubačić

Svetozar Marković, the founder of Balkan socialism, was arrested in January 1874. He was immediately jailed in the Serbian town of Kragujevac. For the police records Marković gave his occupation as a writer; the local authorities recorded that he was "nothing but a tramp." The damp, poorly heated cell of the Kragujevac jail was torture for the young socialist, who was suffering from tuberculosis. The trial against Marković, who stood accused of "press crimes," attracted a large audience. The prosecutor described Marković as a "socialist Messiah" with a venomous pen, recklessly attacking the most important national institutions: the National Assembly, the constitutional laws of the founding fathers, even the king himself. In his speech before the Serbian court, Marković opposed the very essence of the utopia of capitalist modernity: the idea of the sovereign nation-state anchored to a bounded territory, as well as to a certain temporal (linear) and spatial (statist) order.

Marković spoke for the whole day. In a hoarse voice, he proclaimed that socialism is justice, and then collapsed into his chair. It was hard for the presiding judges to maintain order, for the courtroom was filled with peasants from the countryside, workers from the local factory, students, and townsmen, all coming to support the man who stood up against the bureaucrats who took their land and property, who taxed them and harassed them. Serbian peasants knew virtually nothing about socialism, but they knew Svetozar Marković, whom they regarded as a saint.

He was found guilty of all charges but due to enormous public support received a relatively lenient sentence of eighteen months in the state penitentiary in Požarevac. However, prison was a death sentence for Marković. He was dying of advanced tuberculosis, and the Požarevac prison was known in Serbia as the "house of the dead" or a "dry guillotine." He continued to write in prison and in these last months of his life produced some of his most significant works, developing his theory of democratic communalism based on the institutions of *zadruga* (family commune) and *opstina* (village commune) and completing his thoughts on Balkan federalism, imagined as a stateless federation of all Balkan peoples.

He left the prison in November 1874, and immediately began publishing his last newspaper, *Oslobodjenje* (Liberation). In this phase of his work, his ideas were clearly elaborated as internal and social reorganization on the basis of direct democracy and communal self-government, as well as revolution in Turkey and federation in the Balkan Peninsula. His ideas about democratic communalism and stateless federalism unnerved the government, and the police confronted him with two specific charges: "treacherous undertaking" and "spreading hatred against the prince." After giving most of his money to the first school for women in Serbia, he escaped to the Hungarian town of Baja, where he boarded a train to Trieste. It is there, on the morning of February 26, that he died. He was twenty-eight years old. When his body arrived to Serbia, it was greeted by thousands of peasants who came to bid farewell to their beloved Svetozar, some of them shouting at the police to remove their hats in the presence of the saint.

Most of his followers joined the long awaited revolt in Bosnia and Herzegovina, which erupted in July 1875. They played important roles in the so-called Balkan crisis of 1875–1878. The plight of the peasantry, coupled with anti-colonial struggle against the Ottomans, provided fertile ground for socialist agitation. Socialist demonstrations were held throughout Serbia, and on many occasions the red flag was prominently displayed. In 1878, in Kragujevac, five hundred people paraded through the streets, singing the "Marseillaise," shouting

Long live the Republic!
Long live the Commune!
Long live communal autonomy!

and chanting a Serbian "Carmagnole":

Against God and the ruler,
Against the priest and the altar,

Against the crown and the scepter,
And the merchant usurer,
For the worker, for the peasant,
We fight the good fight.

Svetozar Marković belonged to a specific tradition of left radicalism that was at the very center of the global radical culture of the nineteenth century. Indeed, after the magisterial works of the historians of this tradition, such as Ilham Khuri-Makdisi, Sho Konishi, and Benedict Anderson, it is impossible to view the history of nineteenth-century radicalism as a history of North European Marxism.[1] According to Khuri-Makdisi, European scholars relegated this fascinating radical tradition to a mere backstage within the global history of the left. One of the reasons for this oversight, she suggests, is that the politics of this period does not fit the usual description of the "left." One would have been hard-pressed to find revolutionary left in the north of Europe, where social democracy and the Second International were dominant. The revolutionary left was strong in the south, and it was mostly anti-statist, without rigid ideology, notions of class-consciousness or the revolutionary party, or other traditional categories of the bureaucratic left. Before the Russian Revolution and the establishment of party/state-defined movements, the left consisted of a multiplicity of radicalisms, united in the opposition to capitalism and the state. This global movement promoted a political counter-imagination of a transnational shared space external to capitalist modernity: a democratic modernity of cooperation and mutual aid.[2]

Japanese historian Sho Konishi points out the particular nature of organizing inherent to the politics of democratic modernity, which he refers to as the practice of translation.[3] Instead of focusing exclusively and narrowly on the urban industrial working class as a presumed agent of revolutionary change, organizing was aimed at peasants, intellectuals, migrant and unskilled workers, artisans, and artists. Ideas of democratic modernity developed and spread not according to the logic of diffusionism but to that of translation. There was no unidirectional transfer of knowledge from Europe, whether in the form of direct influence, self-colonization, indigenization, or reconfiguration. What we had instead was the multidirectional travel of ideas, with knowledge being altered and added to at each turn. Mutual translation was a practice of definition and redefinition, articulation and rearticulation, in which political concepts were negotiated between languages to produce new concepts. Constructed in this way, translation in practice failed to inspire cultural nationalism. It inspired a sense of transnational sympathy and common experience and a sense that an injury to one is an injury to all.

If the first part of democratic modernity in the long nineteenth century was the practice of translation, the second element was refusal of the state as an exclusive framework for the political organization of society. Democratic modernity was stateless modernity. This, in turn, implied two important revisions. The first one was a relationship to time. In place of the linear thinking common to both Marxist and liberal versions of capitalist modernity, democratic modernity suggested a newly imagined future where the present is a key moment in time and space in which people were to rectify history for the future. Socialism would ultimately be a product of tendencies that are apparent now in the society and that were always, in some sense, imminent in the present. In this restorative historicity, the past was narrated into the future, and the present became the backward past, as a product of capitalist modernity being perceived as barbaric, unmodern, and morally unjustifiable. As formulated in a popular Serbian proverb, you walk into the present with a past ahead of you and the future at your back. Moreover, the new democratic future was to be created as a detour by way of the past.[4]

The second revision concerns space, or an alternative form of a political organization. The alternative to the state form was seen as a decentralized federal organization. The first socialist federalist proposals, elaborated by Proudhon and Kropotkin, are well known; those of Svetozar Marković are less famous but no less original.[5] In a dialogue with Marx and Bakunin, he sought a "balkanized" socialism, defined not as a new economic system but as a new way of life based on communal institutions and instincts rather than upon inexorable historical laws.[6] His broad program outlined a system of local self-government based on the family commune, which he proposed to rehabilitate and improve, and the village commune.[7] He refused to see economic equality as separate from political freedom and argued for communization and decentralization. The problem of bread, Marković concluded, is the problem of self-government. His democratic socialism was ethical and visionary, eclectic and humane. He believed that "female emancipation was one of the foremost tasks of revolutionary socialism."[8] "Far from being incoherent, his revolutionary program rested very firmly on two far-reaching proposals: democratic communalism and horizontal federalism. These proposals were based on the notion of the bureaucracy as a distinct social class.[9]

He valued Marx as the most profound critic of the social and economic development of the industrialized West, but he held Nikolay Chernishevsky and Mikhail Bakunin in the same esteem. His entire life as a revolutionary embodied a search for a method of translation between Western and Russian socialism, in the light of their possible application to the reality of rural Serbia. He never thought much of the Western industrial proletariat as the exclusive agent of social change. He thought Marx's exposition of class struggle was incomplete and eschewed Marx's historical determinism. It is the local conditions, Marković insisted, that will determine the nature of the new cooperative society that the working class will establish in respective regions. European socialism, like socialism in any other territory, would rest on industrial and agricultural associations shaped by local historical and economic patterns.

> Our task is not to destroy capitalism, which in fact does not exist, but rather to transform small patriarchal property into collective property, in order to leap over an entire historical epoch of economic development—the epoch of capitalist economy. . . . In the whole Marxist theory of economic evolution there is only one error, but an extremely important one. The development of capitalist society is the history of Western European society; the laws cited as the laws of development of this society are indeed completely accurate. But they are not laws of human society in general. It is not necessary for every society to pass through all the same stages of economic development as industrial society (for example, England, which Karl Marx had predominantly in view). With this, we wish to say that absolutely no society has to go through the purgatory of capitalist production.[10]

In this sense, as he wrote in 1871, Marxist theory does not provide a "positive basis for the solution of social problems in Serbia."[11] Later, in 1873, he added:

> Marx's program, which the International adopted, is, in the first place, one-sided and inapplicable to almost all nations except England. According to it the International will be in the minority in all countries and will never seize power. Accordingly, the

International must put forward a broad program and not just the struggle of the proletariat with the bourgeoisie, or it will disintegrate and come to ruin in its own bailiwick.[12]

A second area of disagreement with Marx was the history and nature of the state. The state is not inevitable, and it is certainly not desirable, not even in its temporary existence as a dictatorship of the proletariat: "Marx and his group within the International," Marković argued, "concerned itself primarily with economic affairs, while the Russian revolutionary tradition struck deep at the social organization of the state." It was not only capitalism but also the state organization that had a historical and transient character. Instead of the state, he envisioned a directly democratic form of self-government, organized as coordination between communes or local autonomous units whose "primary function would be the regulation of economic life and the organization of work in the interest of society as a whole, for the creation of wealth to be used by the whole society."[13]

Marković provided the final outlines of his democratic communalism in a series of studies that he wrote in Pozarevac prison. The workers' communes were to be the foundation of communalist society, a society where everyone works according to their ability and receives according to their needs. The state will disappear, and the society will become one large commune; this, Marković said, would be "complete communism." Marković defined zadruga, or family commune, as an extended family living on common property, working and consuming jointly. The distinguishing feature of the zadruga was the communal ownership of property.

The second institution upon which Marković proposed to build his democratic communalism in the Balkan Peninsula was opstina. The village commune was an administrative, political, and fiscal entity. He was not blind to the shortcomings of both of these twin pillars of democratic communalism. He recognized that the zadruga was fast disappearing, and that both the zadruga and the opstina had a patriarchal character that was inconsistent with socialism. In his view, the zadruga was declining because of its treatment of women, who felt that this restrictive patriarchal environment was responsible in great measure for their misery. This is why Marković looked at the village commune as a germ, not as a model, of a future society, a communal institution awaiting a socialist reinvention.[14]

Perhaps his greatest contribution to Balkan socialism is his democratic federalist project: a feverish attempt to subdue the separate nationalisms of the Balkan peoples in favor of all-inclusive, directly democratic federalism.[15] He argued for socialist movements that are not only anticolonial with respect to the West and the East but also revolutionary with respect to the Balkan past. Marković was an antiauthoritarian socialist who believed in a pluricultural Balkan Federation organized as a decentralized, directly democratic society based on local agricultural and industrial associations.[16]

World War I marked the end of the first phase of the democratic modernist project. Voices of cooperative/stateless modernity were erased, often killed, and ultimately defeated in the historical struggle between two traditions of the left. The anti-systemic movement of the day adopted a two-step strategy: to take state power, and then, from above, to create a socialist humanity. State-defined and party-defined movements had triumphed after the Russian Revolution in 1917.[17] With immense cruelty, the twentieth century has shown that taking state power is not enough, and that the statist-evolutionist concept of progress, defined as an eschatological end of history, is a dangerous illusion. Hence it is crucial today, in our collective effort to reinvent social emancipation, to distance ourselves from the theoretical traditions that led us to the dead end we find ourselves in. One way to do this is to draw on the central legacy of Marković, which is "balkanization," or regional delinking.

Balkanization, thus defined, implies an active dialectical relationship with the capitalist world-system, a process of selective cutting off and selective engagement, an active insertion capable of modifying the conditions of capitalist globalization. Refusing worldwide capitalist expansion does not necessitate isolation but, rather, the re-articulation of economic and political development in terms relevant to localized needs and concerns. I believe that balkanization—delinking on a regional level—offers an alternative project for the world left that should be further refined to fit new conditions. The place to start is the non-state space of Kurdish Rojava and the theory behind the Rojava revolution.

Like Svetozar Marković, Abdullah Öcalan believes that we live in the time when it is necessary to (re)invent a new kind of national liberation project. In Öcalan's formulation, "[W]hen society and civilisation meet, the main contradiction is between the state and democracy."[18] In this collective effort to reinvent social emancipation, we need to recover, excavate, and reinvent the emancipatory energies and subjectivities of what he calls democratic modernity.[19] Democratic modernity, a process and a project, is conceived not just as an alternative to capitalist accumulation but as an entirely different civilization. The trialectics of democratic modernity includes liberation of nature from capitalism, liberation of democracy from the state, and liberation of women from masculine domination. Another defining element of democratic modernity is the "democratic nation." For Öcalan, the main problem of modernity is the coupling of power and the state with the nation, "the most tyrannical aspect of modernity." Nationalism is not just an obstacle but a form of religious attachment imposed by the nation-state.[20] The revolutionaries in Rojava speak of the democratic nation as an alternative to the statist nation. It is an "organization of life detached from the state," as well as the "right of society to construct itself."[21] The democratic nation is a collective based on free agreement and plural identity. Instead of an ethno-statist nation, an inevitable product of a network of suppression and exploitation, we encounter an innovative conceptualization of a form of collective life

> that is not bound by rigid political boundaries, one language, culture, religion and interpretation of history, that signifies plurality and communities as well as free and equal citizens existing together and in solidarity. The democratic nation allows the people to become a nation themselves, without resting on power and state.[22]

Thus defined, the democratic nation does not require dominant ethnicity or a dominant language. The organization of collective life is based not on a homeland or a market but on freedom and solidarity. Territory is important, and a sense of belonging to a place is only natural, but as a place-based (not place-bound) "tool for life."

As Öcalan suggests:

> [T]he democratic nation is the model of a nation that is the least exposed to such illnesses of being a state nation. It does not sacralize its government. Governance is a simple phenomenon that is at the service of daily life. Anyone who meets the requirements can become a public servant and govern. Leadership is valuable, but not sacred. Its understanding of national identity is open-ended, not fixed like being a believer or a member of a religion. Belonging to a nation is neither a privilege nor a flaw. One can belong to more than

one nation. To be more precise, one can experience intertwined and different nationalities.... With all these characteristics, the democratic nation is once again taking its place in history as a robust alternative to capitalist modernity's maddening instrument of war: nation-statism.[23]

The political expression of democratic confederalism with democratic autonomy, which is a political expression of the democratic nation, is conceptualized as a pluricultural model of communal self-governance and democratic socialism.[24] He provides an elegant definition of democracy as "a practice and process of self-governance in a non-state society.... Democracy is governance that is not state; it is the power of communities to govern themselves without the state."[25]

There is nothing permanent or fixed about the process of direct democracy and democratic autonomy. Democracy abhors timelines. As Öcalan writes in one of his most moving passages, the democratic nation

represents a truth that requires devotion at the level of real love. Just as there is no room for false love in this voyage, there is also no room for uncommitted travelers. In this voyage, the question of when the construction of the democratic nation will be completed is a redundant one. This is a construction that will never be finished: it is an ongoing process. The construction of democratic nation has the freedom to re-create itself at every instant. In societal terms, there can be no utopia or reality that is more ambitious than this.[26]

Abdullah Öcalan has a keen interest in history. He rejects the liberal belief in "natural perversity of mankind." State and capitalism were a radical departure from natural tendencies toward democracy and cooperation, and they developed by crushing cooperative solidarities.[27] However, the state could never prevent people from relating differently to each other and to nature. Furthermore, history has demonstrated that capitalism and the state are inseparable facts and concepts that were developed to prevent direct association among people. In his view, democracy without a state is not a new order but a reconstitution of something that has always been present, that is always in existence, laid to waste alongside the rise of the state. Democracy as self-government was a constructive force that flourished when small parts of humanity broke down the power of their rulers and reassumed their freedoms in "vibrant interstices," relatively autonomous from the intrusive power of the nation-state.

This is why progress assumes a different meaning in the conceptual language of democratic modernity.[28] In this view, capitalist modernity suggests an experience of time as inevitable and linear progress, with an attendant division between nature and culture and an imagined and imposed international spatial hierarchical model.

He calls for radical overturning of the social Darwinism widely promoted by liberal intellectuals and state-centered social sciences. Against the civilization fueled by rationality, possessive individualism, and nation-states, he advocates a democratic civilization created by acts of everyday communism, self-organization, mutual interdependence, and association. Against the utopian finality of a nation-state, he emphasizes actually existing cooperative practices of mutual aid and voluntary association as democratic practices retrieved from both past and present.[29] In agreement with the ideas of Marxist geographer Henri Lefebvre, Öcalan speaks of the "power of everyday life."[30]

It is in this space of everyday life that cooperative society must be reinvented and recovered, power socialized and evenly redistributed, as a democratic nation becomes "once again" a restorative and creative historical force that "re-democratizes those societal relations that have been shattered by nation-statism." Here, Öcalan's thought discloses a curious affinity with the historical sociology of Reinhardt Kosselleck and his notion of the temporality of lived time, or the temporality of possible futures and futures past.[31] Society without the state is not society without history, but it is antagonistic to the capitalist present, resisting what Öcalan terms "societycide."[32] Society becomes ecological society, predicated on the liberation of women, referred to as the "first colony" in the five-thousand-year history of domination.

Progress is spontaneous and free experimentation with new social forms. He opposes the idea of progress and temporality that defines the imagined territorial utopia of liberal modernity. The resistance comes from the places and peoples least exposed to the violence of the modern capitalist world-system. It points to the direction of decentralization, both territorial and functional, as a way to encourage radical new forms of self-government that would return decision-making to local communities in democratic federal institutions.[33] Decentralization, for Öcalan, is a form of social organization; it does not involve geographical isolation but a particular sociological use of geography. For Öcalan, democracy without a state presumes an interwoven network composed of an infinite variety of groups and federations of all sizes and degrees. Federalism is seen as a basic principle of human organization. Defined as such, democratic confederalism is not a program for political change but an act of social self-determination.

This form of balkanization from the world of capitalist modernity is effected through the production of alternative and oppositional conceptions of a non-state space, a recovery/invention of the new/old world that would consist of multiple autonomous micro-societies bound together within mutually agreed upon federal structures.[34] More ambitiously than Svetozar Marković, Öcalan suggests a world federation as a successor to the hierarchical interstate organization of the capitalist world-system.[35] The statist nation would be replaced by a geographical confederation of confederations, in which all affairs would be settled by mutual agreement, contract, and arbitration.

Öcalan maintains that the conditions "are ripe in the twenty-first century to avoid the fate of confederal structures which were eliminated by the nation-states in the mid-nineteenth century, and to achieve the victory of democratic confederalism."[36] If the Kurds are today at the forefront of the struggle for the global democratization of society, that is because the liberation of Kurds is inextricably linked to the liberation of life, to the emancipation of humanity and nature:

> In accordance with their historical and societal reality, the Kurds have vigorously turned towards the construction of a democratic nation. As a matter of fact, they have lost nothing by ridding themselves of a nation-state god in which they never believed; they are rid of a very heavy burden, a burden that brought them to the brink of annihilation. Instead, they have gained the opportunity to become a democratic nation.[37]

Indeed, who could be better poised to pave the way to a state-free modernity than stateless people engaged in a bitter anti-fascist struggle for dignity and life? The stateless socialism of Syrian Rojava becomes, in his words, a model for another Middle East and another possible world of autonomous regions.

Weaving all these different threads together, he arrives at a definition of democratic modernity as an integral organization of democratic nation, communality, and ecology. This "system of liberated life" stands in stark opposition to the capitalist trinity of nation-state, capitalism, and industrialism.[38]

Taken together, the utopian vision promoted by Abdullah Öcalan, a vision of planetary balkanization and planetary confederation, of nature in humanity and humanity in nature, of liberation of women, colonies, and nature, of democratic socialism without a state, of a democratic nation without nationalism, constitutes an insurgent and integral ecology of hope that should be placed in dialogue with the ideas of Svetozar Marković. The left needs to recover a part of its history that was suppressed by various forms of Leninist internationalism. As Edward Thompson was fond of saying, history is forever unresolved: it is a field of unfinished possibilities. We reach back to refuse some possibilities, and we reach back to select and develop others. That is what we need to do today. We need to refuse some historical possibilities. By this I refer to liberal vision of civilization and progress. But I would also emphasize refusing Lenin's vision of party-centered and state-centered internationalism and socialism. National liberation should be understood as democratic liberation from the statist-nation. Socialism should reinterpreted as movement against the state/party form. We should select and develop other unfinished possibilities. We should, as one Japanese exile has said, wake the people from utopian dreams of nation-states and sweep the world clean of capitalism by reviving and inventing the project of democratic modernity.

This essay was written for this book.

Andrej Grubačić is the founding chair of the Anthropology and Social Change Department at the California Institute of Integral Studies, in San Francisco. His interest in world history and anarchist anthropology has influenced his research perspective, which is focused on comparative research of stateless democracies and societies on the world scale. Following Peter Kropotkin and Marcel Mauss, he studies world history as a struggle between institutions of mutual aid. His principal empirical focus is on the autonomous "cracks" peopled by Don Cossacks, Atlantic pirates, Macedonian Roma, Jamaican Maroons, Californian prisoners, Mexican Zapatistas, and autonomous Kurdish communities. This research is included in *Living at the Edges of Capitalism: Adventures in Exile and Mutual Aid* (Berkeley: University of California Press, 2016), co-authored with Denis O'Hearn. The book is a winner of the 2017 American Sociological Association Prize for Distinguished Scholarship.

Notes

1 Ilham Khuri-Makdisi, *The Eastern Mediterranean and the Making of Global Radicalism, 1860–1914* (Berkeley: University of California Press, 2010); Sho Konishi, *Anarchist Modernity: Cooperatism and Japanese-Russian Intellectual Relations in Modern Japan* (Cambridge, MA: Harvard University Press, 2015); Benedict Anderson, *Under Three Flags: Anarchism and Anti-Colonial Imagination* (London: Verso Books, 2007). There is no scholarly consensus when it comes to naming this period in the history of the left. Khuri-Makdisi suggested an interesting but somewhat clunky expression, "global radical culture"; Konishi proposed "anarchist modernity" and "cooperative modernity." I prefer to use the term introduced by Abdullah Öcalan, "democratic modernity"; *Prison Writings, Volume 3: The Road Map to Negotiations* (Cologne: International Initiative, 2012); *Manifesto for a Democratic Civilization: Civilization, Volume 1: The Age of Masked Gods and Disguised Kings* (Porsgrun, NO: New Compass Press, 2015); 2nd revised edition will be published by PM Press in 2021; *Manifesto for a Democratic Civilization, Volume 2: Capitalism: The Age of Unmasked Gods and Naked Kings* (Porsgrunn, NO: New Compass Press, 2017) ; 2nd revised edition will be published by PM Press in 2020.

2 Konishi, *Anarchist Modernity*.

3 Ibid.

4 Ibid.

5 Regional and federalist thinking constitutes one of the key aspects of anarchist political thought. Pierre-Joseph Proudhon, Peter Kropotkin, Élisée Reclus, Murray Bookchin, and Colin Ward recognized region as the basis for the total reconstruction of social and political life. It is the region not the nation that is the motor force of human development, suppressed, attacked, and eroded by the centralized nation-state and by capitalist industry. Anarchist thinkers opted for an alternative organization of socialist society, neither capitalist nor bureaucratic. Rather, they envisaged a society based on voluntary cooperation among men and women working and living in small self-governing communities. A century later, the economist Leopold Kohr published *The Breakdown of Nations* (Cambridge, UK: UIT Cambridge, 2017 [1957]), arguing, once again, that most of the world's problems arise from the existence of the nation-state. For an overview of anarchist federalist and regionalist concepts, see Andrej Grubačić, *Don't Mourn, Balkanize: Essays after Yugoslavia* (Oakland: PM Press, 2011); Andrej Grubačić, foreword to *What Is Anarchism? An Introduction*, ed. Vernon Richards and Donald Rooum (Oakland: PM Press, 2016).

6 There are several collections of Marković's work. In this essay I use the most recent edition of the monumental collection Svetozar Marković, *Celokupna Dela* (Belgrade, RS: Zavod za Udzbenike Beograd, 1995).

7 Ibid.

8 Woodford McClellan, *Svetozar Marković and the Origins of Balkan Socialism* (Princeton, NJ: University of Princeton Press, 1964), 65.

9 The concept of bureaucracy as a separate class, between labor and capital, is widely considered a major contribution to historical sociology. For more

information on the recent history of this concept, see Grubačić, *Don't Mourn Balkanize.*

10 Marković, *Celokupna Dela*, 200.

11 Ibid., 86.

12 Ibid., 145.

13 Ibid., 234.

14 McClellan, *Svetozar Marković and the Origins of Balkan Socialism*; Grubačić, *Don't Mourn, Balkanize.*

15 Grubačić, *Don't Mourn, Balkanize.*

16 Ibid.

17 Grubačić, foreword to *What Is Anarchism?*

18 Abdullah Öcalan, *Democratic Nation* (Cologne: International Initiative Edition, 2016), 63.

19 Öcalan, *The Road Map to Negotiations*; Abdullah Öcalan, *Democratic Conederalism* (Cologne: International Initiative, 2011); Abdullah Öcalan, *Liberating Life: Women's Revolution* (Cologne: International Initiative, 2013); Öcalan, *Democratic Nation*; Öcalan, *Manifesto for a Democratic Civilization*, *Volume 1*; Öcalan, *Manifesto for a Democratic Civilization, Volume 2*.

20 Öcalan, *Manifesto for a Democratic Civilization, Volume 2*.

21 Öcalan, *Democratic Nation*, 21.

22 Ibid.

23 Ibid., 27.

24 Öcalan, *Liberating Life*; there is no doubt that Öcalan's thinking follows and further develops the (con)federalist project of other theorists of democratic modernity, including Marković, Peter Kropotkin, and Murray Bookchin. Öcalan was mainly familiar with Bookchin, whom he read and actively corresponded with during his incarceration.

25 Öcalan, *Democratic Nation*, 62.

26 Ibid., 60. The alternative to capitalist modernity is democratic modernity, with the democratic nation at its core, and "the economic, ecological and peaceful society it has woven within and outside of the democratic nation"; ibid., 28. In opposition to nation-statism, the democratic nation "detaches" itself from the nation-state as a core institution of capitalist modernity; Abdullah Öcalan, *Democratic Confederalism* (Cologne: International Initiative, 2011). This would imply a deliberate fragmentation of the nation-state into non-state communities and townships linked together in complex new federal structures, wherein the mutual relations of its members would be regulated by mutual agreement and social custom.

27 Ibid.; Andrej Grubačić and Denis O'Hearn, *Living at the Edges of Capitalism: Adventures in Exile and Mutual Aid* (Oakland: University of California Press, 2016).

28 This is the real meaning of the curious formulation according to which "the solution to the Kurdish question, therefore, needs to be found in an approach that weakens capitalist modernity or pushes it back"; Öcalan, *Manifesto for a Democratic Civilization, Volume 2*, 20. Öcalan's interpretation of history, just like Marković's, is modern in a very peculiar sense: it is nonlinear and

restoratively historical. History is projected into the future, and the present is seen as a product of backward capitalist modernity; Konishi, *Anarchist Modernity*.

29 Öcalan, *Manifesto for a Democratic Civilization, Volume 2*; Sho Konishi, *Anarchist Modernity*.

30 Henri Lefebvre, *Critique of Everyday Life* (London: Verso, 2014), also see Konishi, *Anarchist Modernity*.

31 Reinhardt Kosselleck, *Futures Past* (New York: Columbia University Press, 2004).

32 Öcalan, *Manifesto for a Democratic Civilization, Volume 2*.

33 For an in-depth conversation on balkanization as a strategy of democratic space-making see Grubacic and O'Hearn, *Living at the Edges of Capitalism*.

34 Grubačić, *Don't Mourn, Balkanize*.

35 Öcalan is quite clear that he sees Kurdish democratic autonomy as a model for the Middle East and the world, as "an emerging entity" that "expands dynamically into neighboring countries"; *Democratic Confederalism*, 36. The name of this emerging entity is democratic confederalism, a project that "promises to advance the democratization of the Middle East in general"; ibid., 20.

36 Ibid., 61.

37 Ibid., 60.

38 Öcalan, *Liberating Life*.

THIRTEEN

Imaginary Dialogues with Öcalan: Updating Critical Thinking

Raúl Zibechi

As a generation that became politically aware in the 1960s, we had the privilege of experiencing a world filled with social upheaval, with permanent and unpredictable changes, with abrupt crises and extraordinary turns. In the words of the historian Eric Hobsbawm, we have lived interesting times. We have lived the times of the Cuban Revolution (1959), the war of the people of Algeria against the French occupation (1954–1962), the heroic resistance of the Vietnamese people who taught the world that even the greatest military power in the history could be defeated.

Some events back then exerted a special influence on us, including the wonderful mobilizations of African Americans in the United States against the laws on racial segregation and the movement led by the Black Panther Party, the most radical and consistent of those turbulent years. The Cultural Revolution in China seemed like a fresh wind against the bureaucracies that in the name of socialism had clung to power throughout Eastern Europe and the Soviet Union and were beginning to show their claws in Mao's land. It taught us that limiting the powers of a bureaucracy that became the new ruling class could only be achieved by mobilizing the people. The young people of Prague, challenging the tanks of the Warsaw Pact in the streets, shared a sentiment similar to that of the young Chinese who waved the *Little Red Book*.

With hindsight we can say that an entire generation of rebels committed to politics was born in the midst of these movements, which left no stone unturned. A feature of the movements of the 1960s and of the world revolution of 1968 is that they started at the periphery of the world-system and found their echo in the center. The events in Paris in May 1968, as well as the large student demonstrations on the campuses of the universities of the United States, would not have been possible without Algeria or Vietnam, for example, but also not without the October 2, 1968, massacre at the Plaza de Tlatelolco, in Mexico.

This is important, because history teaches us that profound movements always begin in the peripheries, and then move to the center, although the Eurocentric culture tends to focus uniformly on the latter. Subcomandante Marcos said it very clearly: "The great transformations neither start from above nor by monumental and epic events but with small movements that seem irrelevant to the politician and the analyst who look at them from above." For Zapatismo, historical changes do not come about through "filled squares or outraged crowds" but through the collectives that organize and coordinate "below and to the left and create another form of politics."[1] This seems to me of utmost importance, because long before we knew of the current Kurdish movement, there had already been small changes that had gone unnoticed by the vast majority of people who consider ourselves anti-capitalist, and we only began to take them into account when they began to appear in the mainstream media. In the case of the Kurdish movement, we in Latin America only began to pay attention in the middle of the 2010s when self-government in Rojava was consolidated, and the media began to focus on this new reality. It is clear that we still have a lot of personal and collective work to do to continue to decolonize and depatriarchalize our critical thinking.

We must not forget that in the 1960s, Marxism-Leninism constituted the common sense of the rebels, here and there distinguished by epithets ranging from Stalinism to Maoism or Trotskyism. Although I've given it a lot of thought, I cannot remember any of my colleagues criticizing Marx's thinking, even though I have to say that some of them were educated in the grassroots church communities, which played an important role in the early 1970s.

At the first political meeting that I attended, a sunny autumn Saturday at the Architecture School in Montevideo, the female comrade (*hevala*) at the meeting of the small group of future militants placed a book titled *Manifesto of the Communist Party* on the table. Although the half dozen of us who participated in that initial event only knew each other passingly from secondary school, none of us were surprised when she said, "I must assume that we are all socialists."

It was the common sense of the time. But not the only one. "Being like Che," the phrase that said it all, was not only about respect for the revolutionary icon fallen a year earlier in combat. It was a promise of life—a promise of giving your own life if necessary—for the revolution that would bring happiness and well-being to the world. We repeated "Being like Che" as a mantra whenever we faced any difficulty, or simply from habit. That's how certain we were that we would fight the enemy, weapons in hand.

I imagine that in Turkey they would have had other fetishized phrases to bolster resolve, disperse fear, and strengthen the fighting spirit. I would like to know what they were, and I imagine that they will relate to the history of the Kurdish people, to the infinity of heroes and heroines that this distant land has given.

We could even imagine playing a game. "We were shouting our support for Cuba and our opposition to imperialism. What about you?"

I imagine that the slogans would be against the Turkish regime, given that succession of military coups delivered with a strange punctuality: 1960, 1971, 1980. . . . I am surprised by the coincidences. In our South America, not to mention the whole of Latin America, there were coup d'états, mass incarcerations and torture, disappearances and paramilitary groups, simultaneously different from and similar to the Grey Wolves, who murdered leftist militants in Turkey.

There must also be a few differences, which I would like hear about someday. I mean the long stories, what it feels like to be part of a people without a state, something that the political currents we belonged to in the 1970s did not theorize, because common sense said that a revolution that was not focused on the state (either to seize it or to annihilate it) was neither possible nor desirable.

What impresses me most about Öcalan's thinking is his ability to change without becoming unfaithful to his goals. Let me explain myself: even the wisest people of my/our generation have shown how difficult it is to move away from what we learned, how persistent the ideas that we internalized in our youth are. Fernand Braudel (whom Apo quotes several times) once correctly stated: "Mental frameworks are also long-term prisons."[2] Moving beyond these theoretical frameworks requires a lot of intellectual courage and a lot of honesty, because it is as if we are looking at ourselves in the mirror and recognizing the limitations of our thinking and our movements.

I have the highest esteem for Öcalan's trajectory, because he did not settle for repeating what he had learned over and over again. He had the courage to take a turn—or several—when things were no longer working according to the old patterns of Marxism-Leninism. He avoided being shipwrecked in orthodoxy. Was Lenin not a heterodox with respect to Marx? And was not Mao with respect to Stalin? Overcoming orthodoxy is not merely a theoretical issue; it is related to ethics, to an attachment to both the truth and to the people.

It is not a theoretical issue, because it makes no sense to cling to a range of ideas acquired in a given context and keep repeating them when the context changes. For revolutionaries, unlike academics, ideas are not an aim in themselves. We do not defend certain ideas to establish their importance or to be recognized as intellectuals. Ideas are just a means. The only purpose is the people, the common people, those below, whatever we want to call the real people to whom we have committed ourselves.

•

When the Zapatistas were just a few dozen fighters and took the first village, they addressed the inhabitants in a dialogue that shows how the theories can be an obstacle to working with the people.

"What did you say to them?" the journalist asked the Subcomandante Marcos.

"Well, the absurdities we had learned, imperialism, social crisis, the correlation of forces, and the situation. Things that nobody understood, of course, and neither did they. They were very honest. We asked them, 'Did you understand?' And they said, 'No.' We had to adapt," Marcos says.[3]

They told him that his words were "very hard," so the Zapatistas decided to talk about the history of Mexico but as an indigenist story, focused on people like those they were talking to. It was the fighters of Indigenous origin who began to explain the history of the country. They appropriated their own history, because they acted as translators, said Marcos, while "we were spectators." The next step was to learn to listen, because they were not only talking about a different approach but also their point of reference, their cultural framework, was different. The result was a hybrid, the product of a clash in which, as Marcos says, "We lost, luckily for us, I reckon."

What was defeated at that meeting was a Eurocentric and patriarchal orthodoxy. It was a necessary defeat, the result of popular embeddedness.

I want to emphasize the important role that women have assumed in Öcalan's writing, *the importance* of focusing on patriarchy as a key mode of domination closely linked to capitalism and colonialism. It is a profound change in critical thinking, because, in the 1960s and 1970s, this was not part of our worldview; we didn't ascribe women a central place. Neither in Marxism nor in Leninism, not even in subsequent currents was this the case. To my knowledge, it is the Kurdish revolutionary movement that is working on the issue of women on the most profound level, women's oppression, an issue that permeates the whole movement and all of its facets and activities.

After these ethical-political considerations, which are the central issue, I would like to address some of the ideas encountered in Öcalan's work since he has been in İmralı prison.

Certainly, it is very difficult to synthesize his ideas and his contributions to the revolutionary movements of the world, because of the enormous diversity of the issues he addresses, because of the broad view of his analysis, but, above all, because he takes as his starting point the rejection of both capitalist civilization and the shortcut that real socialism represented.

This is one of the keys to the profound radicality of his thinking. Öcalan thinks that the crisis of civilization cannot be overcome either through the restoration of fascism or of real socialism. Contrary to what most of the left thinks, it is not about "returning" to a statist socialism that has been improved by the removal of its "deviations" but something much more profound that involves creating something new. It goes without saying that, both theoretically and politically, this radicality bothers classical intellectuals and orthodox militants alike.

However, what calls attention to Öcalan's work in prison is the consistency of thinking that runs through his books. The emancipation of women is a consistent priority, as are the defense of nature and controlling the harmful effects of technology. These are the main conclusions he has drawn from his extensive reconstruction of the history of civilizations, centered on Mesopotamia, on the banks of the Euphrates and the Tigris.

The prominent role attributed to ethics in the construction of a new world is key and goes hand in hand with two other issues that are often left unaddressed in the field of socialist thought: the importance of individuality (which is not synonymous with individualism), since we aspire to a society of free individuals as a precondition for taking responsibility for one's action and the restoration of the role of civil society, which Öcalan defines as the "third domain."

From my point of view, inevitably centered on Latin America, Öcalan manages to go beyond the Eurocentric theories of capitalist modernity, a major achievement that makes his thought indispensable to current emancipatory thinking. He rejects the modern theory of the tabula rasa—that shapes the thinking of the Jacobins as much as the Bolsheviks—according to which the past must be entirely annihilated—and instead hopes to rescue that past as one of the wellsprings of the society of the future, the longed-for "democratic civilization."

This brings me, in general, to the concrete experience of the Indigenous movements on my continent. In particular, Öcalan's work reconstructing history calls to mind for me the words of an Ecuadorian Indigenous leader, a Quichua lawyer who heads Ecuarinari, one of the most important organizations in the country. "We walk in the footsteps of our ancestors," Carlos Pérez Guartambel told me in his village, surrounded by community members who resist mining and defend water and life.

Like the Indigenous Latin American movements, Öcalan's work manages to amalgamate the cultural traditions of the Middle East with a proposal for the total transformation of Kurdish society. While the place from which a discourse, an analysis is developed, from which a theory is being elaborated must be concretely located, this does not hold for Eurocentric thought which strives to turn its own vision into a universal truth. A history that starts from the peoples that inhabited Mesopotamia cannot but enrich the history of all peoples, since its particularities add to the universal, as Aimé Césaire, who just as much refused to get caught up in the "walled segregation of the particular" as he refused to get dissolved "in the universal," pointed out half a century ago. His choice was "a universal depository of everything particular," as his letter to Maurice Thorez in 1956 ends.[4]

It seems to me that both Öcalan's thinking and what has been happening in Rojava in recent years are in tune with what many Latin American social movements are doing. To a large extent this is the case, because both were colonized by the West, and our peoples had to retreat inward to survive, enclosing their communities and their ancestral cultures like "tombs" where it was possible to recreate life.

At least three resonances can be found between these movements. The first regards the nation-state. Different peoples, including the Mapuche of Chile and Argentina, the Nasa of southern Colombia, the Aymara of Bolivia, and the Indigenous peoples of the Amazon and the lowlands, do not identify with the state nor seek positions in state institutions. The new Black movements in Colombia and Brazil are following suit and moving away from the political chess game that is the nation-state. It is not an ideological issue. For most of them, nation-states are not part of their histories and experiences as peoples; they are understood as an imposition of colonialism and Creole elites.

The Rojava Kurds do not intend to build a state. Öcalan considers the nation-state the form of power proper to "capitalist civilization." For the Kurds who share his ideas, the anti-state struggle is even more important than the class struggle, which would be considered heresy by the Latin American leftists who still look back to the nineteenth century. These leftist organizations still consider the state a shield to be used to protect workers.

In fact, the Kurdish leader's thesis is very close to Zapatista practice. The takeover of the state, writes Öcalan, "perverts the most faithful revolutionary," concluding with a reflection that rings true at the centenary of the Russian Revolution: "One hundred and fifty years of heroic struggle suffocated and volatilized in the whirlwind of power"[5]

The second resonance is economic. Zapatistas tend to mock economic "laws" and do not place that discipline at the center of their thinking, as seems evident in the collection of communications of the person formerly called Subcomandante Marcos ("Insurgent Subcomandante Galeano" today). Öcalan, on the other hand, stresses that "capitalism is power not economy." The capitalists use the economy, and force, armed and unarmed, to confiscate the surplus produced by society constitutes the core of the system.

Zapatismo defines the current extractive model—monoculture crops such as soybeans, open-pit mining, and mega-infrastructural works—as "World War IV" against the people, for its use and abuse of force to delineate societies.

Both movements are profoundly critical of economism. Öcalan recalls that "in the colonial wars, where the original accumulation was carried out, there were no economic rules." For their part, Indigenous and Black movements in Latin America feel that they fight against a colonial power, or the "coloniality of power," a term used by the Peruvian sociologist Aníbal Quijano to describe the nucleus of domination on this continent.

In effect, economism, which goes hand in hand with evolutionism, is a plague that contaminates critical movements. Many on the left believe that the end of capitalism will come about by a succession of more or less profound economic crises. Öcalan opposes that perspective and rejects the idea that capitalism came into being as "a natural result of economic development." The Zapatistas and the Kurds seem to agree on Walter Benjamin's thesis that progress is a destructive hurricane.

Contrary to the way of thinking of those of us who have been trained in Marx, he argues that much of the analysis of economic specialists is nothing more than mythological narratives that lay the basis for a new religion: "Political economy is the most falsifying and predatory theory of the fictional intellect, created to cover up the speculative character of capitalism." And he agrees with Braudel in seeing capitalism as negation of the market, because the monopolies rule the prices, which eliminates competition between producers. Going against the grain of traditional approaches, he rejects the notion that the triumph of capitalism was in any way revolutionary, thus siding with Immanuel Wallerstein's analysis that capitalism in comparison to other historical systems did not signify progress.

That is why Öcalan argues that true revolutionary struggle is not expressed by a worker fighting for his rights against his boss but, rather, by a worker resisting being a proletarian and becoming someone who fights against unemployment as much as he does against the condition of being a worker, as this struggle would be more meaningful and ethical for society. The most radical and anti-capitalist tradition of critical thinking, largely forgotten these days, is thus taken up by him.

Third, Latin American movements are close to the concept of "Good Living/Good Life," which they set in opposition to capitalist productivism. The constitutions of Ecuador and Bolivia, approved in 2008 and 2009, emphasized that nature is a "subject of law," whereas previously it was always considered an object for attaining wealth. The notion that we are not just facing a crisis of capitalism but, rather, a crisis of civilization, is slowly gaining ground among the movements.

The Kurdish movement sees capitalism as leading a crisis of modern Western civilization. This analysis allows us to overcome the ideology of progress and development and integrates the various forms of oppression linked to patriarchy and racism, as well as to the environmental and health crisis, and requires a more profound and wider view of ongoing crises.

A civilization goes into crisis when it no longer has the resources (material and symbolic) to solve the problems that it has created. That is why movements so far apart, both geographically and culturally, feel that humanity is on the threshold of a new world.

I think Öcalan has gone much further than other militants of our generation have in their criticism of both Marxism and Marx. When he writes that Marx's work is the result of "a blurring of *reason*," of a positivist and economistic stamp, and that this worldview is responsible for the failure of a century and a half of struggles for freedom and for a democratic society, he not only presents a persuasive analysis but also shows a free spirit that cannot be detained unless it finds the truth.

In this way, he recaptures the insubordinate spirit of Che, who maintained fervent discussions with the Soviet bureaucracy without either weighing the consequences or letting himself be restrained by the bonds tying the revolution to the Soviet Union. Or the rebellious and indomitable perspective of Subcomandante Moisés when he analyzes the Zapatista construction of new worlds, and that of Subcomandante Marcos when he does not make the slightest concession to the reformist and progressive left.

In this way, Abdullah Öcalan is holding up a mirror for the generation of the 1960s, for us to clearly see what we lost in rebellious dignity at the altar of pragmatism and accommodation to the dominant system.

Defeats do not justify stepping back nor is jail a reason to surrender. This dialogue with Öcalan's thought and persistence, with his ability to change without losing track, provides an example for those of us who are still committed to changing the world.

From inside İmralı prison he teaches us that changing the world is something that is impossible to do without changing ourselves, because change—as much as movement—is both single and multiple, and we cannot avoid being part of it.

Montevideo, December 2018

This essay was written for this book.

Raul Zibechi was born in 1952, in Montevideo. At seventeen, he joined the Student Revolutionary Front, the mass front group of the MLN-Tupamaros. In 1975, he was exiled to Buenos Aires and, in 1976, to Spain, where he joined the communist movement working on peasant literacy and participated in the movement against NATO. In the 1980s, he began publishing in the newspapers *Egin* (Basque Country), *Liberación* (Spanish state), *Page 12* (Argentina), and *Mate Amargo* (Uruguay). Since returning to Uruguay he works for the weekly *Brecha*, where he won the Cuban José Martí Prize for his coverage of the piquetero movement in Argentina. Since 1985, he has worked with and in social movements, particularly in Latin America, both in training and in the theoretical analysis of collective action. After the Zapatista uprising of 1994, a way past the Eurocentric heritage of Marxism opened up, beginning an investigation of the contributions of the Indigenous, African American, and mestizo peoples. He has published nineteen books in eight languages in seventeen countries and, in 2017, received an honorary doctorate for his career's work at the Universidad Mayor de San Andrés, in La Paz, Bolivia.

Notes

1 "Coloquio Aubry. Parte I. Pensar en Blanco," Enlace Zapatista, December 13, 2007, accessed July 9, 2019, http://enlacezapatista.ezln.org.mx/2007/12/13/conferencia-del-dia-13-de-diciembre-a-las-900-am/.

2 Fernand Braudel, "Histoire et Sciences sociales: La longue durée," *Annales* 13, no. 4 (October–December 1958): 725–53, accessed September 11, 2019, https://www.persee.fr/doc/ahess_0395-2649_1958_num_13_4_2781.

3 "Interview with Carmen Castillo, October 1994," *Contrahistorias* no. 20 (August 2013): 63.

4 Aimé Césaire, "Letter to Maurice Thorez," October 24, 1956, accessed September 11, 2019, http://abahlali.org/wp-content/uploads/2015/11/153945859-Aime-Cesaire-Letter-to-Maurice-Thorez-1956.pdf.

5 Quotes from Abdullah Öcalan, *La Civilización Capitalista: La era de los dioses sin máscara y los reyes desnudos* (Carcas: Ambrosia, 2017); English edition *Manifesto of the Democratic Civilization: Volume II: Capitalism: The Age of Unmasked Gods and Naked Kings* (Oakland: PM Press, 2nd revised edition, forthcoming 2020).

SECTION IV
Political Philosophy and Political Action

FOURTEEN

Making Connections: *Jineolojî*, Women's Liberation, and Building Peace

Mechthild Exo

When, in January 2018, just a few days before Turkey's attack on Afrin, a *jineolojî* conference took place in Dêrik, Northern Syria, it was announced with the slogan "Defending the Success of the Revolution." Since then, this slogan has acquired a meaning that goes far beyond internal social change. In the light of the war, which is threatening to escalate, I consider in this essay the question of how the negotiation and building peace can become a direct democratic and jineological process.

The etymology of the first part of the word *jineolojî* goes back to the Kurdish word *jin* for "woman," which, moreover, is closely connected to the word *jîn* for *life*. The ending *lojî* is derived from the Greek word *logos*, which means word, cause, reason, or, in analogy, science. This new word and the first ideas about the concept of *jineolojî* come from Abdullah Öcalan, the imprisoned political thinker and chairman of the Partiya Karkerên Kurdistanê (PKK: Kurdistan Workers' Party).

In this essay, I want to address various aspects of jineolojî by "creating connections." First of all, I want to mention the epistemological understanding of jineolojî, which is based on connections and not, as in conventional science, on dissections and separations. The character of jineolojî, as well as that of other feminist, decolonial, and non-Western knowledge systems represents a social and ethical integration and the manifold connections between humans, between humans and nature, between subareas of knowledge, etc. For whom is knowledge produced in these systems and to what effect? Why is this important?

The second connecting aspect results from the holistic approach of jineolojî and creates a bridge between jineolojî, women's liberation, and peace building. Jineolojî and women's liberation are already being situated in relationship to each other in the social process of the women's revolution in Northern Syria, but in Europe connections between jineolojî and women's liberation are only rarely drawn. Similarly, the connection between jineolojî, women's liberation, and the end of the war and a peace process in Syria (and the whole of the Middle East) is rarely addressed. We hear and repeat that a women's revolution is being defended in Rojava, in Northern Syria. We are also conscious of the fact that a direct democratic mobilization is necessary in order to build pressure against a Turkish invasion. But somewhere along the line of our thinking about how a solution to the difficult military and political conflict and the overall threatening situation can be found, the significance of the new science of women seems to get lost. How can we conceive of a peace process as a direct democratic process of gender liberating, restructuring, and increased democratization? How can the adoption of state-centered thinking and a slide into diplomatic power tussles be avoided?

Finally, a third aspect is the interweaving of thoughts about jineolojî, women's liberation, and peace building with the political ideas of Abdullah Öcalan. In this way, I overcome the existing separations: for one thing, the total isolation in prison, for another, the attempt at delegitimizing Öcalan's important thinking and rendering it invisible. It is not just his political analyses, ideas, and concrete proposals that are urgently needed for a peace settlement in the Middle East but also himself as a person. We need to be able to communicate with Öcalan as an important thinker and political negotiator. The peace process must be implemented through comprehensive communication involving all social groups. Each step toward this goal is important, but, ultimately, Öcalan's liberation is a necessity.

The Decolonization of the Forms of Knowledge

Some central points of a jineological criticism with regards to the positivist science conventionally practiced in the West concern what is defined as science, the connection between power and knowledge, and the mechanisms that keep women at a distance from knowledge. Like the society in which it exists, the hegemonic science is Eurocentric and shaped by patriarchy. It primarily serves to preserve the status quo, that is, to keep the West and capitalist patriarchy in power. Global Indigenous movements have turned science into a battlefield of decolonization. The development of freedom-loving research practices that make cross-cultural research without oppression and manipulation possible was described as an important task by Edward Said in his book *Orientalism*, because it opens the option of creating alternatives to the typical presumptuous Western self-assurance achieved by the construction of a devalued Other.[1]

Colonialism and science must be thought of as directly connected. For the colonized of the whole world, research has become one of their many experiences with destructive, colonialist practices. "The word itself, 'research,' is probably one of the dirtiest words in the Indigenous world's vocabulary."[2] With this sentence, Linda Tuhiwai Smith begins her book *Decolonizing Methodologies*, which she wrote from the perspective of the Maori and as a project of the global Indigenous movement. During the UN Decade of the Indigenous Populations of the World (1994–2004), Western scientific epistemologies and methods were massively questioned by Indigenous researchers, and the demand for decolonization was raised. Indigenous communities reject projects involving exploitative research and develop and confidently practice Indigenous research approaches that are anchored in their culture and seize on the problems of their society. One example is Kaupapa Maori research.[3] Parallel to this, in Latin America, the Eurocentric orientation of the universities and the continuation of colonialism in forms of power, such as, inter alia, the colonial character of knowledge, was challenged. Representatives of the group Modernity/Coloniality/Decoloniality demanded epistemic disobedience and a delinking from the colonial power relations within forms of knowledge.[4] The ability to describe and change one's own concepts, criteria, and methods is won in opposition to the claim to universality of the system of knowledge that emerged under the specific historical, cultural, and power political conditions of Europe.

Jineolojî and Relational Epistemology

The colonized of the whole world are decolonizing, in many places and in many different ways, the historical narratives, the descriptions of reality, the political concepts, and much more. To do this, the fundamental understanding of how true knowledge can be produced must be determined anew, primarily by resorting to the respective local traditions and systems of knowledge that were delegitimized and destroyed by colonialism. Thus, among the Aymara in the Andes region in Latin America, knowledge that is imparted nonlinguistically and is instead learned and stored in the body through lived experience or rituals is regaining a higher status: "experiential knowledge that is lived-through and gained *in, from, with* and *within* the world; with and from plants, mountains, lakes, animals, and not least, certain knowledgeable places in the landscape, so called *wak'as*."[5]

Moreover, in many places, reference is made to the feminist critique of science. Parallel to the colonial subjugation of the world by Europe beginning in 1492, within Europe there was a war against the women known as the witch hunt. Women were forced out of the influential social roles they still held (for example in the craft guilds), wise women and women healers were persecuted and killed, and patriarchal repression was intensified. The male-controlled, androcentric sciences developed with the exclusion of the women and as a form of knowledge that centers the male and defines him as the norm. For that reason, feminist theory like decolonial theory has formulated a radical critique of the foundations of science.

Positivist science, which, despite criticism, continues to be the cornerstone of Western science, is rejected. Through its dualist juxtapositions, simplified and hierarchical categories are created and unambiguously delineated from each other: the human being and nature, politics and society, subject and object, etc. Humans and social groups are regarded as objects of research that don't themselves act or think to produce knowledge. They are described and, in the final analysis, manipulated by means of the research results. In the understanding of positivist research, scientists stand outside and above the nature and society that they are researching, which they turn into the passive object of that research. For the researchers, the suspension of all existing forms of integration into social nexuses and other relations in the world becomes the greatest ideal. From a decolonial, feminist, and jineological perspective, this understanding of science is criticized as violent and as an exercise of power.

Instead of isolating parts of phenomena, reducing complexities to small, controllable categories, and separating phenomena from the social or emotional relationships, life circumstances, and corporealities, jineolojî understands research as work with relations and inclusions. Indigenous decolonial research models highlight the multitude of connections within which the research takes place. The issue is relational epistemology; which is to say, it is not an abstract research design implemented from a distance that guides the execution. Rather, the basis of research consists in engaged, committed, and resilient relationships that support the greater collective.

Mutual respectful and trusting relations characterized by care, honest self-revelation, and the acceptance by the research community thus formed of responsibility for each other and the effects of the research are the precondition for the sharing of knowledge and the work on the research question.[6]

Feminist research aims at dissolving the hierarchy between the researcher and the object of research and, in the best case, at arriving at a relationship of mutuality between equal subjects. Nature too should count as an equal subject with dignity that must not be dismembered and destroyed for the purpose of research. In this paradigm, it is necessary to learn to understand the relatedness of all parts, the senses, and the emotions.[7] Concern and empathy instead of neutral noninvolvement are seen as criteria for good research. The notion of objectivity, which ensures science a terrifying degree of authority, along with conformity with the existing power relations, is radically questioned and newly defined. The situatedness of research, the corporeality of the researchers, their cultural and political expectations, their social bonds, relations, and life conditions, and the location of the research all play a role in attaining true and meaningful knowledge.

Decolonial and feminist research demand an end to research as a mostly individualist enterprise that strives to adhere to a purported freedom from values and an indifference to the object of research. It instead calls for research that sees itself as political and consciously partisan and sees both the researchers and the research object as part of the larger social whole and individual problems as the expression of repressive social conditions. The perspective from below must replace the conventional perspective from above. Research ought to serve the interests of the oppressed, particularly women.[8]

Jineolojî is a special kind of science that becomes easier to comprehend against this background. This new science has its roots in the Middle East and is being developed on the basis of the experiences of the Kurdish (women's) movement. It is, however, not a locally or culturally bound specific science but a fundamental project that is already being intensely discussed and coevolved in Europe and in Latin America. Jineolojî takes the exclusion of women's perspectives in conventional science as its starting point and develops an autonomous system of knowledge from the standpoint of women. All historical forms of knowledge, such as mythology, religion, philosophy, and science, are laid out once more in order to understand the—probably five-thousand-year-old—enforcement of patriarchy and other power relations built upon it. "The lifting into visibility and consciousness of the rich social resources of local women's history and culture in the different epochs and communities of the peoples of Northern Syria represents a particularly important source of inspiration and a reference point."[9] The colonial and patriarchal penetration right to the foundations of science is rejected, and autonomous methods, criteria, and concepts are developed. Jineolojî turns against the mystified and elitist expert cult of established science. It is understood as a social project, as a form of research and education that unfolds in the midst of society. "Jineolojî will play a role in encouraging society to realize its own force and its capacity to administer itself. At the same time, the procedures of autonomy [autonomous organizing among women] and the ability to use these will contribute to developing the ABCs of the social sciences from the perspective of the woman."[10]

Science and Education for the Ethical-Political Society

The revolutionary democratization process that was put into motion by the Kurdish movement represents a development in which society increasingly takes responsibility for itself, for all decisions about the matters that concern it, and for the common ethical foundations. Politics is then no longer something distant and superordinated that is managed by others—for example, the government, the state, or the military. The questions and perspectives of the self-organizing, ethical-political society will yield a research and educational mandate that integrates collective experience and social knowledge into its work process.

In the Democratic Federation of Northern Syria, for example, this means the immediate founding of women's communes and education for women in every location newly liberated from the Islamic State (ISIS). Thus, jineolojî stands and emerges in the very midst of society: the research and further development of the science of women in all realms of application is conducted at the Faculty for Jineolojî, University of Rojava, as well as in several research centers. The arising knowledge is disseminated at academies, through other study paths, in schools, and in everyday political communication. It shapes the lifestyle in the women's village of Jinwar and in many other places.

Jineolojî is seen as the "science of and for the women's revolution."[11] With the revolutionary process that has been unfolding in Northern Syria since 2012, which has also been described as a women's revolution, a new, self-organized, direct democratic society is being built. From the beginning, women's organizations played an initiating, constructive, structuring, inspiring, and defensive role. The freedom of the women, the strengthening of their self-confidence, their rights and education, and the work of women in all areas including leadership tasks and armed defense are fundamental aspects of the new social order.

It is becoming clear that education enjoys a very prominent place in the Kurdish movement and is a firmly established building block for all sections of the movement and in the process of self-administration in Northern Syria. Abdullah Öcalan once said that revolutionary processes are at all times primarily educational processes. Part of this is continuous reflection on one's own personality and an assessment of the influence of the dominant relations that are effective within us and that we reproduce. The patriarchal penetration of our modes of thought, our relations, our whole way of life runs deep. All genders must try to come to grips with this, educate themselves, reflect on themselves, and liberate themselves. Öcalan has repeatedly stressed this. The creation of jineolojî as a new science, as well as ideas about the contours of this project, were originally proposed by him. With jineolojî, an understanding of the effects and the possibility of overcoming patriarchy is being worked out. It analyzes the connection between patriarchy, on the one hand, and capitalism and the state, marriage and family, the economy, and natural conditions, as well as health and other areas, on the other hand.

Jineolojî and Women's Liberation in Europe
Jineolojî has already arrived in Europe and is inspiring many women and trans and intersex persons in many countries. After the first big conferences in Cologne (2014), Stockholm (2015), and Paris (2016), international and, then, national and regional jineolojî camps took place over several days in areas and countries such as Italy, Spain, the Basque Country, France, Sweden, and Germany. Jineolojî provides an impetus that reminds people involved in revolutionary women's struggles in Europe to analyze how the social situation and our personality have been shaped by the history of domination in Europe and in the respective countries of the continent and, not least, to discuss how isolation and hopelessness can be overcome through the self-organization.

Internationalists who are in a process of exchange with the Kurdish women's movement are asking questions about what has weakened feminism and women's movements in Europe and where they have gone in the wrong direction. Connections of feminist theory to the women's movement and to the work on radically transforming society have been lost. The reasons for this are numerous. On the road to the academic recognition of feminism, there has been an adaptation to the fundamental institutional and state consensus. Moreover, feminist demands have been co-opted and watered down by the capitalist economic system, and the original critique of economism, androcentrism, and statism has been consigned to oblivion.[12] Feminist scientists no longer justify their work in terms of the concerns and the needs of the women's movements like they did in the 1970s at the women's summer universities that functioned as shared sites of education and discussion. To the degree that this shift didn't simply lead to completely leaving political involvement behind, because gender research supposedly shouldn't be tangled up with politics, change began to be primarily understood as having rights safeguarded by the state. In short, there was an arrangement with the patriarchal state regulatory framework, and any critique of the system that went beyond words on a piece of paper was surrendered.

Jineolojî is an impetus to return to the anti-systemic roots and the radical transformational claim of feminist theory and movement in Europe, to understand past aberrations and to again pursue as a scientific issue the decisive question of how to get rid of the social system that is destroying us.[13] At that time, we all knew that women's research "had to be lateral to all sciences" (as it was formulated at the Bielefeld Sociologists' Convention in 1976). As feminist research, it was necessarily a critique of dominant science."[14] Women's research emerged in the streets and in women's groups that had a political goal and were not in research institutes. By the end of the 1970s, Maria Mies postulated the change of the status quo as the point of departure of feminist scientific research. She claimed that this required participation in liberating actions, and that it would bring about a process of self-transformation.[15]

Jineolojî has assessed and evaluated feminist experience. It links back to many things but also criticizes a number of flaws and mistakes. "Despite the immense knowledge that feminism has built, the latter has still not accepted the role and responsibility to show society the necessity and the dimension of social change."[16] In Europe, feminists haven't succeeded in organizing themselves for the necessary social change or in building alliances. Now there is some hope that jineolojî will provide an important impetus for further developments. The jineolojî institutions in Northern Syria are expressly interested in an exchange of experience and in cooperation with the women's movements and women's researchers the world over.

Peace Building as a Direct Democratic Process

Now I want to build a bridge to questions of creating peace. Is this a presumptuous idea, given the military penetration of Turkey into Northern Syria, which is presently threatening to escalate even further, and given the range of international involvement, negotiations, and power claims in the region? My primary goal here is to direct the reader's attention to the problems inherent in a statist mentality that regards the solution of conflicts as lying primarily in the power negotiations between the actors in the arena of violence. This kind of thinking, oriented around the ordering model of the *state*, dominates (theories and concepts of) international policy and has considerable influence on peace and conflict research, peace movements, and on leftist and feminist discourses. Approaches distancing themselves from this current exist in parallel.

I am trying here to strengthen a different way of thinking and to connect it to jineolojî. Democratic solutions aimed at women's liberation cannot wait until a new regulatory framework has been established through negotiations between state and military actors. Jineological methodology, thinking, and knowledge is needed in all phases, but particularly at times when we are aggressively being pushed in the opposite direction. The imperial attempt at annihilation must also be pushed back through strong epistemologies, concepts, and analyses of our own. In this regard, I am actually referring to the ideas that Abdullah Öcalan formulated in 2009 as a road map for the peace process with Turkey, a process that was unilaterally ended by the Turkish government in 2015.

One of Öcalan's fundamental theoretical assumptions about a peace settlement from the perspective of democratization is that it is necessary to differentiate between theories promoting statist solutions of social problems and the theory underlying a democratic solution. "The state and democracy are realms that have to be dealt with in carefully separated ways." In this, the state is not ignored as a condition and as a negotiation partner: "The major opportunity for democratic theories lies in the fact that they envisage a flexible non-state solution that neither strives for a state nor negates or denies it."[17] But he also says that a solution is an issue that must be addressed by society not by the state, and that any solution must come from society itself.

The social activities being developed in Rojava, Northern Syria, since December 2018, when Turkish president Recep Tayyip Erdoğan began to make concrete threats about smashing the region ruled by self-adminis-tration, indicate the intention to continue to pursue the will of society, while keeping an eye on the war. We can see the people demonstrating in the streets, defiantly assembling in large unarmed crowds at the border to Turkey, and arming themselves as a population for self-defense, but we can also, for example, see them opening a new kindergarten or a new jineolojî research center to promote exactly the construction effort that Turkey wants to attack and destroy. On the occasion of the opening of the jineolojî center on January 8, 2019, the representative of the women's movement, Kongreya Star, said: "[This] is the best response to all threats of attack. The women of Rojava have proven themselves and have occupied their place in all realms of the revolution. Women organize themselves in accordance with the paradigm proposed by Abdullah Öcalan and partici-pate in a decisive way in the construction of a moral and political society."

People defy the attempt by violent state actors to impose their will and their method of warmongering. Jineolojî offers a completely different way to defend yourself. Defense is connected to the process of becoming yourself. This includes the analysis of history to understand which patri-archal, capitalist, individualizing mechanisms have become part of our personality, way of life, and relationship with society. The primary goal in all this is to achieve a free social life connected to nature. On the road to this goal, we need to learn to build strong relationships based on equality that respect differences and regard mutual care as central.

A call by Make Rojava Green Again and the Mesopotamia Ecology Movement for days of action against the threatened attack by Turkey is addressed to ecological activists all over the world who want to become allies in the ecological construction work in Northern Syria. The goal is to prevent the destruction of the necessities of life and nature by spent uranium-rich ammunition, chemical warfare agents, and the burning of forests and oil fields, and to carry on with ecological projects such as refor-estation, establishing protected areas, and preventing dam construction in Turkey. They write: "This is about the defense of hope, life, and humane-ness against fascism." Öcalan describes the promotion and organization of environmental consciousness and the friendship with nature as one of the most important activities in the democratization process.[18] "If ecology and feminism continue to develop, the patriarchal and statist system will be thrown into turmoil."[19] Another example is the demonstration against the impending war that took place in Berlin on December 20, 2018, a protest that was seen as necessary because: "The revolution in the Northern Syria, in Kurdish Rojava, has given all of us more than we can ever give back. It has shown us that another world beyond capitalist modernity is possible; it has given us hope in a time when the left is socially isolated in many countries; it is an island of council democracy, gender equity, and the creation of communal self-administrations right in the midst of a war in Syria that is sponsored by numerous foreign states."

The examples just mentioned reflect an approach to the violent conflict and the intended peace that is based on the theory of a democratic solution. "Not every peace is oriented toward a democratic solution, but every democratic solution guarantees that what evolves will be what we call a 'peace with dignity.'"[20] Öcalan explains that the principle of a democratic solution is always a matter of democratizing civil society as the basis and not to see control of the state as the goal. Here, civil society means a democratic, politically and ethically responsible society, a society that must not be regarded as an appendix to the state.[21]

But in international peace building, the expropriation of democratic social agency is the standard procedure. Since the 1900s, liberal state and peace building have been the normal approach to achieving peace in international politics. Since 2005, a corresponding peace building structure has been created within the UN. A neoliberal market economy within a representative democratic statehood is praised as the guarantee for security and peace and, if necessary, is forcefully implemented either by violent intervention, governance and peace building counselors, or both. This top-down institution building is coupled with a technocratic construction of civil society and presumptuous, pedagogical capacity building programs (citizenship education, gender sensitivity, private investments, and support money management). In all of this, civil society has the function of assisting in building the state in a complementary fashion. Analyses of developments of such peace building efforts in Afghanistan show that autonomously organized direct democratic groups, as well as local democratic and feminist experiences, are actively suppressed and marginalized.[22] The negotiation tables for transitional settlements and peace are staffed with all those representatives (overwhelmingly male) who, from the hegemonic statist and security perspective, are to be taken seriously because of their capacity to exercise violence and power. Lack of democratic orientation or responsibility for serious war crimes and human rights violations are generally not obstacles to participating in the process. Groups that use violence are rewarded with political influence and the other safeguards distributed in power-oriented negotiations. In this sense, the basic framework and the power relations of the new state order are preordained. But this means that this model merely projects the semblance of a democratic orientation coupled with a promise of stability (liberal peace) and sold as salvation and the responsibility to protect. These forms of peace building are characteristic of world politics but, as the example of Afghanistan among many others shows, they will never enjoy legitimacy among the population. On the contrary, ignoring the will of the population and the ongoing multifaceted structural violence of the social conditions this process creates will inevitably engender further conflict.

In its "#RiseUp4Rojava—Call for Global Days of Action on 27 and 28 January 2019" against Erdoğan's declaration of war, the Internationalist Commune writes about the meetings "behind closed doors where regional and imperialist powers are negotiating the future of the peoples of northeastern Syria. . . . In these negotiations we hear the voices of the rulers, talking over the heads of the people of Syria and Rojava. They are concerned only with the redistribution of Syria's wealth and land. Cities such as Idlib and Manbij, whole regions and peoples: all are carved up and traded for one another by the imperialist powers. The people themselves have no voice in this process."[23] But in Rojava, there are strong direct democratic structures, and there is a society whose self-organization is working well despite embargo and war. Moreover, in many parts of the world there are people who, building on their respective struggles and social grassroots organizing, have already created connections with the revolution in Rojava. For all those reasons, peace building will (have to) take a different course than the standard one sketched above.

At this point, both fundamentally different approaches are being practiced simultaneously. On the one hand, there are people pursuing solutions to the conflict that are oriented around dividing up power, while, on the other, there is a pursuit of democratic solutions that continue to advance democratic self-organization. It is clear that the latter path must not be given up under any circumstances. In the recent weeks, after Erdoğan announced an attack was coming, it has become clear that the defense activities developed in the Kurdish areas and here in Europe against the Turkish threat of war clearly rest on the further growth of democracy, the continued development of the democratic, gender-liberatory, and ecological construction of society, with a parallel development in other regions of the world. There are worldwide manifestations of solidarity, as well as a strong interest in continuing to build the revolution and a dignified peace. "Here, we must recognize the building of an alternative to patriarchy and annihilation, and we are sure that this project is one for all people who long for freedom and a different life," the feminist delegation of the German campaign Gemeinsam Kämpfen (Fight Together) wrote from Northern Syria in late December 2018.

According to Öcalan, a peace process must not enforce power-based solutions oriented around the interests of states. This excludes solutions that focus on the division of power. "The democratic solution does not, in principle, deal with the division of power; on the contrary, it even stays away from power."[24] The concentration on power, he says, will lead to a departure from democracy and the lack of participation of the social forces, thereby shaping society as governments or states (or other violent actors) see fit, resulting in anti-democratic conditions. In which case, simply opening of a path toward democratization would not be enough to achieve that goal.

The peace process does not begin with the official launching of negotiations. The character of the future social order is constantly being articulated in very practical ways and should be able to find its place in the negotiation process and affect its outcome—those involved need to continue to work on this. If an acceptable solution is to be achieved, the objective should be a future peace process that serves to establish a framework for the democratization process that is unfolding in numerous disparate places, in many forms, and with different practices. All social groups must be closely involved in negotiations to assure that all segments of the political-ethical self-reliant society play their part. Even now, these social groups are preoccupied with continuing to develop and advance the gender liberation, the ecological developments, and the democracy anchored in the communes and councils. This includes placing consciousness and justice above the principle of strength.[25] "A society cannot live without justice and a conscience."[26] It is necessary to create comprehensive communication networks around the negotiations to prevent governments and UN appointees from turning them into a chess game focused

on the division of power and imposing state- and market-oriented param-
eters, while excluding the population itself.

Peace as a Feminist/Jineological Process

Abdullah Öcalan's political philosophy sees the freedom of the woman
as both the basic condition for the new society and as a stabilizing factor.
This includes an understanding of the need to reverse the significant role
assigned to men in the revolutionary process under patriarchy. Öcalan
assigns a higher revolutionary status to women's liberation in the twenty-
first century than he does to class or national liberation. "The extent
to which society can be thoroughly transformed is determined by the
extent of the transformation attained by women. The level of women's
freedom and equality determines the freedom and equality of all sections
of society."[27] The complete success of the women will be the essence of the
era of the democratic civilization. "Without the equality of the sexes, any
demand for freedom and equality is meaningless and illusory. Just as the
peoples have a right to self-determination, women too should determine
their own fate. This is not a question that can be postponed and deferred.
On the contrary, in the formation of a new civilization the freedom of the
woman will be essential for the realization of equality."[28]

Feminist peace research shows that when gender equality is achieved,
violence decreases.[29] Abolishing gender inequality and dissolving the
dualist system of the male norm and the female Other into the equality of
all sexes without stereotypical assignments of male and female leads to
societies that manage their internal and external conflicts less violently.[30]
Surveys by UN Women (http://www.unwomen.org/en) show that peace
processes in which no women are involved—as is the general rule—clearly
prove to be less durable than those in which women play an active part. In
2000, the UN Security Council adopted UN Resolution 1325, which calls for
the participation of women in peace processes. Nonetheless, the majority
of peace treaties are still concluded and signed without the involvement
of women. There is a statistically marked increase of 64 percent in the
likelihood that a peace process will succeed if groups from civil society,
including women's organizations, participate in decision-making,[31] which
raises the question: Why is the involvement of women in peace negotiations not the standard practice?

However, the participation of women in peace negotiations
demanded here, which has been proven to be an effective way of ensuring

the survival of peace treaties, should not be based on women as biological objects. Their mere participation in frameworks that are deeply patriarchal doesn't bring about change. For example, women have time and again been used to legitimize the presence of Western military forces in Afghanistan, with the feminists in Revolutionary Association of Women of Afghanistan (RAWA) describing the Afghan women who are regularly selected to attend conferences as "dolled-up showpiece women" whose mouths have been sweetened with money and luxuries. "[They] do not want to speak a word about the bitter truth of the situation of women, let alone stand up against, stop and prosecute the real perpetrators of the ongoing disaster in support of their fellow women."[32] According to RAWA, it is impossible for these women to represent the majority of women, as they share the discourse of the murderers in power and, thus, themselves become enemies of the Afghan women. Many of these women are reactionaries connected to Islamist organizations and warlords. A CIA strategy paper published by Wikileaks confirms that (selected) Afghan women are deliberately pushed into speaking positions in order to counter the rejection of the military intervention in Afghanistan by 80 percent of the population in France and Germany.[33] It is, therefore, important that the women participating in peace negotiations are selected in direct democratic processes by organized women's rights groups, and this has been consistently blocked in peace negotiations. Given the separation of civil society from the negotiating bodies, Afghan women's organizations along with numerous other civil society organizations have demanded "that they should be considered as the true agent for the establishment of peace and stability being involved in all decision makings, and not mere victims of circumstances."[34]

Women were also largely excluded from the Astana negotiations on the conflict in Syria chaired by Russia, as well as from the UN-led negotiations in Geneva. They constituted a very small minority, never rising above 15 percent of the delegates present (this at the meeting in December 2017). In 2016, after the Geneva peace negotiations had been going on for four years, an advisory council consisting of twelve women was established. But these women only participated in the negotiations as observers. Moreover, the composition of the women's advisory council is quite doubtful, because, among other things, it includes Islamist women, while women from the self-administered region in Northern Syria have never been involved in the process.

When ways to communicate with civil society were envisaged during the peace negotiations between the Kurdish movement and Turkey in 2013, the Council of the Wise was established—a body largely made up of men close to the Turkish government and handpicked by Recep Tayyip Erdoğan. Öcalan would not accept the exclusion of women's organizations from the peace process and made it a condition for negotiations that representatives of the women's movement participate on a permanent basis at the negotiation table and in the ongoing communication process around the İmralı Delegation that would visit his prison island. On the basis of a decision made by women from the Demokratik Toplum Kongresi (DTK: Democratic Society Congress), the Kurdish women's movement has worked toward democratizing the negotiation process and turning it into a process of social discussion that women play the key role in shaping (Cenî Kurdistan, April 23, 2013).[35] Thus, a Council of Wise Women for the impending "Solution and Negotiation Process" was founded. The DTK women's meeting emphasized that women should actively intervene in developments and should play an important role in working out a new constitution for Turkey, one that would establish the equality of women and a develop a women's policy to fight gender discriminatory, militaristic, and sexist politics. Participants at the women's meeting also made it clear that it was the role of the women "to manage, promote, and control" the process leading to a new and peaceful order "in a partisan fashion as Kurdish women." The meeting also evaluated the worldwide experiences of women in peace negotiations.[36]

Another Kurdish women's movement project with important ramifications for future peace negotiations is the draft proposal for a social contract presented in 2002 for international discussion among women's organizations. In accord with the patriarchal power relations, social contracts have historically been written by men. When drafting peace treaties and new state constitutions whereby the Kurdish movement establishes its self-organization and democratization, the Kurdish women's movement, with its wealth of experience, simply cannot be left out if the process is to lead to a sustainable peace.

The peace process needs both the peace movement and jineolojî if it is to give form to and firmly establish a social liberation that has its roots in gender liberation and women acting as trailblazers in the construction of democratic confederalism and has an ecological consciousness that denies the domination of nature, thereby expressing the will of the people.

Jineological research starts by rethinking the vibrant interconnection of partial areas of knowledge that have been dismembered to once again establish their lively interconnection. Social experience is evaluated as a form of knowledge focused on a dignified, self-determined, just, and caring life, rather than one circumscribed by power, control, interests, profit, and competition. In the process, the capacity is developed to sustain and further work on relationships that center the socially connected character of life and of all living things. This is done as part of rejecting the hegemony of Western Eurocentric ideas and scientific approaches, including positivism. In *The Road Map for Peace Negotiations* this is exactly what Öcalan argues is necessary, not least because the positivist mentality also results in a dogmatic overevaluation of concepts such as *nation* and *state*. Here, jineolojî aids in thinking through, depicting, reflecting, consciously advocating, and continuing to deepen the democratization of society. This is key to any political process that hopes to ultimately force the state to create room for a democratic way of life.

From the experience of our struggle, I know that women's liberation struggle will be faced with extremely fierce resistance as soon as it enters the realm of the political. But without winning in the political space, there can be no lasting achievement. A victory in the political realm does not, however, mean that it is now women who rise to power. On the contrary, the struggle against statist and hierarchical structures means the creation of alternative structures that are not oriented around a state and that lead to a democratic society with freedom for the sexes. In this way, not only women but all of humanity will win.[37]

Every step in the direction of self-organization, of revolutionary education, of the reflection of one's personality, of connecting with all other direct democratic structures in different places and locations represents a move toward strengthening the peace process as a democratic solution. However, we also need a common theoretical basis and methods for developing and passing on the knowledge necessary to build a new society. In this regard, jineolojî can play an important role.

This essay was written for this book. Many thanks to Ina Göken for her careful reading of the essay, her suggestions, and her corrections.

Mechthild Exo is a lecturer on transculturality and international developments at University of Applied Sciences Emden/Leer, Germany, and a member of the Jineolojî

Center in Brussels. She holds a master's degree in Peace and Conflict Studies and was the women's speaker for the German Arbeitsgemeinschaft für Friedens- und Konfliktforschung (AFK: Association for Peace and Conflict Studies) from 2016 to 2018. Her research in Afghanistan on the decolonial critique of liberal peace building allowed her to present the generally overlooked perspective of Afghan feminist and democratic grassroots organizations. Her areas of focus are feminist and decolonial epistemologies and research methodologies, Indigenous approaches to knowledge, and jineolojî. In addition, her teaching focuses on a critique of racism and feminicide and on decolonizing social work. She has been active as an internationalist and antimilitarist since the 1980s.

Notes

1 Edward Said, *Orientalism* (Middlesex, UK: Penguin Books, 1995 [1978]).
2 Linda Tuhiwai Smith, *Decolonizing Methodologies: Research and Indigenous Peoples* (London: Zed Books, 2008), 1.
3 Ibid.
4 Walter D. Mignolo, *Epistemischer Ungehorsam: Rhetorik der Moderne, Logik der Kolonialität und Grammatik der Dekolonialität* (Vienna: Verlag Turia + Kant, 2012).
5 Anders Burman, "Places to Think with, Books to Think About: Words, Experiences and the Decolonization of Knowledge in the Bolivian Andes," *Human Architecture* 10, no. 1 (January 2012): 101–20, accessed September 12, 2019, https://scholarworks.umb.edu/humanarchitecture/vol10/iss1/11/ (italics in the original).
6 Smith, *Decolonizing Methodologies.*
7 Maria Mies, "Feministische Forschung, Wissenschaft—Gewalt—Ethik," in *Ökofeminismus: Die Befreiung der Frauen, der Natur und unterdrückter Völker*, ed. Maria Mies and Vandana Shiva (Neu-Ulm: Verein zur Förderung der sozialpolitischen Arbeit, 2016), 64.
8 Ibid.
9 Andrea Benario, "Von der Jineolojî-Konferenz zum Widerstand in Efrîn," *Kurdistan Report* no. 196 (March–April 2018): 23–28, accessed July 10, 2019, http://civaka-azad.org/von-der-jineoloji-konferenz-zum-widerstand-in-afrin/.
10 Jineolojî Komitee Europa, *Jineolojî* (Neuss: Mezopotamien Verlag, 2018), 88.
11 Ibid., 23.
12 Nancy Fraser, "Feminismus, Kapitalismus und die List der Geschichte," *Blätter für deutsche und internationale Politik* 8 (August 2009): 43–57, accessed July 10, 2019, https://www.blaetter.de/archiv/jahrgaenge/2009/august/feminismus-kapitalismus-und-die-list-der-geschichte.
13 John Holloway, "Resistance Studies: A Note, a Hope," *Journal of Resistance Studies* 1, no. 1 (2016): 12–17.
14 Mies, "Feministische Forschung," 48.
15 Ibid.
16 Jineolojî Komitee Europa, *Jineolojî*, 47.
17 Ibid., 26.

18 Abdullah Öcalan, *Jenseits von Staat, Macht und Gewalt* (Neuss: Mezopotamien Verlag, 2010), 202; English Edition *Beyond State, Power, and Violence* (Oakland: PM Press, forthcoming 2020).

19 Ibid, 203.

20 Abdullah Öcalan, *Gefängnisschriften: Die Roadmap für Verhandlungen* (Cologne: Pahl-Rugenstein, 2013), 26.

21 Ibid., 34.

22 Mechthild Exo, *Das übergangene Wissen: Eine dekoloniale Kritik des liberalen Peacebuilding durch basispolitische Organisationen in Afghanistan* (Bielefeld: transcript, 2017).

23 Internationalist Commune Rojava/Democratic Federation of Northeast Syria, "#RiseUp4Rojava—Call for Global Days of Action on 27 and 28 January 2019," Kurdiatan Solidarity Network, accessed July 10, 2019, https://kurdishsolidaritynetwork.wordpress.com/2019/01/04/riseup4rojava-call-for-global-days-of-action-on-27-and-28-january-2019/.

24 Öcalan, *Gefängnisschriften*, 35.

25 Ibid., 40.

26 Ibid., 31.

27 Abdullah Öcalan, *The Political Thought of Abdullah Öcalan* (London: Pluto Press, 2017), 94.

28 Abdullah Öcalan, "Die Revolution ist weiblich," Civaka Azad, accessed July 10, 2019, http://civaka-azad.org/die-revolution-ist-weiblich-2/.

29 Mary Caprioli, "Gendered Conflict," *Journal of Peace Research* 37, no. 1 (January 2000): 51–68.

30 Simone Wisotzki, "Gender in der EU-Friedens- und Sicherheitspolitik," in *Hoffnungsträger 1325: Resolution für eine geschlechtergerechte Friedens- und Sicherheitspolitik in Europa*, ed. Gunda-Werner-Institut für Feminismus und Geschlechterdemokratie in der Heinrich-Böll-Stiftung (Königstein: Ulrike Helmer, 2008), 46–51.

31 Desirée Nilsson, "Anchoring the Peace: Civil Society Actors in Peace Accords and Durable Peace," *International Interactions Empirical and Theoretical Research in International Relations* 38, no. 2 (April 2012): 243–66.

32 "Afghan Women Burn in the Fire of the Oppression of the Occupiers and Fundamentalists," RAWA, March 7, 2013, accessed July 10, 2019, http://www.rawa.org/rawa/2013/03/07/rawa-statement-on-iwd-2013-english.html.

33 CIA Red Cell, "Afghanistan: Sustaining West European Support for the NATO-led Mission—Why Counting on Apathy Might Not Be Enough," March 11, 2010, accessed July 10, 2019, https://file.wikileaks.org/file/cia-afghanistan.pdf.

34 "Civil Society Resolution: Statement on the Peace Process and the Formation of the High Peace Council," accessed July 11, 2019, https://www.boell.de/sites/default/files/assets/boell.de/images/download_de/worldwide/Civil_Society_Resolution_Eng.pdf.

35 Cenî Kurdistan is an organization established in 1999 by Kurdish and Turkish women living in Europe with a focus on involving women in the peace process in Turkey and throughout the Middle East, see Cenî Kurdistan, accessed September 29, 2019, ceni-kurdistan.com.

36 "Frauenbeschließen Aktionsplan für Friedens- und Demokratisierungsprozess in der Türkei" (press release), Civaka Azad, April 23, 2013, accessed July 11, 2019, http://civaka-azad.org/?s=ceni+23.04.2013.
37 Öcalan, "Die Revolution ist weiblich."

FIFTEEN

Öcalan as Thinker: On the Unity of Theory and Practice as Form of Writing

David Graeber

I want to write a few words on the status of Abdullah Öcalan as a thinker. He has written voluminous works; but outside the Kurdish movement, the world appears to have had a very difficult time figuring out what to make of them. There seems to be confusion even over such apparently basic questions as what sort of thinker Öcalan is.

Certainly, his output is nothing if not prolific. During his time in prison in particular he has created a body of theory that really does not fit into any obvious intellectual category, ranging from essays on the mechanics of direct democracy, the possibility of a sociology based in quantum physics, to a multivolume world history focused on the Middle East. The range and sophistication are especially remarkable when one considers almost all of these writings were composed with no access to the internet, using as research materials only the three books his jailers permitted his lawyers to convey at any given time—or that, legally, he was only allowed to publish them by offering them as testimony before a court in which he stood accused of treason.

Still, outside of certain very specific radical circles, this body of work has been almost completely ignored. There has been almost no engagement by other scholars with his ideas. In this essay, I want to consider why this is and, ultimately, make the argument that Öcalan's works make many intellectuals uncomfortable, because they represent a form of thought that is not only inextricable from action but that also directly grapples with the knowledge that it is.

•

Let's start with my initial question: What sort of thinker is Öcalan?

Admittedly, there is always something a slightly aggressive in an attempt to categorize another's thought. In ancient Greek, the word "categorize" meant "to publicly accuse," and even to "pin something down" suggests an act of violence—like attaching a dead butterfly to a piece of cork board underneath some kind of handwritten label. Generally, if you want to dismiss an intellectual, you place him in some category—oh, he's just a positivist, a postmodernist, a neo-Kantian. If you want to really honor that same person, you create a new category out of their name: Foucauldian, Rawlsian, and so forth. It is thus fitting testimony to the success of Öcalan's thought in Kurdistan and within the Kurdish diaspora that if one describes someone as an "Apoist," everyone knows what you are talking about—but there is no larger category of thought in which to place Öcalan himself.

Outside Kurdish circles, however, this has made it all the easier for intellectuals to simply ignore him. If you search Öcalan's name on JSTOR, the most widely read compendium of academic articles in English, you will immediately turn up 448 hits; if you pick your way through them, however, you will discover that not a single one of them is primarily addressed to his ideas: almost all of them are about the history of the Partiya Karkerên Kurdistanê (PKK: Kurdistan Workers' Party), Turkish politics, the question of terrorism, and legal questions raised by his imprisonment and trial. He is seen as an object of study but never an interlocutor. Even when he is an object of study, it is almost never for his actual ideas: for instance, among those 448 articles, there is only one that so much as mentions his engagement with the ideas of Murray Bookchin—and that one, only to acknowledge it as an element in the political evolution of the PKK. The same can be said of his key political concepts, such as "democratic confederalism" (mentioned in 1 of 448), "democratic modernity" (0 of 448), "jineology" (0 of 448—in fact, the existence of *jineolojî*, the Kurdish movement's *science of women*, has never been acknowledged in any English-language article on JSTOR), etc. The silence is really quite impressive, considering how regularly movements inspired by such ideas have been at the very center of world news events, many of them, daily and even breathlessly reported in the international press.

No doubt much of this is simply one of the many cascading effects of the Turkish government's successful campaign to have the PKK placed on various international "terror lists"—which in the contemporary world is about as violent a form of categorization possible. This campaign corresponded precisely to the moment when the PKK, largely under Öcalan's initiative, renounced both separatism and offensive military action of any kind and attempted to initiate a peace process with the Turkish regime; if proof is required for how destructive such a designation can be, one might only cite here the fact that almost no one, even many of those sympathetic to the PKK, actually knows this. But it seems almost a moral principle on the part of Western opinion makers, intellectuals included, that if someone is designated "terrorist," their ideas cannot be taken seriously. Even to speculate on the motives of a terrorist is seen as validating their actions, which must always be represented as a product of blind rage or irrational hatred. This habit of thought has caused all sorts of dilemmas for the international media—most dramatically when the PKK guerrillas successfully broke the siege of Mount Shengal in Iraq and saved thousands of Yezidi civilians from genocide at the hands of ISIS, and the Western press, which had previously made the genocide front-page news, suddenly either dropped the story or pretended the Yezidis had been rescued by someone else—but it seems to have influenced the perceptions of the academy as well. Most academics are, at least in political terms, an inherently cowardly lot. When in doubt, it's easier just not to say anything.

•

Still, I think there are deeper forces at play. Academics don't really know what to do with a thinker who isn't either part of the academy or, at least, in some sense playing the academic game. And, increasingly, that game is the only game in town.

It wasn't always so. Much of the most creative thought in the world—not only in Europe and America but Asia, Africa, and Latin America as well—has taken place outside of universities. Creativity tends to emerge from spaces in between (this is probably one reason the Kurdish movement has been so intellectually creative; Kurds tend to be in between everything), and the most innovative and memorable thinking has, at least from the time of the French Enlightenment, emerged from the nexus of art, journalism, and radical politics rather than from university lecture halls. There is a reason why "avant-garde," used to refer to those exploring new artistic territory, and "vanguard," used to refer to the political leadership of a revolutionary party or movement, are the same word (the only difference is that one is French and the other is English). Both go back to a debate in the early nineteenth century between Auguste Comte and Henri de Saint-Simon about whether artists or social scientists would be the priests of the newly emerging industrial civilization, those who would provide it with its vision and strategic direction. No one at that time, even Comte, imagined such visionaries would be university professors.

Over the course of the twentieth century, college campuses came to be increasingly politicized, a process that culminated in what Immanuel Wallerstein calls "the world revolution of 1968," when outright insurrections broke out in universities everywhere from Paris to Tokyo to Mexico City. (The PKK, of course, has its origins in this student ferment as well.) What we have seen in the half century that followed might best be understood as a determined campaign by political and academic establishments to ensure nothing remotely like that can ever happen again. Campuses have been neutralized; intellectuals effectively defanged. This was done not by expelling radical thinkers from the university system (with the exception of a handful who go too far in trying to translate their ideas into action—it's always necessary to make the occasional symbolic sacrifice to remind people of unspoken limits) but rather by incorporating them. By the dawn of the twenty-first century, virtually all significant intellectual work was expected to take place within the academy. Even artists and journalists—at least if they have any intellectual ambitions—are expected to spend at least some time on academic grants or in academic lectureships, which means, of course, submitting themselves to the discipline of grant writing and peer review. And all this has happened (and this part is crucial, actually) at exactly the same time as universities themselves have become increasingly anti-intellectual. I mean this in the sense that they have been gradually redefined as institutions that are not *primarily* about scholarship or intellectual life at all: having the time to read, to think, and to debate ideas is now largely seen as at best an indulgence occasionally granted as a reward for an academic's real work, which is not just teaching but fund-raising, administration, box-ticking rituals, and self-marketing.

Academics are not only expected to avoid political engagement, they literally don't have the time.

•

Actually, the first statement was imprecise. It's not precisely that academics are expected to avoid politics. It's more that they must only engage in carefully regulated ways. Here one might divide those engaged in social inquiry of one form or another into two broad groups. On the one hand, we have what might be called "power disciplines," like economics or international relations or anything employing "rational choice theory." Anyone who works in a university in such fields is largely engaged in training cadres to take part in national or global bureaucracies of one sort or another (ministries, policy think tanks, banks or other multinational corporations, planet-wide institutions like the UN or IMF, and so forth). In other words, such disciplines are there to support existing power structures. While scholars working in such fields might claim to be objective and apolitical, these claims to value-freedom tend to be, as Max Weber emphasized, ways of positioning themselves politically in order to be better to influence policy.[1] On the other side, we have what might be called the "critical disciplines." These range from literary theory to cultural studies to anthropology, history, perhaps half of sociology, or anyone who is likely to regularly refer to the work of Michel Foucault. These are the disciplines the 1960s radicals were effectively folded into after the sixties ferment wound down. Those in the "critical disciplines" almost invariably define themselves as radical leftists and as opposed to the structures of power maintained by the first group; but the more they do so, the more they tend to see real-world political engagement of any kind as suspect. Such matters are ringed about by endless concretions of fear and guilt. One form this takes is the refusal to believe that anyone who has taken any sort of effective political action in the world can also make important contributions to human thought. At best, they can be an object of analysis. They cannot be seen as engaging as equals in the development of ideas.

It is hardly surprising, then, that contemporary intellectuals for the most part have no idea what to do with the ideas of Abdullah Öcalan. He is a thinker who started out in a university context as a student activist but has since moved steadily away from it. In fact, his trajectory is diametrically opposed to most of those who have come to define what I've called the "critical disciplines." He has continually refashioned his ideas around pragmatic considerations and the need to rally real people to real action, without ever sacrificing theoretical sophistication. What's more, while many have made similar attempts, Öcalan's has been unusually successful. It's hard to find another theorist of the last fifty years who has taken philosophical and social scientific ideas and adapted them in such a way that he's been able to inspire millions of people to try to treat one another differently. Yet it seems like the intellectual class is unable to take those ideas seriously for that very reason.

•

When I say that Öcalan's ideas, sitting as they do outside the academy, appear to defy existing categories, I should emphasize that this is true only to an extent. In one sense, Öcalan might, at first glance, seem a familiar figure of a sort. After all, he was, at one point in his intellectual career at least, the leader of a Marxist party. Leaders of Marxist parties are expected to write works of theory. This is one way that Marxism, as a political movement, is somewhat unusual: it is perhaps the only social movement created by a PhD, and it has always been theory-driven, organizing itself internally around a series of "great thinkers"—in a kind of peculiar exception to its erstwhile hostility to any great-man theory of history. This remains true to this day. One still finds Leninists, Maoists, Trotskyists, Stalinists, Gramscians, Althusserians, or even those who have dedicated their life to expanding on the ideas of Rosa Luxemburg, George Lukacs, or Henri Lefebvre. Marxism, though, forms a kind of alternative intellectual world of its own, with its own complex debates and terminologies, only intersecting at certain points with the academy.

As I have often remarked, in this respect Marxism stands in dramatic contrast to its great nineteenth-century rival, anarchism. While Marx in his own lifetime did intellectual battle with anarchists like Proudhon and Bakunin, and while anarchism's history has not lacked for "big-name thinkers" like Kropotkin, Malatesta, Magon, or Voltairine de Clayre, not to mention contemporaries like Starhawk or Noam Chomsky, none of them aspired to or attained the same intellectual ascendancy. When Marxists denounce one another, when they "categorize" one another in the bad Greek sense, it's largely as adherents to some rival school of thought, almost invariably identified with some great male thinker— Leninists condemn Maoists, Troskyites call their rivals Stalinists, and so on—anarchists almost never condemn one another as "Bakuninites" or "Maletestians." When they divide themselves into sects and set about attacking one another, it's generally on the basis of adherence to some rival form of revolutionary organization or practice: as platformists, insurrectionists, mutualists, pacifists, individualists, syndicalists, and so forth.[2] One can observe the same difference in debates: Marxists might issue bitter condemnations of one another for holding a different position on the revolutionary status of the peasantry or the relative importance of alienation and exploitation in Marx's analysis of capitalism, but anarchists, when they engage in similar heated debates, almost always argue about some form of action (When is it okay to break a window? Must one condemn someone who assassinates a head of state?) or question of revolutionary organization or decision-making process (Do we use consensus or majority vote?). I've known people to have been kicked out of Marxist groups for departing from the party line on the origins of language. There is no real equivalent in anarchist or anarchist-inspired organizations, which tend to embrace a certain ideological multiplicity.

In other words, Marxism has tended to be a theoretical discourse about revolutionary strategy, while anarchism has tended to be an ethical discourse about revolutionary practice.

This is obviously not a hard-and-fast distinction, but I think it's an important one—not least because it helps us understand any number of historical phenomena that might otherwise have remained obscure. It makes it much easier, for instance, to explain how these different poles of revolutionary thought have come into relation with the academy. As I've noted above, in terms of founders of Marxist schools of thought (Leninists, Maoists, Gramscians, Althusserians. . .), one can proceed almost seamlessly down the line from heads of state to French professors. Admittedly, the former are seen as a bit outré from the academic standpoint. Nowadays Mao Zedong is still respected as a classical Chinese poet, but his *Little Red Book* is largely a figure of fun; to cite Lenin as a theoretical source in an academic paper (let alone Stalin or Enver Hoxha) would seem bizarre. But purged from any likelihood of real-world consequences, Marxism can live and thrive in the academy. Academics are perfectly comfortable with warring sects. In many ways the sensibilities of academic sectarianism and revolutionary sectarianism have come to inform each other so much that they sometimes seem barely distinguishable. In contrast, since anarchism without real-world consequences is basically nothing, it has never been able to find a way to fit in. One might observe here, for instance, that despite the fact that almost all the gods of poststructuralism (an intellectual movement that has come to be very much driven by a "great-thinker" model), whether Michel Foucault or Gilles Deleuze or Jacques Derrida, declared themselves anarchists at some point in their intellectual history, almost none of their latter-day academic avatars are aware of this—or, if they are, act as if it has no particular social or political significance. A cynic might say this is because it doesn't, since such professions did not influence anyone's social or political action in any way; a more generous assessment would be that it had no effect on the way their ideas were received in the academy itself.[3]

●

Öcalan did not precisely abandon Marxism for anarchism, though his general intellectual trajectory has definitely been to move in the direction of the antiauthoritarian tradition of which anarchism has always been a part. He started his intellectual career in the world of sectarian Marxist thought, gradually transcended it, and, ultimately, has left it almost entirely behind. But doing so (and he, obviously, is not the only one to have made such a journey, even if each does it in her own particular way) tends to create its own sort of intellectual crises. Because it's not entirely clear what, if one abandons the vanguardist model, the role of an intellectual, let alone an intellectual leader, would be. If one's job is not to lay down the party line, then what, precisely, is it? Is it simply to provide as clear an analysis of the political, economic, or social situation, so as to allow democratic movements to collectively decide what to do about them? Is it to discover subtle forms of power and domination that might lie invisible in daily life or to try to understand the appeal of the values or forms of desire that support them? Is it to reexamine the past for forgotten social possibilities or to speculate about those that might exist in the future? Should one write works for the general public and, thus, figure out how to translate otherwise obscurantist theoretical language into accessible terms that can inform democratic debate, or is it better to play the academic game, even if it means writing in abstruse jargon, so as to give intellectual respectability to ideas that would otherwise be dismissed as plebian rantings? Just framing the question this way makes it obvious that there is no one right answer to this question. Indeed, imagining there should be only one right answer is itself a symptom of the vanguardist habits of thought with which we are trying to break. But knowing that doesn't make the task any easier.

Öcalan's problem was all the more acute, because he was not precisely in a position to reimagine himself whole cloth; he was still the head of a political movement, a figure whose history and writings were already a source of guidance and inspiration for millions of human beings. This placed him in the paradoxical situation. You can't simply order people to question authority. On the other hand, to try to destroy his own authority entirely—as, say, Louis Althusser tried to do when he wrote his famous confession that he'd never actually read volumes 2 and 3 of *Capital*—would not really have done anyone much good.[4] In fact, a case could be made that it would have been profoundly self-indulgent, since it would have meant squandering a unique historical opportunity.

The quality of Öcalan's writings—particularly those written since his imprisonment—can best be seen, I think, as a very self-conscious effort to grapple with this common problem (how to move from the theoretical vanguard of a top-down movement to providing intellectual support to a bottom-up one) in this extremely unusual form. This would appear to be the first time in history that the leader of a vertically organized political movement of the sort whose leader is always seen as the "first theorist" has decided to use his theoretical writings as a way to convince his followers to reject that model. There was no real precedent for how to do this. He was pretty much forced to make it up as he went along.

•

What I want to do in the rest of this essay is to examine some of Öcalan's writings in this light.

Now, I've said that Öcalan was facing a common problem in an unprecedented form. Insofar as he was abandoning Marxism and embracing more antiauthoritarian politics, there are, of course, plenty of precedents for how one proceeds. The first step, generally speaking, is to announce a series of theoretical breaks with Marxist orthodoxy: the concept of alienation or the priority of class struggle or the declining rate of profit. Öcalan has made a whole series of such breaks. The danger here is how to do so without either establishing some new orthodoxy or sinking into a nihilistic relativism that will make it impossible to make moral arguments of any sort. What's called "68 thought" in France—for instance, Deleuze, Foucault, Derrida...—began as a movement to break free of the shackles of Marxist orthodoxy and ended up largely bouncing back and forth between both of these bad options or, alternately, embracing both at the same time. Öcalan makes it clear he wishes to avoid falling into either trap. Let's consider in this light one of his key ruptures with Marx, over the nature of the commodity and the labor theory of value. In *Manifesto for a Democratic Civilization, Volume 1*, he first brings up the issue by writing: "Here I have to note I do not share Karl Marx's concept of *commodity*. The opinion that the exchange value of a commodity can be measured by the workers' labor has initiated a conceptualization period fraught with disadvantages."[5]

This particular passage is from a work mainly about the emergence of civilization in the ancient Middle East, and the book goes on to argue first of all that the commodification process begins not with forms of labor but with the gradual transmutation of earlier gift economies and the reduction of social relations into impersonal relations of exchange—a process that, he observes, was made possible primarily by lending money at interest (an observation that, I might add, converges quite nicely with my own observations on this subject in *Debt: The First 5,000 Years*).[6] If *all* social relations are commodified, society would simply disintegrate.

Commodification, he continues, severs not only relations between people but between those people and their natural environment, leading to "ecological disaster":

> This happened because of the profound distinction which has been made between material and moral values, which form a natural unity. In a way this severing has cultivated the seeds of poor metaphysics. By leaving the material without spirit and the spiritual without matter, the path was being paved for the most confusing dichotomy encountered in the history of thought. Throughout the history of civilization the bogus distinctions and discussions that have divided every aspect of life into either materialism or morality have destroyed ecology and free life. The concept of inanimate matter and an inanimate universe combined with an incomprehensible spiritualism are occupying, invading and colonizing the human mind.[7]

This is a critique of commodification very much in the spirit of Marcel Mauss and the anthropological tradition inspired by him, which argues similarly that the creation of impersonal markets and the corresponding emergence of universalizing "world religions" (which developed in tandem with impersonal markets with uncanny consistency in India, China, and the Eastern Mediterranean alike in the middle of the first millennium BCE) was what made our familiar distinctions between egoism and altruism, materialism and idealism, body and soul, possible to begin with. If so, then alienation would appear to occur first—to use the appropriate Marxist jargon—in the sphere of circulation rather than that of production.

But there are other problems:

I have some doubts about another aspect of Marx's concept. I am quite doubtful that social values (including commodities) can be measured. Commodities cannot be regarded as a mere product of abstract labor but, rather, as a combination of many non-countable non-natural properties. To claim the opposite paves the way for fallacy, extortion and theft. The reason is clear: How are we to measure the total amount of non-countable labor? Moreover, how are we to measure the labor of a mother at birth and that of the family that raises the worker? Then, how are we to measure the share of the whole society in which this object called "value" is realized?[8] Hence, exchange value, surplus value, labor-value, interest rate, profit, unearned income and so forth are all forms of theft through official and state power. It may be meaningful to develop other measures or new forms of a gift economy to replace the exchange system.[9]

Obviously almost every issue raised in this passage is a heated matter of debate within the Marxian tradition, starting with whether Marx actually intended to propose a theory of price formation in the first place and proceeding through a whole series of feminist debates about whether "reproductive labor" produces value for capital (i.e., Silvia Federici's position) or whether the whole point of the value system in capital is to define certain forms of work as "real value-producing work" and to de-validate others (i.e., Diane Elson's position).[10]

In a way, the position Öcalan is taking here bears a good deal of similarity to that taken by Michael Hardt and Antonio Negri from the *Labor of Dionysus* to their celebrated *Empire*—perhaps not entirely surprisingly, considering they are both activist intellectuals coming out of the Marxist tradition but writing work in dialogue with antiauthoritarian social movements (and Negri also spent a certain portion of his intellectual life in prison). Still, I think the differences are, if anything, even more revealing. Öcalan has taken the insights of feminism and used them to reimagine five thousand years of political economy, to argue that true social value was never something that could be measured and that any attempt to do so was always already a form of violence; Hardt and Negri argue instead that it was the rise of feminism itself, in the 1970s, that rendered "the law of value" obsolete.

It might be useful to quote some of the passages where they originally lay this out.

> Marx thus conceived the labor theory of value in two forms, from two perspectives—one negative and one affirmative. The first perspective begins with the theory of abstract labor.... The quantity of value expresses the existing relationship between a certain good and the proportion of social labor time necessary for its production.[11]

This approach, they emphasize, is concerned with how the system orders itself and, therefore, uses the language employed by the political economist in Marx's day. But there's another form the labor theory of value can take and sometimes does take in Marx's work: a more radical form. Workers are constantly struggling to establish what labor power actually is, and this is a dynamic, antagonistic, political struggle. One effect of that struggle has been to establish women's unpaid work as a legitimate form of labor:

> The relationship between labor and value is thus not unidirectional. As numerous scholars have recognized over the last thirty years... what counts as labor, or value-creating practice, always depends on the existing values of a given social and historical context; in other words, labor should not simply be defined as activity, any activity, but specifically activity that is socially recognized as productive of value. The definition of what practices comprise labor is not given or fixed, but rather historically and socially determined, and thus the definition itself constitutes a mobile site of social contestation. For example, certain lines of feminist inquiry and practice, setting out from an analysis of the gender division of labor, have brought into focus the different forms of affective labor, caring labor, and kin work that have been traditionally defined as women's work. These studies have clearly demonstrated the ways in which such forms of activity produce social networks and produce society itself. As a result of these efforts, today such value-creating practices can and must be recognized as labor.[12]

It's for this reason, they explain, that the "law of value" no longer applies; social values can no longer be measured; feminism has opened the way to a postmodern society in which new forms of value producing cooperation have emerged outside of the factory and workplace, from subcultures to the internet, invading our daily existence, and identity politics replace class politics, because it's the production of those identities that is now the most important form of labor. The values they produce are "beyond measure." In fact, they go even further: what we are really witnessing is the emergence of communism (aka "society") within the shell of capitalism. No longer masters of producing value, capitalists are reduced to simply appropriating, privatizing, patenting, and extracting rent from the use of things they never really created in the first place. This can only be accomplished through a fusion of capital and state power, a fusion that they ultimately come to label "Empire." The emergence of Empire, in turn, means power has come to define reality itself:

> The political must also be understood as ontological owing to the fact that all the transcendental determinations of value and measure that used to order the deployments of power (or really determine its prices, subdivisions, and hierarchies) have lost their coherence.... Empire constitutes the ontological fabric in which all the relations of power are woven together—political and economic relations as well as social and personal relations.... Every fixed measure of value tends to be dissolved, and the imperial horizon of power is revealed finally to be a horizon outside measure.[13]

Many have found such grand declarations seductive and inspiring—we are living in a giddy new age, we are already creating communism when we surf the web, anything is now possible—but in many ways, what they're arguing seems completely ridiculous. Are Hardt and Negri seriously arguing that only factory labor produced value in 1845, because, at that time, most male factory laborers thought it did, and their wives were not allowed to weigh in on the matter? Do they really believe that "affective" or caring labor did *not* produce society before feminists made it impossible to ignore by putting it, as it were, on the political table? It's hard to imagine they would hold these positions explicitly. And, indeed, they largely avoid taking on such questions directly; but the entire thrust of their argument is that this would have to be the case.

For me, what Hardt and Negri propose is the very definition of a postmodern argument. If historical change brings to the fore certain aspects of, say, capitalism or the state that one was not previously aware of, what does one do? Does one reexamine history in that light and come up with a new theory of what capitalism or the state has always been; or does one simply declare that the world changed entirely sometime around 1975, and we are living in a totally new reality? (This may sound silly, but it's almost precisely what Hardt and Negri and a host of other scholars actually do. And they call that new system "postmodernity.") Öcalan's procedure is the opposite. He takes the first option. If feminism—including, in his case, the tireless efforts of female guerrillas in the PKK to have women's issues accepted as primary concerns and not something to be addressed "after the revolution"—has made certain aspects of capitalism impossible for him to ignore, his response was to reimagine what capitalism was in the first place. Even in his volume on capitalism he introduces the problem by taking things straight back to ancient Mesopotamia:

> At this point, I think it is necessary to rethink Marx's treatment of the labor theory of value.... The view that human labor is the basis of exchange value is highly disputable; this is true also for Marx's analyses. Whether defined in terms of concrete or abstract labor, exchange value always has a speculative aspect. To illustrate, let us presume that the first merchant from Uruk, in one of his colonies along the Euphrates, tried to exchange stones and metal compounds in return for pottery. What would have determined the exchange value?[14]

It might well be, he continues, (it often was) that a merchant might jack up prices by creating an artificial scarcity, even by destroying valuable resources or commodities. Destroying things involves labor too, of course, but no one would seriously suggest that a division of Sumerian soldiers sacking and burning a rival city to neutralize a competing wool producer and preserve their merchant's monopoly were working harder than the women who actually spun and wove the wool! One suspects in the back of Öcalan's mind here is the story of the British East India's suppression of the Indian cloth industry, which was accomplished by military force, but which also opened world markets for British cloth exports and, hence, made possible the industrial revolution—a revolution that, he argues, itself paved the way for the emergence of the labor theory of value to justify such conquests in the eyes of British workers.

It is easy to understand how a Kurdish revolutionary from Turkey might not feel he really has the luxury of viewing capitalism as somehow independent from the imperial violence it unleashed on the rest of the world, and how he might instead embrace, as Öcalan does, the tradition of Fernand Braudel and Immanuel Wallerstein, which argues capitalism was a system of speculation and trade before it became a system of production. But the contrast with Hardt and Negri is revealing. Öcalan is arguing that capitalism *began* in the way that Hardt and Negri claim it is now finally ending. Ultimately, capitalism is simply a continuation of a long tradition of violent patriarchal expropriation.

> [Its] birth can be described as the modern link of the tradition whereby a band of looters gathered by and around the strong man seizes the social values generated by mother-woman. Capitalism is the act of groups with advanced speculative intelligence who would not abstain from using violence when necessary and frequently. They are the early capitalists of England, the Netherlands, and, prior to them, of Italian city-states like Genoa, Florence, and Venice; they were intertwined with the state, and, like members of a sect, had their own special lifestyles.[15]

In other words, where Hardt and Negri see capitalism, once a purely productive force, now spent, reduced to a sheer thuggish brutality, stealing the products of our loves and passions, Öcalan insists it was always so. The greatest trick the capitalists played on us was to convince us it was ever anything else:

> Just as with the initial Uruk merchants' religions, the construction of a new version of the mythological narrative was given to what they called the political economists, who were really the inventors of the religion of capitalism. What was being constructed was nothing but a new religion, with its own sacred book and intricate sects. Political economy is the most fraudulent and predatory monument of fictive intelligence, developed to disguise the speculative character of capitalism. The English classical school of political economy came up with just the right bait: the labor theory of value. I really do wonder why they decided on this notion. I suspect a main reason was to distract the workers.[16]

And, he adds, noting that it causes him "great sorrow" to have to say it, "Even Karl Marx could not refrain from taking this bait."

•

Now, speaking just for myself, I think Öcalan is going a bit far here: it seems to me that the labor theory of value can be said to reveal a deeper truth, that the world we inhabit is largely our own creation, and insofar as Marx did fall into a trap set by the political economists of his day (which to a certain extent, I would agree he did), it was in seeing value-creating labor as necessarily "productive" rather than a matter of caring, tending, maintaining, and nurturing. Still, I didn't introduce these themes primarily to work out the difference between Hardt and Negri's position, Öcalan's, and my own. In fact, I had something of an ulterior motive in citing the passages that I did at such length. I did so, because I also want to draw attention to the profound difference in their prose styles.

The mode of exposition, I think, cannot be entirely divorced from what it is that's being exposed. Let us consider the matter more closely then.

•

Hardt and Negri are employing what might be called the classical Marxist high style: one which not only relies heavily on technical language drawn from a variety of philosophical traditions but operates in constant reference to received sources of intellectual authority. This starts, of course, with the need to first lay down the correct reading of Marx. They follow by noting the weight of intellectual authority ("numerous scholars have recognized...") and end up arguing that certain writers—feminist ones in this case—actually play a key role in constituting the realities they describe. This kind of language makes sense if you assume, as they do, that intellectuals like Marx or his latter-day interpreters are at least to some degree simply the voice of social movements: they crystallize an emergent insurgent common sense. This is how it is possible to argue that Marx's labor theory of value was true when the workers' movement embraced it but that housework is now constitutive of value, because feminist scholars and activists have forced society to recognize it as such.

But, of course, such intellectuals don't just tell people—even revolutionary people—what they already think, they also play a role in molding and shaping that emergent understanding. To a certain degree they could even be said to bring new realities into being just by pointing out that they are there. Hence, the combination of declarative statements ("productive labor is this," "empire is that"...), injunctions ("should not be defined as," "must be recognized to be," "must be understood"...), and the strategic use of passive voice to describe historical processes that appear to be happening largely of their own accord ("every fixed measure of value tends to be dissolved, and the imperial horizon of power is revealed"...). The results often read like something halfway between an academic essay and a political manifesto. The language of science seems constantly on the verge of slipping into the language of prophecy. Sometimes it clearly does. But for the authors this is not a problem: just as the Hebrew prophets, according to Spinoza, effectively created the Hebrew people by "organizing the desires of the multitude" around a certain vision of history, so too, Hardt and Negri argue, can revolutionary thinkers in the present day bring a revolutionary subject into being,[17] like some massive, ferocious, and wonderful demon, by correctly calling out its name.

•

This is precisely the path that Öcalan has chosen *not* to follow.

The problem with Hardt and Negri's approach, of course, is that it is still effectively vanguardist. Obviously, they are trying to shake off the old explicitly vanguardist model where the "great theorist" comes up with the strategic analysis for the masses to follow, but it's not entirely clear how successful this effort is. True, the fact that they are not the leaders of such a movement but are just writing as if they were gives them a lot more leeway in this regard. Öcalan, again, does not have the luxury. He actually is the leader of a revolutionary movement that started out organized on vanguardist principles. As a result, he is careful to write in a way that simply cannot be used to create that sort of doctrinal authority.

Let us return to Öcalan's prose, then, and consider how it departs from what I've called the Marxist high style.

The first and most obvious way is that Öcalan takes care to always place himself, personally, in the picture. To some extent, of course, this is an effect of the circumstances under which his most recent works were written. The only reason Öcalan was allowed to publish these books at all is that, legally, he was entitled to offer testimony explaining the context for the crimes of which he was accused; all of the books he has written from his island prison were, as noted above, statements addressed to a Turkish court. But clearly this isn't the only reason. The *Manifesto of the Democratic Civilization* reads much less like a manifesto than a unique combination of history, autobiography, and theoretical reflection, each driving the others. Childhood fantasy blends into mythic visions and these into rage at current injustice, in a way that perhaps only makes sense in the writings of a man who has spent decades in a prison cell contemplating the nature of human freedom:

I always thought the peaks of the mountains to be the sacred throne of the gods and goddesses and its skirts to be the corner stones of heaven that they created in plenitude, and always wanted to wander around in them. As a young boy, because of this, I was described as "mad for the mountains." When I much later learnt that such a life was reserved for the god Dionysus and the free and artistic groups of girls (called the Bacchantes) who travel before and behind him, I really envied him. ... When I was still at my village, I always wanted to play games with the girls of my village. I never approved of the dominant culture's way of shutting women behind doors. I still want to engage with them in unlimited free discussions, in games, in all the sacredness of life. ...

I remember how I have always saluted the free women of these mountains with the morning breeze of goddesses and in remembrance I try to "add meaning to myself." I also remember the unique anger I have always felt against men—family, clan and state—for the deaths of truck loads of south-eastern women who died in car crashes on their way to other regions for seasonal work. How is it possible that they fell this low from being the descendants of the goddess? My mind and soul have never accepted their fall.[18]

To return to Öcalan's analysis of the commodity, in this light, the first thing that leaps out is its emotional quality; the second, the care he takes to head off any possibility that the depth of his emotions, the absolute nature of his rejection of existing forms of power, should turn into any form of absolute prescription of what is to be done.

Commodification "paves the way for fallacy, extortion, and theft."[19] Applied to society as a whole, its logic becomes an unmitigated disaster: "the mental acceptance of the society's commodification is to abandon being human. And this is beyond barbarity."[20] The prospect of life within a system defined by such logic fills him with "disgust." Revolutionaries employing the high style tend to avoid this sort of language or, at best, use it very sparingly.

Some would argue that Öcalan is simply being unusually honest. John Holloway calls this "the scream."[21] Radical theorists, he observes, may write as if their descriptions of the contradictions of global capitalism are a result of reasoned contemplation, as if having made careful examination of the workings of the system and discovered its laws of motion, they were finally forced to the conclusion that something is terribly wrong. But it isn't really true. In every case, the analyst begins with a deeply emotional, gut feeling that something is terribly wrong. A scream of horror, even, at the violence and suffering and sheer insanity of the world we see all around us. This is always what comes first. We begin with that horror, and then try to apply the tools of reason to understand how such a world is possible. If this is the case, the passions Öcalan expresses are always there, they are, as it were, the burning fuel propelling the motor of the argument. Öcalan has just made the unusual decision to reveal them.

I think what Holloway says is true; but by bringing the passions to light, Öcalan's work might also be said to illustrate how even this formulation is incomplete. After all, Holloway is not just talking about horror but about indignation. Why do we recoil before injustice? Why are we able to recognize it as "injustice" at all? This cannot be purely spontaneous, like someone who recoils before the sight of a body being torn apart. If it were, we could just as easily conclude the world is a horrible place and turn to heroin or become Seventh Day Adventists. It has to be based on some deep felt feeling that none of this is necessary, that a society that was not founded on such horrors *could* exist. The image of the free girls playing in the mountains, making up rules as they go along, then, is the necessary foundation for the outrage at their later unnecessary deaths. Our universal experience of maternal care, in which reason and emotion, morality and economics, mind and body, have not yet been prized apart, is the necessary foundation for our indignation at the imposition of a market logic. We could never see the system as inhuman unless we had a deeper sense of what being truly human might entail.

For all the passion he expresses—or, perhaps, because of the very intensity of that passion—Öcalan takes care to largely avoid the kind of flat, declarative statements and injunctions so characteristic of the Marxist high style. He has "some doubts" about Marx's labor theory of value. It is "highly disputable." Insofar as it is wrong, it is fraud, theft, and extortion. But it's not *entirely* certain it is wrong. This means it might be right. It's just unlikely. Commodification is violence. Taken to extremes it denies us our very humanity; the most truly human aspects of value creation (childbirth, maternal love, sociality...) could not, he implies "should never," be quantified. But other aspects possibly could. Just not the way they are presently quantified. It's possible we might have to invent some new form of measurement. Or, if not that, then we might have to invent "new forms of gift economy" that refuse the logic of quantification entirely. But what they would precisely look like is unclear. Öcalan is careful to leave the matter open. This is an invitation to think creatively, and many in the Kurdish movement have indeed begun to take such questions up.

•

One might object: But, in the end, is this so different from Marx? Marx might not have expressed a lot of doubts, but he made his passions clear enough, and he too refused to set out prescriptions as to what economic arrangements in a free society would actually be like. True, but one could also argue that Marx's refusal partakes of the very absolutism that Öcalan is trying to shun. At least this is the way most later Marxists interpreted it: a total revolution means we can know nothing of what comes after the dictatorship of the proletariat, so it is pointless to even try to imagine the kind of problems we might face. In historical retrospect all this is more frightening than reassuring. Öcalan, in contrast, is not a totalizing thinker and, therefore, does not think in terms of total ruptures. Capitalism is nothing fundamentally new. It is just a new constellation of tendencies that have existed since at least the Bronze Age. Therefore, the questions we need to ask are not entirely beyond our capacities of imagination. We can start thinking about them, even if we cannot really know where such thoughts will end.

For a revolutionary, for anyone actively engaged in political struggles, really, anything one writes is necessarily a kind of political intervention. An essay or book, even a blog post, is always a direct action. It is meant to have an impact on the world, not just to state a truth but to state it in a certain manner to a certain audience in such a way as to lead them to act differently than they had before. In embracing the antiauthoritarian tradition, Öcalan is also embracing a rejection of any utilitarian calculus that would argue that the ends justify the means, but instead insists that, insofar as it is possible, the form of one's intervention should itself be a model for the world one wishes to create. Direct action, as I have myself phrased it in the past, is the defiant insistence on acting as if one is already free. A man in prison can only do this through words. It seems to me what Öcalan is doing in his writing is not just to call for a society that undoes the work of commodification, that ongoing violence that constantly shatters the original unity of reason, morality, and what he calls "emotional intelligence," but to also write in a way that attempts to refigure what a restoration of such a unity might be like. This is why he's so careful to both reveal the passions driving his commitments and to systematically refuse the language of command.

This is why so many of his key interventions take the form of suggestions, disruptions, confessions, and narratives that resist being read in any biblical or ex cathedra form. It is necessary to create a new language, avoiding both pure rationalism and "incomprehensible spirituality," lest we fall into the same trap as previous revolutionary movements that ultimately created nothing but an unholy synthesis of both:

> It is with pain and anger that I have to admit that the noble struggle that has raged for the past one hundred and fifty years was carried out on the basis of a vulgar, materialist positivism doomed to failure. The class struggle underlies this approach. However, the class—contrary to what they believe—is not the workers and laborers resisting enslavement, but the petit bourgeoisie who has long ago surrendered and became part of modernity. Positivism is the ideology that has formed this class's perception and underlies its meaningless reaction against capitalism.[22]

But positivism, he says, has also become an idol and Marxism a form of religion—if a religion that makes sense only to the professional managerial class who have, inevitably, therefore, ended up actually managing past Marxist dictatorships. The form of writing Öcalan employs is an attempt to find an initial way to move beyond that.

•

Is it a successful attempt? It's hard to say exactly how success in such matters should be measured. Certainly, Öcalan's works have played a key role in inspiring one of the most widespread movements of real-life revolutionary transformation in recent memory.

One might offer many cautions. Does not the subjective element, the emphasis on Öcalan's personal history and emotions, open up the danger of a classic revolutionary cult of personality? It's understandable that antiauthoritarian visitors are often made more than a little uncomfortable by the constant portraits of Öcalan displayed in homes and offices in places like Rojava, or the references to "our leader." It's also clear that authoritarian and antiauthoritarian tendencies are very much at war within the movement, as they inevitably must be, perhaps, in any real mass revolutionary movement (as opposed to those perfect movements that only exist in our heads). In this context, Öcalan exists as a kind of halfway figure, even a kind of living martyr—the old living leader whose image is displayed in political contexts, in a political world full of images of the heroic dead. As a prisoner of his enemies, he remains somehow halfway between. So he is also the intellectual leader who advises his followers to reject all the certainties that ordinarily flow from the role of an intellectual leader, the patriarch who calls on men to kill the patriarch within them, the ultimate figure of authority who encourages young men and women to look with skepticism on anyone who claims to know better than they.

•

It might be curious to ask ourselves how much time would have to pass or what would have to happen for the intellectual world to treat Öcalan's ideas in the same way that they do those of Walter Benjamin, Georges Bataille, Simone de Beauvoir, or Frantz Fanon—to name a few politically engaged scholars who were neither party leaders nor academics—or even a theorist/comedian like Slavoj Žižek. But in a way this is an idle question. Academics—at least critical academics—are increasingly engaged in writing works that sound like they are meant to change the world, in an institutional context designed to ensure there is almost no possibility they might actually do so. Since Öcalan's words really are, before anything else they might be, a form of political action, their ultimate meaning can only be known by what they do.

This essay was written for this book.

David Graeber is an anthropologist and activist who currently resides in London. Trained in Chicago, he spent two years doing fieldwork in Madagascar before returning to work in Yale, then later Goldsmiths and the London School of Economics, where he is currently a professor. A participant in the global justice movement and later Occupy Wall Street, as well as other social movements, Graeber has written on a variety of topics, ranging from the nature of politics, debt, value, democracy, bureaucracy, and, most recently, the modern plague of useless employment. He is a long-standing friend of the Kurdish freedom movement.

Notes
1   This is the argument of "Science as a Vocation," in *From Max Weber*, ed. H.H. Gerth and C. Wright Mills (Oxford: Oxford University Press, 1946).

2   True there is a bit of a fuzzy middle ground on either side: green anarchists, who have been among the most sectarian, are sometimes referred to as "Zerzanites," though I'm not aware of any who embrace that name themselves, and the most antiauthoritarian Marxists—say, autonomists or situationists or council communists—will tend to identify themselves with forms of practice rather than some founding thinker's name. It's also significant that even those strains of Marxism that resist the "great-man" model tend to be reimagined in this way if attempts are made to incorporate them in academic debate: so, for example, in the oos Italian post-workerism was treated as if it came almost entirely from the brains of Michael Hardt and Antonio Negri.

3   There is, obviously, still something of the old radical reading circles that exist outside both the academy and sectarian Marxism that still center on the overlap between art, activism, and journalism, and such authors are still very much favored there. But much of it is now simply a diminishing penumbra on the academy.

4   Louis Althusser, *The Future Lasts Forever: A Memoir* (New York: New Press 1996). Anyway, Althusser's confession didn't really work. When people decide they want adopt you as a god simple self-abnegation will rarely be adequate to stop them.

5   Abdullah Öcalan, *Manifesto for a Democratic Civilization, Volume 1: Civilization: The Age of Masked Gods and Disguised Kings* (Porsgrunn, NO: New Compass Press, 2015), 127; 2nd revised edition will be published by PM Press in 2021.

6   David Graeber, *Debt: The First 5,000 Years* (Brooklyn, NY: Melville House, 2012).

7   Öcalan, *Manifesto for a Democratic Civilization, Volume 1*, 127–28.

8   Similarly, in volume 2: "How shall we then define the reward for a mother's labor of carrying the proletariat for nine months and then nurturing him or her until he or she is fit to work? And how do we determine the owners and how do we reward all those who, over thousands of years, had contributed to the construction of production tools, which now have been stolen by the capitalists? Let us not forget that, in not a single case the value of the tools of production is equal to what it is sold for at the market. Even the technical inventions used in a modern factory are the products of thousands of people's collective creativity. How are we to determine the value of their labor and whom are we to pay?"; Abdullah Öcalan, *Manifesto for a Democratic Civilization, Volume 2: Capitalism: The Age of Unmasked Gods and Naked Kings* (Porsgrunn, NO: New Compass Press, 2017), 76; second revised edition will be published by PM Press in 2020.

9   Öcalan, *Manifesto for a Democratic Civilization, Volume 1*, 128.

10 Silvia Federici, *Revolution at Point Zero: Housework, Reproduction, and Feminist Struggle* (Oakland: PM Press, 2012); Diane Elson, ed., *Value: The Representation of Labor in Capitalism* (London: CSE Books, 1979).

11 Michael Hardt and Antonio Negri, *The Labor of Dionysus: Critique of the State Form* (Minneapolis: University of Minnesota Press, 1994), 8.

12 Ibid., 8–9.

13 Michael Hardt and Antonio Negri, *Empire* (London: Harvard University Press, 2000), 364.

14 Öcalan, *Manifesto for a Democratic Civilization, Volume 2*, 72.
15 Ibid., 66.
16 Ibid., 73.
17 Hardt and Negri, *Empire*, 65.
18 Öcalan, *Manifesto for a Democratic Civilization, Volume 1*, 91.
19 Ibid., 128.
20 Ibid., 127.
21 John Holloway, *Change the World without Taking Power: The Meaning of Revolution Today* (London: Pluto Press, 2002), 1.
22 Öcalan, *Manifesto for a Democratic Civilization, Volume 1*, 94–95.

SIXTEEN

Rojava or the Art of Transition in a Collapsing Civilization

Fabian Scheidler

The achievements of the Kurdish liberation movement in Northern Syria are not only highly important for the freedom struggles in this region but also for the transition period that we are facing on a global scale. Five hundred years of violent expansion of the capitalist Megamachine have brought both societies and the planet to the brink of collapse.[1] The Capitalocene has led to the sixth mass species extinction in the history of the earth. We are losing 1 percent of our fertile soil each year. The UN Food and Agriculture Organization predicts that the world has only sixty harvests left on this path. However, this seems overoptimistic, given that biodiversity loss and climate chaos are proceeding at a much faster rate than even the grimmest forecasts considered possible ten years ago. When the glaciers of the Himalaya are gone, up to 1.5 billion people in Asia, who depend on the melting water, will be bereft of their livelihoods. The same is true for coastal communities devastated by rising sea levels and storm surges and for large parts of the Middle East and Africa that risk becoming uninhabitable in the coming decades due to extreme heat and drought. All this is happening on a planet where forty-two men possess as much as the poorest half of world population. This grotesque inequality not only stokes social and political chaos but also causes extreme economic instability to the point of systemic breakdown.

When we combine this short survey with the almost complete refusal of global elites to even acknowledge that there is a systemic crisis—let alone to act accordingly—we are facing a perfect storm. What could lie ahead of us in the coming decades is nothing short of the collapse of a civilization. However, as James C. Scott pointed out, the breakdown of a civilization is not necessarily equivalent to the annihilation of the people involved. Failing systems break up into smaller often less hierarchical forms of organization.[2] Sometimes systemic collapse can even lead to more freedom and greater well-being for the majority, as was the case when the Western Roman Empire disintegrated and both slavery and the ravaging mercenary armies largely disappeared from Europe for centuries.

The difference today, however, is that the current system is much more dangerous than the Roman Empire was. It is, indeed, by far the most violent and dangerous civilization that has ever existed since the first structures of power and domination emerged in Mesopotamia five thousand years ago. And it might turn out to be even more destructive when breaking apart. Western civilization has bestowed upon us fifteen thousand nuclear warheads and six hundred million small arms, which could quickly turn against everybody. Furthermore, a globalized industrial society is much more vulnerable to deteriorating supply mechanisms due to economic or ecological disruptions than an agrarian society such as Rome's. Therefore, today's transition strategies must not only deal with political and economic reorganization but also with the question of how to respond to sudden system failures, supply bottlenecks, and the spread of violence.

For these reasons, learning from Rojava could turn out to be essential for survival. For people in Rojava have dealt with both anomic violence and the breakdown of supply chains in a remarkable way. Under the most extreme conditions, attacked by ISIS from one side and Turkey from the other, in the crossfire of almost a dozen local, regional, and geostrategic wars, the women and men of western Kurdistan were able to create an island of self-determination and true democracy that has become a beacon of hope for people all over the world. Cut off from global and interregional supply chains, they have started to build an economy based on cooperatives and collective decision-making.

This is all the more amazing, as war tends to impose a militaristic, hyper-hierarchical logic on even the most emancipatory movements, squashing self-organization for the sake of military effectiveness. The historic examples for this are legion, reaching from the Russian Revolution to independence movements in the Global South and countless postindependence guerrillas. Even if the war was won, it was, in a sense, still lost, because the winner had become confusingly similar to his adversary. However, as in the case of the Zapatistas in Mexico, the people of

Rojava have learned from this history in a profound way. Inspired by the writings of Abdullah Öcalan (who, in turn, draws from feminist theory, Murray Bookchin, Immanuel Wallerstein, and others), they have begun to challenge not only a specific formation of power, such as capitalism or a particular state, but also the roots of domination.

This is all the more important, as capitalism is not the only system that subjugates people and nature. When it breaks apart, locally or globally, new power structures may emerge that turn out to be as bad, or even worse, than the previous one, using different means to achieve the same ends, i.e., maintaining privileges, wealth, and power for a few. Practicing the art of transition in a collapsing civilization implies anticipating what new forms of domination might arise in the upheaval (or which older forms might be revived) and challenging them at their roots.

Challenging the Four Tyrannies

All systems of domination in the past five thousand years have been based on four pillars of power, which I call the Four Tyrannies.[3] Each of these is challenged by the Kurdish project of democratic confederalism. The first tyranny is physical power. It is found in patriarchal family structures, slavery, mafias and warlord systems, and, in its most consolidated form, in states (which sometimes emerge from mafias and warlord systems). In the modern era, the main function of the state has been to make sure that the wheelwork of capital accumulation runs smoothly, by conquering new territories, crushing resistance movements, forcing people into wage labor or slavery, protecting trade routes, asserting property rights for the wealthy and heavily subsidizing corporations, today in the order of trillions of dollars each year. Without states doing all of this, capitalism could not work for a minute. A lot of leftist movements have dreamed of conquering the state in order to change its functions, and to eventually even dissolve it. However, when they have succeeded in taking over power, the inner logic of state apparatuses usually overwhelmed them, leading to different variations of George Orwell's *Animal Farm*.

One of the most momentous decisions in the history of the Kurdish movement was to abandon the goal of creating a state. Instead of focusing on this single objective and subordinating all other struggles as mere "side contradictions" to this goal, a much more holistic approach could be pursued, simultaneously addressing different forms of domination that arise, both from outside the community and internally. The issue of overcoming patriarchal structures, for example, could no longer be postponed until "after the revolution" but was to be confronted at all levels immediately. This would also play a key role in preventing imposition of a militaristic logic on the society.

Overcoming Structural Violence
The second tyranny, or pillar of domination, is structural violence. It has been manifest since the first Mesopotamian city states in land privatization and concentration, debt relationships, the concept of private property, written law codifying and cementing inequality, and, finally, in the institutions of modern capitalism. Today, the endless accumulation of capital, which is the determining principle of the Megamachine, is primarily institutionalized in the biggest five hundred corporations, which control 40 percent of world GDP. These institutions are monstrous not only for their size and power but also for their inner logic. Their only rationale, enshrined in their legal construction, is to turn the world of living beings, of matter, and even of human relationships into commodities, and finally into chains of numbers on a bank account. Death by abstraction is the vanishing point of their operation—a moonlike planet with a lonely computer screen displaying endless rows of zeros.

The Kurdish movement challenges all these forms of structural violence at their root. Hundreds of cooperatives have been created: in textile production, food processing, and other sectors, with private property being partly replaced by commons-based principles. Free education and health care structures are also being developed. The goal is to establish an economy that is based on needs not profits, permanent growth, and accumulation.

Unraveling the Myths of Civilization and Modernity
The third tyranny challenged by the people of Rojava is ideological power, which legitimizes and "naturalizes" the physical and structural violence upon which every system of domination is based. This layer of domination can manifest itself in different ideological systems, authoritarian religion, scientism, and Western universalism among them, and has historically been institutionalized in numerous spheres, including architecture, the arts, schools, universities, and the media. When the first states consolidated in Mesopotamia, the elites developed a mythology that both mirrored and legitimized their power. The metaphysical universe came to be

dominated by a ruling male god, who, like an earthly ruler, disposed of a kingdom and a throne, whose will was to be obeyed ("thy will be done"), and who determined life and death. When the zenith of worldly dominion was finally reached in the Roman Empire, it culminated in the notion of the omnipotent God found in Christianity and the other monotheistic religions.

Later, in early capitalist modernity, the one and only God was key to justifying the subjugation and extermination of colonized peoples, whose souls were to be saved, even if they died in the process. With the "Age of Enlightenment" the vesture of this missionary ideology changed, but the substance remained the same. Now, it was "civilization" that had to be brought to the "savages," just as Christianity had been brought to the pagans. Later, other concepts served the same goal, including "progress," "development," and, today, "Western values."

The Kurdish liberation movement challenges this mythology on two different levels. First of all, the "myth of civilization" is deconstructed. We all have this image in our heads that the so-called "Stone Age" (which after all makes up 95 percent of human history) was marked by barbarians cluelessly running around, slaughtering each other with clubs, and dying at the age of thirty. Civilization then ended this age of misery and barbarism, restraining violence, bestowing culture on the primitives, and lifting mankind to a higher living standard. Historically, however, all of this is dead wrong. According to anthropologic and historical evidence, Neolithic cultures in the Middle East were less hierarchic, less violent, and much more equal in terms of both gender and economic relations than the state-based cultures of the following eras.[4] People were even much better nourished. Civilization—in the sense of hierarchically organized military states—gave us ziggurats, pyramids, and the written word, along with war, oppression, slavery, and eventually ecocide.

The second myth unraveled by the Kurdish movement—the "myth of modernity" (or the West)—has a similar structure. According to this narrative, modernity with its shining light led us out of the dark Middle Ages five hundred years ago and still continues on this path. However, all the gruesome things we are usually told were part of the Middle Ages, such as the Inquisition, torture, draconian punishments, and witch hunts, reached their climaxes in the capitalist era not in the Middle Ages. In fact, these measures were part of the strategies of the new ruling classes to crush resistance movements.[5] At the same time, European expansion overseas led to the annihilation of non-Western cultures and to a chain of genocides. Since then, capitalist modernity has unleashed an unprecedented spiral of violence and exploitation around the globe that may well lead to the destruction of humanity and even the planet.

Challenging the mythology of both civilization and modernity is key to creating a new narrative for a postcapitalist society that does not fall back into older forms of domination. However, as Kurdish activists stress, this does not mean rejecting everything that has been invented in the course of the past five thousand or five hundred years. The strength of the Kurdish movement is that they combine a thorough radical analysis with down-to-earth pragmatism.

The Tyranny of Linear Thinking

In the course of history, the first three tyrannies have created yet another one: the tyranny of linear thinking. Linear thinking is the assumption that the world functions according to predictable laws of cause and effect and is therefore controllable. As in antiquity the concept of a ruling God was shaped according to the model of earthly dominion, in the modern era the ruling God served as a blueprint for the modern man who tamed the earth through science and technology. In both the theological and technocratic versions of omnipotence, we find the idea that nature—including human nature—can and must be controlled. Just as the king commands his subjects and God his creatures, the engineer likewise commands nature to obey his will.

However, living systems do not work according to the logic of order and command. They are hypercomplex and nonlinear by nature. Each intervention can cause unpredictable chain reactions. This is true for both human societies and nonhuman nature. When I try, for example, to control a river in a linear way by shoring up the banks and damming the flow, it may one day react in an unexpected way and suddenly overflow with unprecedented flooding.

The application of linear thinking to living systems has left a trail of devastation across the planet. Industrial agriculture is a case in point. It is based on linear concepts of maximizing output and profit, killing pests, and pumping up groundwater. The results are depleted soils and water resources, shrinking yields, and multiresistant pests.

The Kurdish revolutionary movement has begun to tackle this fourth tyranny, both intellectually and in practice. In spite of the enormous difficulties posed by war and economic isolation, agricultural coopera-tives have begun efforts to convert industrial farming to ecologically sound production methods based on the idea of cooperating with complex living systems instead of trying to dominate them.

Contradictions

Of course, the project of transition in Rojava is rife with contradictions. Oil drilling, for example, continues in the region, although the movement aims at an ecological transition. Oil is still needed both for internal use and as an export commodity in order to pay for essential import goods. The issue of statehood is another example. Trying not to be a state proves almost impossible when surrounded by states. Not only because many of these states either try to destroy or exploit Rojava, but also because a self-administered region needs to have some sort of relationship with states in order to allow for a minimum of exchange of people and goods across borders. The current solution found to that problem is what David Graeber called a "dual power structure."[6] It has some sort of central administration that is able to make agreements with states; however, these agencies have no physical power over the population. Police forces are controlled by local councils not by the central administration. Thus, two parallel struc-tures are established, with the councils being not merely at the base of a pyramid but permeating all levels of society.

Another contradiction is that, although it challenges all forms of dom-ination, especially patriarchy, the Kurdish autonomy movement has a leader, who also happens to be a man: Abdullah Öcalan. However, without the writings of Öcalan as a point of reference, it would have been very difficult to develop the coherent strategy and practice found in Kurdistan.

A lesson to learn from all of this is that there are no solutions without contradictions in the world as it is. Every solution has to emerge from, respond to, and be adapted to local circumstances and traditions. There is no such thing as "purity" in this process.

Defending Rojava

The Kurdish autonomy project in Rojava is in acute danger. After the brutal invasion of Afrin by Turkish troops and the subsequent "ethnic cleansing" in early 2018, more Turkish assaults are looming. Western governments have been and still are furnishing Turkey with the weapons that are being used against the Kurds, for example German Leopard tanks and British helicopters. At the same time, these governments are preventing the Yekîneyên Parastina Gel (YPG: People's Protection Units)—which defeated ISIS—from getting the weapons necessary to defend the Kurdish population from a possible genocide by Turkish high-tech forces and their Islamist henchmen.

In this situation, international support for Rojava is crucial. Further arms transfers to Turkey and the continuing maintenance of these weapons by NATO must be stopped. Western governments have to be pressured not to look the other way when Turkey next intrudes in Rojava. If borders, territory, and human rights are as sacred as Western governments constantly claim, then any new Turkish aggression should be met with fierce opposition and sanctions. Defending Rojava is defending the hope for a livable future on a planet that desperately needs hope.

This essay was written for this book.

Fabian Scheidler lives in Berlin, Germany, where he works as a writer for print media, television, and theater. In 2009, he cofounded the independent newscast Kontext TV (www.kontext-tv.org), producing regular broadcasts on global justice issues; guests have included Noam Chomsky, Vandana Shiva, Immanuel Wallerstein, Amy Goodman, Silvia Federici, and many others. Fabian Scheidler's book *The End of the Megamachine. A Brief History of a Failing Civilization*, published in German in 2015, was selected as a top ten of future literature and went on to be a bestseller. Noam Chomsky commented: "The topic couldn't be more important. A very valuable and surely timely contribution." The English version will be published by Zero Books in 2020. For more information, see www.end-of-the-megamachine.com.

Notes

1   The term "Megamachine" was coined in Lewis Mumford, *The Myth of the Machine*, vol. 1 (San Diego: Harcourt, 1967); also see Fabian Scheidler, *The End of the Megamachine: A Brief History of a Failing Civilization* (London: Zero Books, forthcoming 2020).

2   See James C. Scott, *Against the Grain: A Deep History of the Earliest States* (New Haven, CT: Yale University Press, 2017).

3   Scheidler, *The End of the Megamachine*.

4   Scott, *Against the Grain*.

5   See Silvia Federici, *Caliban and the Witch: Women, the Body and Primitive Accumulation* (Brooklyn, NY: Autonomedia, 2004).

6   "David Graeber: From Occupy Wall Street to the Revolution in Rojava," speech at the conference "Challenging Capitalist Modernity" in Hamburg, April 2017, Kontext, accessed July 18, 2019, www.kontext-tv.de/en/node/2861.

SEVENTEEN

When Öcalan Met Bookchin: The Kurdish Freedom Movement and the Political Theory of Democratic Confederalism

Damian Gerber and Shannon Brincat

As is well-known, diverse forms of "communalism" or "democratic confederalism" have developed throughout parts of Kurdistan.[1] These self-managed forms of sociopolitical life are a direct expression of the Kurdish people and their regional circumstances. Yet they are also, in part, traceable to the visionary ideas of Abdullah Öcalan—a key figure in the Partiya Karkerên Kurdistanê (PKK: Kurdistan Workers' Party) and now the Kurdish freedom movement—and, in turn, one of his deepest influences, Murray Bookchin. Bookchin was a libertarian socialist and political theorist who developed the theory of social ecology in the 1960s as a response to what he perceived as the failures of the revolutionary projects of both Marxism and contemporary anarchism. Central to social ecology is the insistence that ecological crises arise from social pathologies, in particular, the consolidation and, eventually, colonization of political life by hierarchies, such as patriarchy, capitalism, and the nation-state. As an outgrowth of Bookchin's anthropological research into the relationship between ecological crisis and systems of hierarchy, "communalism" was proposed as a realizable political goal that involved decentralized social organization through direct democratic and ecological principles.[2] Öcalan, especially after his imprisonment in 1999, adopted key aspects of Bookchin's thought into his own political model of "democratic confederalism." This is not to conflate Bookchin with Öcalan nor to suggest that their models mirror each other. Nor is this to overstate Bookchin's influence on the Kurdish freedom movement, which has any number of unique internal (cultural and historic) and external (particularly geostrategic) influences irreducible to the purely theoretical. Nevertheless, during their brief correspondence in 2004, Öcalan stated that his "worldview" stands close to Bookchin's, especially in regards to the theory and practice of municipalities. Moreover, he admitted that alongside Immanuel Wallerstein, Bookchin was the writer with whom he was most "currently engaged," emphasizing that his own work was not an academic exercise but the work "of someone searching for practical ways out of the crisis the Middle East and the Kurds are in."[3] The connection between Bookchin and Öcalan therefore runs far deeper than their shared theoretical and normative ideas, going to the very core of the transformation of the Kurdish freedom movement toward the practice of "democratic confederalism."

The influence of Bookchin's communalism in the Kurdish freedom movement has been noted by many scholars, including well-known theorists like Slavoj Žižek and David Graeber, and, Kurdish specialists like Joost Jongerden and Ahmet Hamdi Akkaya.[4] However, despite this clear linkage, no one has yet undertaken a systematic analysis of how the ideas of Bookchin have been taken up in the thought of Öcalan and the Kurdish movement generally or the areas in which these ideas have been modified—even rejected—in favor of local conditions, geopolitical shifts, and the necessities of the Kurdish struggle. This article provides a theoretical analysis of Öcalan's adoption of Bookchin's idea of communalism in the form of democratic confederalism and the tensions and obstacles facing this process, both conceptually and in practice.[5]

The first part of the paper explores the social and historical framework developed by Öcalan and its relation to Bookchin's thought. Here, we engage with the key texts from both theorists that have informed the geopolitical and strategic outlook of Kurdish democratic confederalism. Specifically, we look to Bookchin's critique of hierarchy as informing the shift in the Kurdish freedom movement away from nationalism, tribalism, and capitalism toward a social ecology premised on gender equality, direct participation, and semi-autonomous confederation. In the second part, we examine the spatial dimensions of democratic confederalism by analyzing Öcalan's critique of nationalism and concept of democratic civil society. In particular, we look at how Öcalan's concept of political space draws on Aristotle's understanding of humanly scaled communities and how Kurdish democratic confederalism reimagines political life as *ethical space* in which the development of civic education is provided with the degree of institutional support necessary for the flourishing of ethical self-governance. In the final part, we examine the geopolitical implications of this theoretical shift in the Kurdish freedom movement. We argue that despite the challenges facing the movement, its respect of traditions for autonomy and traditional cultures of anti-statism may prove to be a sustainable model of praxis for, even a prefiguration of, the vision of a secular and non-hierarchical democratic confederacy in the Middle East.

The Theoretical Foundations of Democratic Confederalism

In 2002, the PKK dissolved itself, transcending its aim of statehood under a new paradigm: democratic confederalism.[6] This "democratic system of a people without a state" aimed for the "construction of a democratic, ecological, and gender-liberated society" throughout Kurdistan within the Koma Civakên Kurdistananê system (KCK: Union of Kurdistan Communities).[7] In July 2011, democratic autonomy was announced by the Demokratik Toplum Kongresi (DTK: Democratic Society Congress—the umbrella organization of the Kurdish movement involving all groups and individuals in civil society) proclaiming communal powers, democratic participation, self-determination, and self-organization *within* the borders of Turkey.[8] The shift was fundamental. This transition marked a revolution *within* the revolution. The PKK of the 1970s and 1980s had maintained a classical communist party organizational structure, seeking national liberation through a separate nation-state for the Kurds and fighting a war with Turkey to this end. The goal was the realization of the core principle of international society that was the mainstay of decolonization—self-determination—in a struggle buttressed by justifications of national liberation and the overthrow of imperialism. Yet after his capture in 1999, Öcalan was compelled to be critically self-reflective on the movement's previous failures and its aims, turning openly toward the thought of Murray Bookchin, among others. So decisive was Bookchin's influence that Öcalan directed the PKK to move away from its Leninist focus on capturing a nation-state toward Bookchin's outline of "communalism" (also termed "democratic municipalism"), broadly defined as the creation of semi-autonomous, direct democratic, and regional cantons united in a confederal structure administered by popular and revocable delegates and policed by citizens' militias and a citizens' army. While the movement has not yet achieved strict autonomy outside the state or world capitalism,[9] both the organizational form and the political aims of the movement have nevertheless been utterly transformed in this shift.

Rather than a Kurdish state, the movement now aims for "autonomy, femi-nism, ecological stewardship, cooperative economics, and ethnic, linguis-tic, and religious pluralism" *within* existing borders—thus changing the very basis of the previous geopolitical struggle. This shift in aims has corresponded to a shift in organizational form away from political parties to a social movement involving the direct self-management of communal life by the villages and neighborhoods, confederated in a voluntary asso-ciation. Rather than a seizure or creation of state power, only the right of self-defense is deemed consistent with the emancipatory political goals of this new democratic confederation that is premised to coexist *within* present territorial demarcations.[10]

Democratic confederalism (or "democratic autonomy," a term that is often used interchangeably by Öcalan) is said to promise the "rebirth" or "renaissance" of the Kurds—and potentially the entire Middle East.[11] Like Bookchin, Öcalan defends the potential in Enlightenment thought for the supersession of barbaric practices through democratic decision-making based in the social life and cultural values of Kurdish society.[12] History is Janus-faced rather than teleological, however, holding prospects for both a common humanity *and* barbarities.[13] It is creating the social conditions for such common humanity that the movement strives for—what Bookchin describes as the "general human interest" that "cuts across the particu-laristic interests of class, nationality, ethnicity, and gender"[14]—to emerge by overcoming all hierarchical and parochial forms, whether located in the folk, tribe, or nation. This shift toward universal democratic values in the Kurdish movement corresponds to a wider movement in the language of the revolutionary left since the 1970s away from "national liberation" toward a universal human rights paradigm.[15] For Öcalan, this shift has led to two *new* potentialities in the Kurdish movement. On the one hand, there is the potential for the autonomy of minorities by the acceptance of different cultural identities within a given territory that can revivify democratic processes within the existing borders of Turkey (and by impli-cation also Iraq, Iran, and Syria).[16] On the other hand, this "new politi-cal manifesto" or "third way" that ties political, cultural, and economic development to direct democratization promises a new emancipatory horizon for the region as a whole[17]—it could "ignite sparks" everywhere.[18] This shift has been expressed in the changes to the 2000 program away from a "federation of" to the "democratic union of" the Middle East, in which democratic unity of the Kurds with all neighbors is to be based on confederal structures and multilateral agreements.[19] This programmatic shift expands confederalism from a national and regional form to one operating on an interstate level.[20] Hence the concept of "space" in Rojava as a transcendental and basically transnational concept rather than delimited by geographic "places."[21]

Öcalan's *The Roots of Civilisation* marked this radical reconceptualization of space by tracing the ethical agency and developmental impetus of the Kurds as representative of a wider, transnational emancipatory interest.[22] This was at odds with the typical historical representation of the Kurds as either collaborationists or victims of foreign oppression—both phenomena of a divided society in Öcalan's estimation—that served to confine the movement to a space between conspiracy and liberation.[23] The importance of Öcalan's alternative historicism is that it provided a critical reflection on the nature and potentials of the movement within concrete conditions that could account for both the exploitation and co-optation of the Kurdish people but also the dialectic of resistance and transformation rooted in language, culture, and place. It is these older sociocultural structures that bridge the modern democratic "turn" with local practices largely handed down from the Neolithic Age, which uniquely positions the Kurdish freedom movement as the product of a continuous struggle for emancipation from local elites and imperial powers over time.[24] For Öcalan, despite capitalism and the state, despite pre-feudal and feudal structures, and despite tribal and aristocratic privileges, "the population has preserved its instinctive understanding of freedom, equality and fraternity"—a "will for freedom."[25] This is both a strength and a challenge: these older social forms provide a robust social basis of cohesion and resilience, and yet some traditional practices challenge the necessity of developing institutions of civil society for the freedom of *all* humanity, regardless of class, gender, or ethnicity. As Lenin protested, there can be no expectation of "a 'pure' social revolution."[26] That is, these historically inherited forms of hierarchy—in gender relations, tribal structures, and privileges of chiefdom in Kurdish society—constitute the particular conditions in which the project of democratic confederalism must contest and emerge.

These particular historical obstacles to democratic confederalism are not merely temporal. For Bookchin and Öcalan, the problem is *hierarchy* regardless of its institutional form or source of legitimacy. In this conception, hierarchy is a *social* term that takes on various institutionalized forms (all of which are unique to human society),[27] and hierarchical differences have been established through systems of status long before classes or the state emerged.[28] Tribal structures in Kurdistan have been caught in this contradiction in that they embody localized institutions of organization and forms of social recognition, some of which are also parochial, limited, and unequal. Nevertheless, this potential in traditional forms of society has long been deemed an important bastion against capital and colonialism. For example, Marx saw the communal forms in India, Algeria, Latin America, and Russia as possessing vitality and resistance.[29] Similarly, Sylvia Federici has extolled the communal property relations and the cooperative, for, as she claims: "*it is not where capitalist development is the highest but where communal bonds are the strongest* that capitalist expansion is put on halt and even forced to recede."[30] What Bookchin similarly emphasizes is that the institutionalized practices in older societies—specifically, socialization, the "irreducible minimum," complementarity, and usufruct—all tend to *curtail* hierarchy.[31] At the same time, this does not romanticize the potential in the *aşiret* by overlooking its practices of vendetta, petty tyrannies, and patriarchal customs. As Öcalan determines, the tribal structures in Kurdistan have tended to ossify elite rule, hindering intellectual and cultural renewal.[32] Quite simply, they are no longer adequate to express the social freedom of the Kurdish people. The *value* of historical social entities (like clans and stateless nations) can be reclaimed as "component entities" of developed nations if democratized.[33] Similarly, communitarian social formations, which at times have yielded nurturing, ecological, and liberatory values, are seen as part of a legacy of a socialism that is in need of "completion" through a renewed democratic direction.[34]

Öcalan and Bookchin argue that the problems of hierarchy are exacerbated by nationalism—the acknowledgement of which caused a dramatic shift in the political aims of the movement. For Öcalan, bourgeois nationalism is as incapable of expressing the type of freedom sought by the population, as were older forms of political community that were equally anachronistic, elitist, and hierarchical.[35] So too was the dogmatism of "real socialism," which Öcalan has since compared to that of the Sumerian hieratic society, characterized by "the negation of equal rights and freedom."[36] Those movements that had held on to such political solutions fixated on authoritarian ends—reifying or forgetting these as institutions *of* hierarchy—rather than pursuing a lived social freedom that transcends the spatial and ideological limitations of the nation-state. For

Öcalan, hierarchies are merely the protections of particular interests pre-served through power.[37] For Bookchin, similarly, the impetus of any hier-archical form is to *contain* the body politic, to control and rule it, rather than express its will. So while there may be no uniform ruling class, the state is nevertheless a professional system of coercion that administers through its monopoly of violence.[38] Such coercive administration is "inor-ganic," an "excrescence of society that has no real roots in it, no respon-siveness to it."[39] But this relation of hierarchy to society is then mystified: divisions are seen as personal not social. That is, real social conflicts are concealed by appeals to a fictional social harmony in which hierarchy goes on largely misdiagnosed, even mollified.[40]

Yet, at the same time, Öcalan appreciated that such elements of society could not simply be wiped away.[41] The task has been to dissolve them organically through new institutional forms permeating civil society—changing the roots of "daily life" by removing hierarchy and resocializa-tion. For Öcalan, each of these older social forms must be "pressed" to "join the democratic change" while remaining rooted in society.[42] In this way, the tyrannies of custom may be willingly abandoned and replaced by the community with new forms of solidarity. For Bookchin, this "general human interest" that cuts across "class, nationality, ethnicity and gender" can be "embodied" in the nonhierarchical demands of women, minorities, and all oppressed groups for the recognition of their differences within a *substantive* "equality of unequals."[43] Grounded in a social demand for the recognition of difference, a wider possibility emerges for a "sweep-ing social movement" to emerge from the bottom up, that has become the guiding principle of "democratic autonomy."[44] Ross reports, for example, that Kurds have been enthused about the virtues of participatory non-hierarchical self-government, because it has been able to produce a social stability that is woven from the bottom up rather than imposed from the top down.[45] The key, as explained by Öcalan, lies in freeing the Kurdish movement from even "*thinking* in hierarchical structures."[46]

On the basis of Bookchin's critique of hierarchy, Öcalan's decisive reorientation of the Kurdish movement away from nationalism, the state, and tribalism is readily understandable. Nationalism is exposed by Öcalan as "serving," among other things, the "colonialist divide-and-rule strategy," regional fragmentation, and the maintenance of a specific ruling class.[47] For Öcalan, the solution was not a denial of ethnicity, the social significance of place, or state secession on the grounds of an ethnic or civic nationalism but democracy, grounded in a wider confederalist notion of space. The "essential objective" of the movement became the democratization of the Turkish Republic as "a voluntary association" in which all minorities are to be recognized as free and equal citizens.[48]

The Spatial Dimensions of Political Community and Democratic Confederation

A key influence in "democratic confederalism" has been the influence of classical social life. Models of direct democracy and the ethical substance of Hellenic life have provided both Bookchin and Öcalan with a fertile contrast to the geopolitical imagination of statism and capitalist modernity. A key example of these values is Aristotle's concept of "human scale" actively taken up by Bookchin and evident within the organizational frame of democratic confederalism, which is primarily based on creating assemblies at the local level and coordinating them horizontally through confederations.[49] For both Bookchin and Öcalan the reorganization of community along direct democratic lines revolves around the creation of *ethical* space—a space of face-to-face communities, where people remain on familiar terms and responsible for one another's livelihoods, secured through deliberation and administrative functions. As Aristotle made abundantly clear in his ethical and political works, such a notion of the political community (polis) was a far cry from the institutional nexus of the centralized nation-state of modern times.[50] According to Alasdair MacIntyre, the Hellenic democratic polis reflected a social "context" in which "moral judgments were understood as governed by impersonal standards justified by a shared conception of the human good" and paved the way for a "moral economy" shaped by the needs of the community rather than a "market economy" shaped by commodification.[51] Aristotle's remarks in *Politics* on the advantages of democratic ethical spaces run directly through Bookchin and Öcalan and are central to democratic confederalism. Of particular importance is how the human scale of community public space is meant to lead to the virtue of the "multitude," a reciprocity of good character in which members of society are assured that "their character is as good as his."[52] This mutuality is a product not merely of consensus or popularity but is produced by the rhetorical reasoning, heated debate, and relational characteristics of the Athenian polis. Through election by lottery and through assembly debate in particular, the social body becomes distinct as an agent of deliberative reasoning as opposed to the highly manipulated "preferences" or ephemeral "opinions" that inform representative government.

Furthermore, rotational powers, delegation rather than representation, and election to executive and administrative positions mitigates moneyed special interests and corruption. The importance of delegation, in the form of representatives who are immediately recallable and serve only administrative functions, was a key feature of the DTK that Öcalan has described as a "project for the democratic organization of society."[53] All policy-making decisions are reserved for the local community at the neighborhood and town levels, and the DTK meets as a general assembly with 40 percent elected officials and the remaining from grassroots organizations elected in public general meetings in their locales.[54] In this way, communalism is a dialectic of place and space: a synthesis of localized places (such as neighborhood assemblies) necessary for human scale, integrated into a wider network (confederation) of delegated power, functioning as a spatial totality. Most notably, whereas this is discussed only as experimental and theoretical in Bookchin's communalism,[55] it has now been concretely developed within the practices of the Kurdish freedom movement.

Communalism's vision of a revolutionized municipality, taken up in such diverse ways throughout Kurdistan, is grounded in a belief in the value of democratic amateurism as a superior means of social organization than bureaucratic specialization. While the capacity for civic life in the polis is now too distant to be a regulative ethic, Bookchin believed that it could be reinvigorated through a distinct form of social education, a rupture in thought away from hierarchy, to one in which all individuals were made capable of self-management and the mutual recognition of this capacity with and between all social members.[56] As Bookchin affirmed, "Every revolutionary project is, above all, an *educational* one."[57] Öcalan's shares this emphasis on education as the lodestone of ethical space. For example, his reliance on the Aristotelian notion that "education of mind without the heart is no education at all" and "virtue-ethics" in the pursuit of truth, firmness and flexibility, innovation, analysis, and sagacity in the "Education Programme and Traits of the Party Militant" bears a close resemblance to Bookchin's emphasis.[58] More deeply, however, this emphasis on education is related to the rejection of "mentalities and relations of subservience," for it is only through such civic awareness that democratic confederalism can be actively supported.[59]

As stated by Jongerden and Akkaya, democratic autonomy and confederalism are not a mere formal and legal arrangement but are premised on the competencies and practices of the people themselves.[60] Öcalan has been keenly aware of the necessity for supporting such educational processes as a form of phronesis for the success of democratic autonomy as a whole. As Öcalan describes it, the goal of education is "to enable the people willingly to accept even difficult duties,"[61] part of which means bearing through geopolitical conflict, whether with ISIS or with the Turkish forces.

The Future of Kurdish Communalism: Tensions, Challenges, Opportunities

One of the greatest political challenges of the struggle for democratic confederalism lies within the political geography of the movement and its relations to its neighbors. The consolidation and expansion of the movement will bring it beyond the familiar horizons of the cantons, leading inevitably to the question of how to extend democratic autonomy to non-Kurdish cultural communities that do not necessarily share enthusiasm for the secularism, women's liberation, and non-statist forms of political administration of this "new" republic.[62] For example, the opening up of new administrative areas as a result of recent military victories, such as in the Sinjar province, brings with it the prospect of integration into a wider democratic confederation and the winding back of traditional hierarchies that deter persecuted ethnic and social groups from full democratic participation. Yet the political geography of the Middle East, as elsewhere, has been prefigured on religious and nationalist hierarchies that pervade the state, the village, and the patriarchal family. One of the greatest dangers to the democratic confederalist movement, therefore, is the prospect of a dualistic mentality emerging out of a nationalistic privileging of Kurdish cultural identity, a development already foreshadowed in the governing body of Kurdish Iraq.[63] In other words, a nationalistic focus upon Kurdish identity could culminate in a political division between Kurdish and non-Kurdish areas that may even be reflected in future military and administrative distinctions. Such distinctions would quickly lead to new forms of hierarchy and statism, rather than embracing the potentials of ethical space envisioned by democratic confederalism.

This geopolitical conflict of ideologies is already at a juncture. On the one hand, the pursuit of military *imposition* of democratic communities—including the forced municipalization of private property, the dissolution of local hierarchies, and even possibly a mandatory integration into a Kurdish federation—and on the other, the pursuit of a necessary level of respect for local and traditional communal autonomy, in which the inclusion of new areas within a democratic confederation strictly confined to voluntary agreements between cantons. The former may undermine the integrity of the democratic confederalist project; the latter would risk fracturing the movement and regional infighting. A most pressing factor that may drive this dialectic in a more militaristic direction is the presence of undercover ISIS terrorists and sympathizers in many villages and townships newly occupied by the Kurdish militias.[64] The tension, then, between a forced integration into a wider confederal structure and a voluntarist emphasis on communal "autonomy" is of enormous significance for Kurdish communalism and forms a substantial bridge between communalist theory and praxis.

Bookchin observes that "the danger that democratized municipalities in a decentralized society would result in economic and cultural parochialism is very real and can only be precluded by a vigorous confederation of municipalities based on their material interdependence."[65] Similarly, for Bookchin, anything less than the municipalization of property—including direct municipal control over economic policies—would favor the nationalization, collectivization, or privatization of property, thus reinforcing either the material foundations of a nation-state or of a competitive market economy.[66] This might imply the need for Kurdish militias to forcefully municipalize the economies of newly won provinces should they meet with local resistance in the form of established hierarchies. Indeed, it has recently been argued that overcoming the gross inequalities found in the Middle East, where several oil monarchies control 70 percent of wealth, is a lynchpin to defeating ISIS and terrorism in general.[67] And despite Bookchin's uncertain stance on whether the *coercion* of non-democratic, autonomous, or avowedly hostile polities into a municipal confederation is ethically permissible, his late writings leave no doubt about the need to seize power in order to create new institutions. As he wrote, "power cannot be abolished: it is always a feature of social and political life. Power that is not in the hands of the masses must inevitably fall into the hands of their oppressors."[68] These insights indicate the need to take seriously Bookchin's stress upon education for civic virtue, as the ideal ethical *process* of transforming hierarchical and autarchic municipalities into non-hierarchical and confederated ones.

In spite of these aforementioned challenges, Kurdish communalism has begun to find its own innovative solutions. From praxis has emerged significant qualifications upon theory. We offer one example regarding the integration of new communities or townships into a democratic confederation that has so far emphasized the importance of respecting local traditional attitudes that might favor decentralization and local autonomy, rather than the coercive overcoming of these potentially incompatible political geographies. Öcalan has stressed that military force should be employed only for the self-defense of democratic civil society against the incursions of surrounding states but not in the pursuit of broader aspirations of regional hegemony. As he affirms, "They will become cross-border confederations" if or when the "societies concerned so desire."[69] For Öcalan, democratic confederalism lives and dies by virtue of its demonstration or "proof" of its capacity for solving the most pressing civilizational problems, such as inequality, suffering, and domination.[70] This helps to clarify why, for Öcalan and the Kurdish freedom movement, traditions of local autonomy and anti-statism are viewed as a vital cultural reservoir in building popular *support* for a wider democratic federation, rather than as limitations to be swept away coercively.[71] What is viewed as decisive is not the potential "backwardness" of the precapitalist villages or autonomous townships but, rather, the *potentialities* of their long-lived traditions of resistance to the hierarchical and centralizing structure of nationalism and statism. In this respect, the Kurdish freedom movement takes a long-term view of the integration of communities into a wider, federated structure of power on a voluntary basis—with a view to gaining *cultural* support for *voluntary* communalist transformations—rather than pursuing the short-term gains of a coercive subjugation of existing power structures. In these ways, the Kurdish freedom movement is distinguished by its prefigutive sociality—its institutions and practices are to be established cooperatively so that in the course of actually achieving its aims, its activities realize the standards or "way of being" that they are contributing to.[72] This Kurdish praxis is a vital addendum to Bookchin's thought that should continue to qualify communalist political theory in the future.

In this context, the promise of a Kurdish "transconstitutionalism" is greatest.[73] Transconstitutionalism could instill formalized relations through core principles and basic content accorded to *all* members of the confederation as the "minimum requirements" for freedom to emerge. This is a view that Öcalan seems to tend toward,[74] positing human rights, social participation, and material necessities as the minimum content of democratic confederalism. Yet this would not be presented as some "superlegal code" over local forms but, rather, as a question of social organization with local differentiations to be debated through respectful dialogue within the confederated polities. Arguably, this has been reflected in aspects of The Social Contract of the Rojava Cantons in Syria (2015)[75] as a form of decentralized federalism that builds upon the de jure Syrian Constitution in order to hold it to account as a "free, sovereign and democratic state." For Öcalan, there is no reason why people of different genders, faiths, or origins could not be citizens under one "common administrative roof."[76] Should the Kurdish freedom movement prove successful militarily and socially, it could achieve an "ecological community [that] would municipalize its economy and join with other municipalities in integrating its resources into a regional confederal system."[77] But discussing the potentials and problems of transconstitutionalism leads beyond the boundaries of Bookchin's thought and into another suite of questions.

This essay, an edited version of an article published in *Geopolitics* (October 2018), appears with kind permission of the authors.

Damian Gerber is an independent academic. As well as articles published in *Antipode* and *Thesis Eleven*, he is the author of *The Distortion of Nature's Image: Reification, the Ecological Crisis and the Recovery of a Dialectical Naturalism* (Albany: State University of New York Press, 2019).
Shannon Brincat is a senior lecturer in Politics and International Relations at the University of the Sunshine Coast, Australia. His most recent manuscript, *The Spiral World*, traces dialectical thinking in the Axial Age. He has been the editor of a number of collections, most recently *From International Relations to World Civilizations: The Contributions of Robert W. Cox and Dialectics and World Politics* (London: Routledge, 2017).

Notes

1   Other names for this process include "libertarian municipalism" and "democratic autonomy." We adopt "democratic confederalism" as the umbrella term for the forms of self-management and direct democracy in the Kurdish freedom movement. We are indebted to the work of TATORT for their reports on these autonomous projects; TATORT Kurdistan, *Democratic Autonomy in North Kurdistan: The Council Movement, Gender Liberation, and Ecology*, trans. Janet Biehl (Porsgrunn, NO: New Compass Press, 2013).

2   For commentaries on Bookchin's work, see John P. Clark, *Renewing the Earth: The Promise of Social Ecology: A Celebration of the Work of Murray Bookchin*

(New York: Green Print, 1990); Brian Morris, "The Political Legacy of Murray Bookchin," *Anarchist Studies* 17, no. 1 (Spring 2009): 95–105, accessed September 12, 2019, https://go.gale.com/ps/anonymous?id=GALE%7CA214471669&sid=goo gleScholar&v=2.1&it=r&linkaccess=abs&issn=09673393&p=AONE&sw=w; Janet Biehl, *Ecology or Catastrophe: The Life of Murray Bookchin* (Oxford: Oxford University Press, 2015).

3   Private correspondence between Murray Bookchin and Abdullah Öcalan, April 11, 2004 and May 5, 2004, courtesy of Debbie Bookchin. Representatives of Öcalan contacted Bookchin in April 2004 to organize a dialogue that involved a number of exchanges of written correspondence; also see Biehl, *Ecology or Catastrophe*.

4   Slavoj Žižek, "Kurds Are the Most Progressive, Democratic Nation in the Middle East," KurdishQuestion.com, October 22, 2015, accessed July 12, 2019, http://kurdishquestion.com/oldarticle.php?aid=slavoj-zizek-kurds-are-the-most-progressive-democratic-nation-in-the-middle-east; David Graeber, "Why Is the World Ignoring the Revolutionary Kurds in Syria?" *Guardian*, October 8, 2014, accessed July 12, 2019, https://www.theguardian.com/commentisfree/2014/oct/08/why-world-ignoring-revolutionary-kurds-syria-isis; Joost Jongerden and Ahmet Hamdi Akkaya, "Born from the Left: The Making of the PKK," in *Nationalisms and Politics in Turkey*, ed. Marlies Casier and Joost Jongerden (London: Routledge, 2011), 143–62.

5   Our emphasis is on tracing the influence of Bookchin on Öcalan's published political theory and working through the tensions that manifest in this exchange. We discuss examples of the actual practices of democratic confederalism in Kurdistan for illustrative purposes only. A full analysis would require a systemic *book length* treatment. For a more detailed account of the political practices in Kurdistan as related to democratic confederalism, see TATORT Kurdistan, *Democratic Autonomy in North Kurdistan*.

6   Abdullah Öcalan, *Democratic Confederalism* (Cologne: International Initiative, 2011).

7   This is the umbrella and grassroots organization that includes all forms of communities, councils, and collectives implementing democratic confederalism and embracing the Kurds in Turkey, Iran, Iraq, and Syria.

8   TATORT Kurdistan, *Democratic Autonomy in North Kurdistan*, 209–11.

9   Ibid., 16.

10   Öcalan, *Democratic Confederalism*, 28–29.

11   Klaus Happel, quoted in Abdullah Öcalan, *Prison Writings, Volume 2: The PKK and the Kurdish Question in the 21st Century* (Cologne: Transmedia Publishing, 2011), x.

12   See Abdullah Öcalan, *Prison Writings, Volume 3: The Road Map to Negotiations* (Cologne: International Initiative, 2012); also see Murray Bookchin, *Remaking Society* (Montréal: Black Rose Books, 1989), 18; Murray Bookchin, *The Next Revolution: Popular Assemblies and the Promise of Direct Democracy*, ed. Debbie Bookchin and Blair Taylor (London: Verso, 2015), 194.

13   Bookchin, *Remaking Society*, 180.

14   Ibid., 166–69.

15 See Jon Piccini, "Human Rights and the Left," in *Upswell* no. 2 (May 2015), accessed October 3, 2019, https://medium.com/@JonPiccini/human-rights-and-the-left-1e6a740a3db.

16 Öcalan, *Prison Writings, Volume 2*, 152.

17 Ibid., 62.

18 Ibid., xviii.

19 Ozum Yesiltas, "Democratization and Ethnic Conflict: Transformation of Turkey's Kurdish Question," in *Nationalism and Intra-State Conflicts in the Postcolonial World*, ed. Fonkem Achankeng (Lanham, MD: Lexington Books, 2015), 277.

20 Öcalan, *Prison Writings, Volume 2*, 62.

21 See Zeynep Gambetti, "Politics of Place/Space: The Spatial Dynamics of the Kurdish and Zapatista Movements," *New Perspectives on Turkey* 41 (Fall 2009): 43–87.

22 Abadullah Öcalan, *Prison Writings, Volume 1: The Roots of Civilisation*, trans. K. Happel (London: Pluto Press, 2007).

23 Öcalan, *Prison Writings, Volume 2*, 98, 100.

24 Ibid., 28; Abdullah Öcalan, *War and Peace in Kurdistan: Perspectives for a Political Solution of the Kurdistan Question* (Cologne: International Initiative, 2012), 8–25.

25 Öcalan, *Prison Writings, Volume 2*, 49.

26 V.I. Lenin, "The Discussion on Self-Determination Summed Up," *Sbornik Sotsial-Demokrata* no. 1 (October. 2016), Marxists Internet Archive, accessed July 12, 2019, http://www.marxists.org/archive/lenin/works/1916/jul/x01.htm.

27 Bookchin, *Remaking Society*, 62.

28 Ibid., 61.

29 Marx's 1881 drafts and 1879 notes on Sewell and Kovalevsky as discussed in Kevin Anderson, *Marx at the Margins* (Chicago: University of Chicago Press, 2010), 233ff.

30 Sylvia Federici, "Marx, Feminism and the Construction of the Commons," in *Communism in the 21st Century*, vol. 1, ed. Shannon K. Brincat (Santa Barbara, CA: Praeger, 2015), 184.

31 The "irreducible minimum" refers to the material needs of the individual as satisfied by the community; Bookchin, *Remaking Society*, 64.

32 Öcalan, *Prison Writings, Volume 2*, 28.

33 Abdullah Öcalan, "Briefly on Socialism," YPG International, July 21, 2016, accessed July 13, 2019, https://ypginternational.blackblogs.org/2016/07/21/briefly-on-socialism-abdullah-ocalan/.

34 Ibid.

35 Öcalan, *War and Peace in Kurdistan*, 28; also see A.K. Özcan, *Turkey's Kurds: A Theoretical Analysis of the PKK and Abdullah Öcalan* (London: Routledge, 2005), 5.

36 Öcalan, *Prison Writings, Volume 2*, 51.

37 Michael M. Gunter, "Interview; Abdullah Öcalan: 'We Are Fighting Turks Everywhere,'" *Middles East Quarterly* 5, no. 2 (June 1998): 82; Öcalan, *War and Peace in Kurdistan*, 35; Öcalan, *Prison Writings, Volume 2*, 34–35.

38 Bookchin, *Remaking Society*, 66–67.
39 Murray Bookchin, *The Rise of Urbanization and the Decline of Citizenship* (San Francisco: Sierra Club Books, 1987), 243.
40 Bookchin, *Remaking Society*, 72–73.
41 Abdullah Öcalan, *Seçme Yazılar*, volume 6 (Cologne: Weşanên Serxwebun, 1995); cited in A.K. Özcan, *Turkey's Kurds: A Theoretical Analysis of the PKK and Abdullah Öcalan* (London: Routledge, 2005), 161.
42 Öcalan, *Prison Writings, Volume 2*, 41.
43 Ibid., 65.
44 Ibid., 169.
45 Carne Ross, "Power to the People: Rojava, Anarchism, and Murray Bookchin," *Financial Times*, October 23, 2015, accessed July 18, 2019, https://www.carneross.com/index.php/2015/10/26/power-to-the-people-rojava-anarchism-and-murray-bookchin-financial-times-24-oct-2015/.
46 Öcalan, *Prison Writings, Volume 2*, 34.
47 Ibid., 18, 73.
48 Ibid., 18, 79–80, 91, 150.
49 Janet Biehl, "Report from the Mesopotamian Social Forum," New Compass, October 5, 2011, accessed July 13, 2019, http://new-compass.net/node/265.
50 Aristotle, "La Politica," in *The Basic Works of Aristotle*, ed. Richard McKeon (New York: Modern Library, 2001), book 3.
51 Alasdair Macintyre, *After Virtue: A Study in Moral Theory* (Notre Dame: University of Notre Dame Press, 2007 [1981]), ix.
52 Macintyre, *After Virtue*.
53 TATORT Kurdistan, *Democratic Autonomy in North Kurdistan*, 27.
54 Ibid., 33.
55 See especially Bookchin, *Remaking Society*, 95–126.
56 Bookchin, *The Rise of Urbanization and the Decline of Citizenship*, 250–51.
57 Bookchin, *Remaking Society*, 197.
58 Özcan, *Turkey's Kurds*, 164ff (171–72).
59 Öcalan, *Prison Writings, Volume 2*, x–xi.
60 Ahmet Hamdi Akkaya and Joost Jongerden, "Reassembling the Political: The PKK and the Project of Radical Democracy," *European Journal of Turkish Studies* 14 (2012), accessed July 13, 2019, https://journals.openedition.org/ejts/4615.
61 Öcalan, *Prison Writings, Volume 2*, 124.
62 Ibid., 30, 152.
63 Wes Enzinna, "A Dream of Secular Utopia in ISIS' Backyard," *New York Times Magazine*, November 24, 2015, accessed July 13, 2019, http://www.nytimes.com/2015/11/29/magazine/a-dream-of-utopia-in-hell.html?_r=1.
64 Ibid.; also see Rebecca Collard, "The Rise of ISIS Sows Distrust Between Kurds and Sunni Arabs," *Time*, August 26, 2014, accessed July 13, 2019, http://time.com/3182347/kurds-sunni-arabs-iraq-isis-erbil/.
65 Bookchin, *The Next Revolution*, 137.
66 Ibid.; also see Andy Price, *Recovering Bookchin: Social Ecology and the Crises of Our Time* (Porsgrunn, NO: New Compass Press, 2012), 225–26.

67 See Thomas Picketty, "The All Safe Is Not Enough," *Le Monde*, November 22–23, 2015.

68 Bookchin, *The Next Revolution*, 143.

69 Öcalan *Prison Writings, Volume 2*, 32.

70 Ibid.

71 See Janet Biehl, *Kurdish Communalism* (interview with Ercan Ayboga), New Compass, October 9, 2011, accessed July 13, 2019, http://new-compass.net/article/kurdish-communalism.

72 MacIntyre, *After Virtue*, 175.

73 See Marcelo Neves, *Transconstitutionalism* (Oxford: Bloomsbury, 2013).

74 Öcalan, *Prison Writings, Volume 2*, 78, 156–57.

75 The Social Contract of the of Rojava Cantons in Syria, accessed September 12, 2019, https://civiroglu.net/the-constitution-of-the-rojava-cantons/.

76 Ibid., 60–1.

77 Bookchin, *Remaking Society*, 194–95.

EIGHTEEN

Re-enchantment of the Political: Abdullah Öcalan, Democratic Confederalism, and the Politics of Reasonableness

Patrick Huff

Introduction

In this essay I read Öcalan's thought through key Western intellectual interlocutors, including Friedrich Nietzsche, Immanuel Wallerstein, Theodor Adorno, Murray Bookchin, and Fernand Braudel. Grounding his life history in the context of the long struggle for Kurdish freedom, I sketch his intellectual trajectory from childhood through the formation of the Partiya Karkerên Kurdistanê (PKK: Kurdistan Workers' Party) to his imprisonment by the Turkish state. Throughout his life Öcalan has creatively engaged with an impressive range of Euro-American thinkers and intellectual traditions. Öcalan has sought solutions to the problems of Kurdistan, the wider Middle East, and the world. I argue that his innovative political project amounts to a re-enchantment of the political. I show, however, that this re-enchantment is not an embrace of magical thinking but rather a politics of reasonableness instituted in the forms of democratic confederalism and the democratic nation.

An Interpretive Challenge

Engaging Öcalan's body of work is a challenging task. Öcalan's richly metaphoric narratives combine history, archeology, critical theory, social ecology, and philosophy of science, aimed at inspiring popular revolutionary praxis. Any scholarly engagement with Öcalan's oeuvre should recognize three crucial points: 1) for the last twenty years Öcalan has been a political prisoner, held by the Turkish state under torturous conditions; 2) Öcalan is not a conventional scholar, and his aims are revolutionary rather than those of formal scholarship; 3) my examination of Öcalan's intellectual engagement with Western thinkers is in no way meant to reduce his highly original work to a derivative status. Instead, I show the creative intellectual synthesis Öcalan develops throughout his writings. As David Graeber observes, "What Öcalan is doing here is taking the same pieces and putting them together in a different way. In so doing he is taking the lead from his native Kurdistan."[1] Öcalan easily fits the figure of the Gramscian organic intellectual, a revolutionary theorist arising from and capable of articulating subaltern interests.[2] Though his writings are inextricably grounded in the Kurdish historical experience, with an unswerving commitment to free Kurdistan, he embraces internationalism and cross-cultural solidarity. The roots of Öcalan's intellectual trajectory can be found in his early life history.

Part I: A Biographical Sketch

Öcalan was born on April 4, 1948, in Ömerli, a small rural village in Turkey's Southeastern Urfa Province. Twenty-five years earlier, in 1923, the Treaty of Lausanne established the borders of modern Turkey and—like the earlier Sykes-Picot Agreement hatched by Europe's imperial powers—cemented the dismemberment of the Kurdish nation. Kurds were given minority status within the nation-states of Turkey, Iraq, Syria, and Iran. Emerging from the ruins of the Ottoman Empire, the Turkish Republic undertook a crash course modernization program, guided by Mustafa Kemal Atatürk, founding father of the republic. Extreme nationalism was promoted as a unifying ideology alongside industrial development. Adopted in 1925, the Turkish constitution defined citizenship in strictly ethnic terms: citizens were Turkish by definition.[3] For Kurds like Öcalan and other minorities this meant engagement in civic life required the denial of their identities. Minorities that insisted on their own existence, despite their constitutional erasure, were marginalized and repressed. Turkey's modernization and integration into the developing world-system was in full swing by the time of Öcalan's birth. As he observes:

> My life story coincides with the beginning of the 1950's when the drive of global capitalism of the era reached its peak. On the other hand, my place of birth is the most fertile land in the upper part of Mesopotamia—the Fertile Crescent enveloped by the Taurus-Zagros mountains—the location where the remnants of the oldest and most

deep-rooted mentalities can still be found, and where the Neolithic Age and the initial urban civilization existed for very long periods: These are the mountain skirts that bore the civilization.[4]

Throughout his writings Öcalan draws connections and enduring sociohistorical continuities from the deep past to the present. Öcalan's thought tends toward the long view. Revolutionary transformation requires understanding the historical context of the present situation. Öcalan's preoccupation with Mesopotamia's ancient past also seems to reflect a desire to recover from the historic erasure of Kurds.

Against his mother's wishes, Öcalan left his village at a young age.[5] His reflections on this are somewhat ambivalent. On the one hand, Öcalan writes, "I am quite certain that I was right not to give in to the village society." However, on the other hand, he immediately follows by stating, "But I was wrong in believing that capitalist modernity could offer an alternative to this way of life. Earlier in my life I made the huge mistake of radically breaking with the village society." I should note that in Öcalan's terminology "capitalist modernity" includes the Marxist-Leninism he now disavows. Further considering village society, Öcalan explains, "even though it had not been democratized, it was far removed from fundamental stages such as nation-state and industrialization."[6]

In contrast to the village, Öcalan's assessment of urban civilization is less ambivalent. He writes, "I think city society, which, like a magnet pulled me away from village society, is the main locus of our social problems. The city-state-classed civilization and the societal form it has caused are the main culprits not only of society's internal decay but also its detachment from nature."[7] Öcalan's affinity for rurality and nature should not be read as advocating neo-primitivism. Öcalan's critique of modernity is primarily a critique of the meaninglessness and unethical nature of the social relations inherent in capitalist modernity. In contrast, Öcalan's political aim is to develop a basis for ethical and meaningful life, a life in close communion with other humans and nature. Capitalist modernity's political form has substituted meaningfulness with instrumental rationality. On this account, Öcalan praises Nietzsche's trenchant critique of modernity, suggesting that Nietzsche "can almost be called the prophet of the capitalist era."[8] Likewise, Öcalan observes that Max Weber "underlined the material characteristics of the civilization when he described rationality as the reason behind the disenchantment of the world."[9] Öcalan, however, does not share Weber's sense of pessimism about the possibility of overcoming this condition of rationalized disenchantment.

Affected by his rural childhood, Öcalan's earthly and life-affirming disposition is closer to Nietzsche than Weber. Reminiscing on his childhood wandering the mountains, Öcalan recalls:

> [A]s a young boy, because of this, I was described as "mad for the mountains." When I learnt much later that such a life was reserved for the god Dionysus and the free artistic group of girls (the Bacchantes) who traveled before and behind him, I really envied him. It is said the philosopher Nietzsche preferred this god to Zeus and that he would even sign many of his works as the "disciple of Dionysus." When I was still at my village, I always wanted to play games with the girls of my village. Although this did not conform to the religious rules, I have always thought that this was the most natural thing. I never approved of the dominant culture's way of shutting women behind doors. I still want to engage with them in unlimited free discussions, in games, in all the sacredness of life. I still say an unconditional "no" to the slavery and bond that smell of possession and that is based on power relations.[10]

For Nietzsche, Dionysus is a metaphor for the affirmation of life and humanity's healthy growth (overcoming). Dionysus stands as a symbolic reference to human potential for creation and destruction, particularly in regards to cultural values. As Douglas Burnham explains, "Growth, and in particular growth in the expression and feelings of power, requires both creativity (the devising of new life practices and values) and destruction (of existing practices and values, including those in the self)."[11] Öcalan's struggle has accomplished a revolutionary revaluation of existing values, his devastating critique of patriarchal culture being a prime example.

Öcalan's Political Coming of Age

In Turkey, during the late 1960s, multiple sectarian tendencies of the student left fought outright battles with each other over ideological squabbles. The "Kurdish Question" was one of many points of factional dispute. The Dev-Genç, the Federation of Revolutionary Youth, an umbrella group, was perhaps the most sustained coordination effort among the various radical tendencies of the Turkish left. Öcalan, then a student of political science, found himself in the ideological hotbed of Ankara University.

Öcalan recalls, "In Ankara in 1970, I joined the fearless revolutionary youth. The killings of Mahir Çayan and his friends at Kizildere (March 1971) and the execution of Denis Gezmiş and his comrades (May 1972) called on us honest sympathisers to continue their legacy."[12] Developing a Guevarist strategy, Gezmiş, a student leader, formed the Türkiye Halk Kurtuluş Ordusu (THKO: People's Liberation Army of Turkey) to wage guerrilla war against the Turkish state. Likewise, Çayan led a splinter group, the Türkiye Halk Kurtuluş Partisi-Cephesi (THKP-C: People's Liberation Party-Front of Turkey). These revolts, though short-lived, inspired a generation of radicals and influenced Öcalan's own strategic analyses. By 1974, a small cadre of militants had gathered around Öcalan. "We gathered a group of a dozen young people, all from similarly poor families. Some of them were of Turkish descent and had joined us for their internationalist stance," Öcalan recalls.[13] This cadre would go on to become the PKK. Throughout this period the small militant cadre focused on building the intellectual, ideological, and physical capacity for struggle, but not necessarily armed struggle. However, the 1977 assassination of Haki Karer, a beloved organizer for the group, finally spurred the formation of the PKK. Ostensibly a rival faction killed Karer, but it was clear that Turkish intelligence had planned it. In Öcalan's recollection this was the moment that fully radicalized the group. "Our political platform and the name of our organization, PKK, was set up and decided upon as an immediate consequence of his murder. We all regard it as his legacy."[14]

The PKK and After

The PKK's founding party congress was held in November 1978. It was composed primarily of poor and working-class youth following a rough ideological hodgepodge of Marxism-Leninism and Kurdish nationalism. Öcalan recalls, "our knowledge was obtained from a few books only, which we discussed and understood at beginner's level. Obviously, this insufficient understanding led to flawed analyses both of history and the current situation."[15] Öcalan's writings are filled with this kind of practical self-critique, expressing a genuine desire to learn and grow from mistakes. This characteristic reflection and adaptability has been key to the group's survival and success. Despite initial ideological shortcomings, the PKK proved itself to be highly capable at popular organizing. Unlike other revolutionary groups, the PKK centered the "Kurdish Question," the existential status of Kurds in Turkey and the wider diaspora.

This won the organization wide popularity among marginalized and often brutalized Kurdish populations. As Paul White explains, "This emerging new movement faced an ideological climate in which the state and Turkish nationalists denied the very existence of the Kurdish people generally—and readily resorted to violence in an effort to stifle the movement."[16] Willing and able to meet force with force, the PKK targeted particularly hated landlords and other collaborators with the Turkish state in some of their first guerrilla actions. They were bold and disciplined but not particularly well trained. In 1980, PKK cadres attended militant training camps in Lebanon. That same year, a military coup took power in Turkey. On this, according to White, "The party's Second Congress . . . set the PKK's military strategy, comprising three phases: defense, balance, and offense. Reminiscent of Mao's strategy of protracted war, this envisaged an armed struggle proceeding in stages from asymmetrical guerrilla attack up to conventional war."[17] In 1984, the PKK went to war with the Turkish state. The PKK was very effective, but as it grew it began to lose sight of its principles. Today Öcalan is very critical of this period:

> [M]any of the negative practices adopted during the formation phase of the PKK from real socialist praxis or from the system around us now came to light. Many activists also increasingly neglected our socialist ideology, which they had not internalized satisfactorily in the first place. Cadres affected by traditional Kurdish identity began to feel like little Nimrods because of the military and political power they suddenly had. Others with strong feudalist traits assessed everything against their own qualities and ideas. To obtain their purposes, they played intensely on others' primitive nationalism. With their feudal mentality, backed by primitive nationalism, they became ever more brazen. They pillaged and destroyed what numerous activists and supporters had accomplished. All in all, between 1987 and 1997 the PKK lost much of its original character and structure.[18]

Success was a double-edged sword. Growing mass popular support was undermined by internal fragmentation and corruption. Öcalan is unambiguous in his critique of the basic failure of strategy and vision. "[T]he essential reason for the shortcomings of the early PKK was its concept of the state and its approach to violence," Öcalan explains.[19] The PKK has, however, demonstrated a strong capacity for self-criticism and correction. By the 1990s, a thoroughgoing process of reform was underway.

The PKK made overtures toward a peace process, declaring a unilateral ceasefire in 1998, the year Öcalan was captured and rendered to Turkey. Another ceasefire was declared in 1999 and was formally maintained until 2004.[20] Meanwhile, through his prison writings, Öcalan continued his ideological reevaluations. Öcalan found a kindred spirit in his encounter with the work of American libertarian socialist Murray Bookchin.[21] Bookchin's philosophy of social ecology, with its decentralized stateless municipalism, contributed to Öcalan's turn from the nation-state, inaugurating his project of political re-enchantment.

Part II: Political Re-enchantment

Öcalan's intellectual project—what I characterize as the re-enchantment of the political—is a complex conceptual framework. Historicism stands out as a crucial aspect of his mature thought. Öcalan sees enduring continuities between the Neolithic Age, antiquity, and the present. This is not a static view of history. Clearly, Öcalan believes revolutionary historical transformation is possible. For Öcalan, however, it is necessary to locate the deep roots of historical oppressions before they can be effectively dismantled. Öcalan identifies three historical epistemological systems—myth, hierarchical religion, and scientism—that make truth claims about the world and guide meaningful action. These "methods," as he calls them, structure sociohistorical meanings and practical action.

Öcalan's Use of History

To appropriate Eric Wolf's phrase, Kurds are a people without history.[22] Their history, in other words, has been obscured and marginalized by powerful states and empires.

Öcalan's celebration of Kurdish historical agency and cultural achievements should not be confused with a narrow nationalism. Öcalan's disposition is internationalist and revolutionary.

Instead of the typical manifesto schematically outlining immediate demands, a reader of Öcalan's mature writings will find a rich and subtle diagnostic analysis linking contemporary social maladies to their deep roots in enduring historical continuities. Öcalan's more immediate political goals and strategies can be understood through his long-term historical analyses.

Öcalan's historical analyses are indebted to the works of Fernand Braudel, Immanuel Wallerstein, V. Gordon Childe, and Robert J. Braidwood.

In particular, Braudel's concept of *longue durée*, the long-term, is crucial; likewise for Wallerstein's world-system, a spatial or geographic corollary of the longue durée.[23] The archaeological work of Childe and Braidwood has been very influential as well. Childe's theory of the Neolithic Revolution as a period of transition from nomadic hunting and gathering to settled agriculture and animal domestication is significant to Öcalan's analyses.[24] The transition from the Neolithic to the Bronze Age marked the development of the first states. Braidwood's archaeological excavations along the Taurus-Zagros mountain ranges, which geographically define the northern arch of the Mesopotamian plain, showed this region to be among the earliest sites of plant and animal domestication.[25] Significantly, the geographic arch of these mountains defines the traditional Kurdish homeland. From Öcalan's perspective this establishes Kurds as key contributors to the Neolithic Revolution. Recent archaeological evidence supports the contention that ancient peoples of the hilly flanks were precocious domesticators, at least in terms of animal domestication.[26] Linking these ancient peoples to contemporary cultures must be approached, however, with great circumspection, especially given Western Asia's status as a genetic and cultural crossroads.

Öcalan identifies the Neolithic transition with the emergence of not only the proto-state but concomitantly with the rise of the patriarchal enslavement of women. For Öcalan, this stands among the gravest historical wrongs whose consequences civilization still suffers. The subjugation of women in the patriarchal family forms the basis for the dominating hierarchy of the state form. Öcalan uses the ancient three-tiered Sumerian ziggurat as a metaphor for this enduring hierarchical social institution.[27] One can find a parallel in Braudel's metaphor of economic history as being structured as a three-story house, material life at base, then markets, and, finally, capitalism.[28] Braudel argued that historians must make use of short-, medium-, and long-term analytical frames. Historical change is constant, but particular structural relations may change at different tempos.[29] The notion of these differential temporalities informs Öcalan's views. For instance, patriarchy endures despite many other social changes over the last five thousand years. Öcalan juxtaposes the rise of patriarchy with what he believes to have been a previous era of widespread matricentric societies; a period of relative egalitarianism that Öcalan dubs "primordial socialism" or "natural society."[30] The history that came after "natural society" is punctuated by what Öcalan characterizes as two sexual ruptures. He predicts a needed third sexual rupture. The first sexual rupture—the rise of patriarchy and the state—came about through an alliance of three figures, proto-priests arising from shamans, the strongman hunter, and elder males. Taken literally this seems to be a far too simple and linear view of a highly complex and spatial, temporally, and heterogeneous historic process. Öcalan, however, seems often to make use of an abbreviated rhetorical style, heavy on metaphor and analogy. The second sexual rupture sees the intensification of patriarchy as the monotheistic religions—Judaism, Christianity, and Islam—sacralized women's subjugation. The third sexual rupture, as Öcalan sees it, will need to remedy this situation. To this end Öcalan calls, metaphorically, for the revolutionary necessity of "killing the dominant male."[31] Öcalan explains:

> [M]an is a system. The male has *become* a state and turned this into dominant culture. Class and sexual oppression develop together; masculinity has generated ruling gender, ruling class, and ruling state. When man is analysed in this context, it is clear that masculinity must be killed.[32]

This call for a radical revaluation of gender roles and relations is now being answered by the Kurdish women's movement and within the revolutionary structures of Rojava.

Öcalan's Methods: Myth, Meaning, and a Critique of Scientism

Öcalan identifies three "methods"—mythology, hierarchical monotheistic religion, and positivist scientism—that have historically constituted particular "regimes of truth," à la Foucault.[33] Öcalan believes the mythological method, associated with the Neolithic Age still holds important insights. He explains, "The mythological approach is environmentally oriented, free of notions of fatalism and determinism and conducive to living life in freedom. Its fundamental approach to life is one of harmony with nature."[34] The mythological method is a necessary and generative element of historical interpretation. Öcalan asserts that "[t]he mythological method should be given back the prestige it lost when it was discredited by monotheistic religious dogma and by the scientific method; method alleging to bow to absolute laws." In a seemingly contradictory move, however, he criticizes science as contemporary mythology. "[T]here are indications that many of the current scientific theories that are seen as the antipode of the mythological approach are themselves nothing but mere mythology."[35] Examining this seeming contradiction actually reveals a deeper consistency in Öcalan's thought.

Mary Midgley has articulated a position similar to Öcalan's. Though neither writer was aware of the other their theoretical similarities are illuminating nonetheless. Midgley explains, "Myths are not lies. Nor are they detached stories. They are imaginative patterns, networks of powerful symbols that suggest particular ways of interpreting the world. They shape its meaning."[36] In both Midgley and Öcalan's accounts mythology is not timeless or detached from reality. Rather, it is deeply historical and present in daily life. "But really such symbolism is an integral part of our thought-structure. It does crucial work on all topics, not just a few supposedly marginal areas such as religion and emotion, where symbols are known to be at home, but throughout our thinking."[37] This realist conception of myth holds that mythology can be adaptive or maladaptive based on its contribution to human and ecological flourishing. Mythic notions may serve a perfectly useful, and even an emancipatory, purpose in one historical context but become oppressive in another. For instance, Midgley, like Öcalan, is critical of Enlightenment "myths" of individualism, domination of nature, and the omnicompetence of science as having outworn their usefulness. In some respects, *myth* is similar (though with important differences) to Foucault's *discourse*, Castoriadis's *social imaginary*, Barthes's *mythologies*, and Horkheimer and Adorno's *Dialectic of Enlightenment*, wherein the authors critique instrumental rationality as a particularly pernicious mythology.[38]

Öcalan calls the era of religious authority "the age of disguised king and masked gods" and capitalist modernity "the age of naked kings and unmasked gods." A troubling feature of this latter age is its embrace of positivist scientism with its epistemological dualism, its strict subject-object dichotomy. This duality catastrophically separates humanity from nature and makes both humanity and nature into objects of rational manipulation. Characterizing his own critical approach, Öcalan explains, "It is not an endeavor for an alternative method but rather an endeavor to find a solution to the problems that a life detached from the values of freedom creates."[39] Öcalan's solution seems to entail a practical open-ended holism and a realistic social intuition that at its core values and affirms the complex unity of life. Öcalan is concerned with the human being and the dynamic multitiered and interpenetrating relations of the individual and society and nature.

Öcalan contra Weber

Max Weber did not celebrate disenchantment as an unambiguous good. He simply saw it as an unavoidable consequence of modernity, though with troubling implications. Summarizing Hennis's (1989) assessment, Lassman explains, "Underlying all of Weber's political thought is the problem of the continuing existence of the free human being under modern conditions of rationalization and disenchantment."[40] Weber presented his thesis in two essays titled "Science as a Vocation" and "Politics as a Vocation."[41] He diagnosed the loss of meaning and guiding values as a fundamental condition of modernity and sketched the political consequences of this disillusionment or devaluation of values.

For Weber, science seems a ready substitute for the loss of overarching values, but he finds the methodology ultimately unable to provide its own warrant precisely because it can say nothing of values and meaning. Nevertheless, belief in the scientific mastery of the world was persuasive and seductive. The rationalized bureaucratic state stands as the inescapable political corollary of positivist scientism. Weber's diagnosis of the modern condition was not completely original. Nietzsche had already called attention to this dilemma. Expressing his affinity for Nietzsche, Öcalan observes that "[t]he great philosopher Nietzsche (it would be right to call him the strongest oppositional prophet of the capitalist era) was the first to notice the dangers associated with the 1870 declaration of the German nation-state."[42] Nietzsche, however, does not share Weber's pessimism. Like Öcalan, Nietzsche affirms the possibility of meaningful life against rationalistic pessimism and political nihilism.

Nietzsche, too, sought the re-enchantment of life against the mediocrity of modernity.

The Radical Reasonableness of Öcalan's Project of Political Re-enchantment

Öcalan recognizes modernity's disenchantment but rejects its inevitability. The bureaucratic state form is not the end of history. For Öcalan, like Bookchin,[43] history is an open-ended struggle entailing a legacy of both domination and freedom. Öcalan's project of re-enchanting the political is not a call to return to a reliance on superstition, religious authority, or folkloric magical thinking. It is not political primitivism or neoromanticism. Öcalan values and celebrates the real achievement of previous eras and believes those achievements should be recovered if they can contribute to meaningful life. Öcalan values the wisdom contained in ancient mythology. Recuperation of this wisdom is an element of Öcalan's project of re-enchantment but does not reflect a simple desire to return to a pristine past. The force of Öcalan's thought is directed instead toward the present and future. The Hegelian concept of *aufheben*, the simultaneous movement of preservation, change, and progressive transformation, is helpful here. Öcalan's project is preservative as well as transformative.

Öcalan's sees ethics and morality as immanent to his conception of political form. Politics, for Öcalan, exists in substantial ethical praxis rather than formal or abstract right. The political is not outside or above society but immanent to it. Murray Bookchin perhaps the strongest influence on Öcalan's mature thought, draws an important distinction between politics and statecraft. Statecraft entails: "the exercise of its monopoly of violence, its control of the entire regulative apparatus of society in the form of legal and ordinance-making bodies, and its governance of society as a means professional legislators, armies, polices forces, and bureaucracies."[44] In contrast to statecraft, "[p]olitics, conceived as an activity, involves rational discourse, public empowerment, the exercise of practical reason, and its realization in a shared, indeed participatory, activity."[45] Here Bookchin and Öcalan's projects of political re-enchantment significantly coincide:

> In calling for the "re-enchanting" of humanity, I refer—playfully—to the importance of recognizing humanity's *potentiality* for creating a rational, ecologically oriented, aesthetically exciting, and a deeply humane world based on an ethics of complementarity and a society of sharing.[46]

I understand Bookchin's use the term "rational" in the quote above as being closer to what I describe below as "reasonableness," rather than instrumental rationality. I develop this crucial distinction in detail in the next section.

A Political Philosophy of Reasonableness

Öcalan's conception of democratic confederalism and democratic nation amounts to what I call a politics of reasonableness. Öcalan has developed a political form capable of expressing reasonableness rather than statist rationality. Unlike political rationality, political reasonableness necessarily assumes an integral place for values, ethics, and morality. This is a defining feature of what I call the re-enchantment of the political. This is not a regression to prescientific magical thinking but rather a progressive expansion of political reason, commensurate with morals and values rather than antithetical to them. I am not suggesting this as a kind of ethical voluntarism; Öcalan is not simply issuing moral exhortations for his followers to be good. This is crucial: Öcalan's innovation is in the political *form* itself. By *form* I mean the totality of relations described under the headings of democratic confederalism and democratic nation. Öcalan explains that democratic confederalism is a non-state social paradigm and a cultural organizational blueprint for a democratic nation.[47] These are, ultimately, the building blocks of democratic modernity. "Our project of 'democratic modernity' is meant as an alternative draft to modernity as we know it. It builds on the democratic confederalism as a fundamental political paradigm. Democratic modernity is the roof of an ethics-based political society."[48] Thus, in its grandest possibility, democratic confederalism is the molecular form of an epic civilizational transformation, one grounded in a politics of reasonableness rather than statist rationality.

The Neglected Legacy of the Politics of Reasonableness

Reason integrates and balances both rationality and reasonableness. At least since the seventeenth century, however, reason has lost its balance; with the ascent of political and economic rationality, traditions of reasonableness have been marginalized.[49] Rationality begins with the "I," as in the abstract individual of Descartes's famous proposition "cogito, ergo sum"—I think, therefore I am. This abstract egoism easily translated into the figure of *homo economicus*, the rational self-maximizing man of economic philosophy. In contrast, a sense of what I call political reasonableness is expressed in the social premise of African philosophy: I am because we are and, since we are, therefore I am.[50] Where rationality is egoist and calculative, reasonableness is immanently social and deliberative. David Graeber has pointed to the Occupy Wall Street movement as an example of political reasonableness. He explains:

> Consensus is an attempt to create a politics founded on the principle of reasonableness—one that, as feminist philosopher Deborah Heikes has pointed out, requires not only logical consistency, but "a measure of good judgment, self-criticism, a capacity for social interaction, and a willingness to give and consider reasons."[51]

Tim Sprod draws a close link between reasonableness, autonomy, and ethical practice. Sprod characterizes reasonableness as being critical, creative, committed, contextual, and embodied.[52] As Anthony Simon Laden explains, "Reasoning, so understood, is a species of conversation.... It is a form of relating to others that can be contrasted with non-reciprocal forms of interaction such as commanding and obeying, ignoring or manipulating."[53] Reasonableness is immanently social. In contrast, by *rationality* I suggest a mode of praxis that is calculative, abstract, formal, mathematical, quantitative, a priori, asocial, ahistorical, abstract universal, and supposedly value-free. Rationality is concerned with measurement, prediction, and control. Rationality is the goal of all bureaucracy and technocratic politics. Alternatively, by *reasonableness* I indicate a praxis that is relational, interpersonal, situational, contextual, qualitative, particular, adaptable, dialogic, and capable of dealing with uncertainty. Reasonableness entails openness to experience and change. Reasonableness may be stable but not static. Reasonableness is inescapably value-laden. Reasonableness is closely tied to notions of fairness, accommodation, and moral concern.

The Radical Reasonableness of Democratic Confederalism

Reasonableness is best understood as embedded in forms of social relations. Of course, an individual may be considered reasonable, usually for displaying good social judgment. The characteristics of reasonableness that I have been explicating are similar to what Öcalan calls "emotional intelligence," or, perhaps, more precisely the balance of "analytical" and "emotional" intelligence in reason.[54] Reasonableness, like rationality, can be embodied in and expressed through political forms. The bureaucratic state form embodies and expresses the principle rationality. I argue that, in contrast, the non-state social paradigm of democratic confederalism expresses the principle of reasonableness. An important distinction, however, is that, unlike rationality, the substantive reasonableness content of a particular form cannot be fully prescribed beforehand but must be worked out in concrete practice. The institutional form facilitates the principle of reasonableness but cannot predetermine its substantive content. Öcalan recognizes this when he describes democratic confederalism as "open toward other political groups and factions. It is flexible, multi-cultural, anti-monopolistic, and consensus-oriented. Ecology and feminism are central pillars."[55] The substance of a politics of reasonableness must flow from the real life of the society in which it is implemented. Democratic confederalism, Öcalan explains, "rests on the historical experience of the society and its collective heritage. It is not an arbitrary modern political system but, rather, accumulates history and experience. It is the offspring of the life of the society."[56] This is not an endorsement of conservative traditions. Rather, as Öcalan sees it, a revolution cannot create a new society. "It can only influence the ethical and political web of a society. Anything else is at the discretion of the ethic-based political society."[57] Again, this is not to advocate parochialism. To the contrary, the society of the democratic nation is premised on the coexistence and participation of diverse groups and associations of peoples. Öcalan explains, "While the state's nation pursues homogenized society, the democratic nation mainly consists of different collectivities. It sees diversity as richness. Life itself is only possible through diversity. The nation-state forces citizens to be uniform; in this regard, too, it is contrary to life."[58] Quest for a meaningful and rich life is a core concern of Öcalan's political project of re-enchantment, and ethics and morality are integral elements of its definition.

Moral and Political Society

Throughout his writings Öcalan returns repeatedly to Adorno's famous statement: "Wrong life cannot be lived rightly."[59] The question of life's wrongness and how one might or might not be able to live rightly raises ethical and moral issues. Adorno is not so much concerned with particular ethical precepts as much as he is concerned with the ethical *form* of life.[60] For Adorno, like Öcalan, the form of capitalist modernity, its totality of relations, constitutes wrong life. Thus, the effort to live rightly in capitalist modernity is necessarily a revolutionary effort. An important difference between Öcalan and Adorno, however, is that where Adorno was pessimistic about revolutionary prospects, Öcalan looked forward to the task of changing the form of wrong life so society could live more rightly. With the changed form Öcalan envisions a "moral and political society." As he explains:

> Politics and democracy, in the true sense, are identical concepts. If freedom is the arena in which politics expresses itself, then democracy is the modus operandi of politics within that arena. The trio of freedom, politics and democracy cannot be devoid of a moral base. We can also define morals as the institutionalized or traditional form of freedom, politics and democracy.[61]

The proliferation of diverse autonomous social structures, organizations, and communities within society with direct participation in local decision-making process is an antidote to the alienation of the "wrong life" so pervasive in capitalist modernity.

Conclusion

In this essay I have read Öcalan's thought in relation to key Western intellectual interlocutors, including Nietzsche, Weber, Wallerstein, Adorno, and Bookchin. I contextualized Öcalan's ideological development through a sketch of his life of revolutionary struggle. I examined the ways in which Öcalan combined his situated life experience with a deep historical and geostrategic outlook, synthesizing Braudel's notion of the longue durée and Wallerstein's world-system theory. I have shown how Öcalan's historicism, with Adorno, allowed him to critically diagnose the alienated "wrong life" of capitalist modernity and, with Weber, its disenchanted institutional rationality. Öcalan, unlike Adorno and Weber, has not drawn pessimistic conclusions from this state of affairs. He has, with Nietzsche, sought a life-affirming overcoming and revaluation of existing conditions. I have shown that Öcalan's project is one of political re-enchantment, the re-embedding of meaning, values, and ethics into the political form. I have argued that—far from a return to magical thinking—Öcalan's project of re-enchantment develops a new politics of reasonableness realized in the political forms of democratic confederalism and the democratic nation.

This essay was first presented at the ERPI 2018 International Conference "Authoritarian Populism and the Rural World" at the International Institute of Social Studies (ISS) in The Hague, Netherlands.

Dr. Patrick Huff is a social anthropologist and associate lecturer in the Department of Geography, Environment and Development Studies, Birkbeck University, London. His research interests include social movements, radical politics, feminism, political economy, and political ecology. He is a member of Brighton Kurdistan Solidarity and the Kurdistan Solidarity Network, UK.

Notes

1 David Graeber, preface to Abdullah Öcalan, *Manifesto for a Democratic Civilization, Volume 1: The Age of Masked Gods and Disguised Kings* (Porsgrunn, NO: New Compass Press, 2015), 16; 2nd revised edition will be published by PM Press in 2021.
2 Steve Jones, *Antonio Gramsci* (London: Routledge, 2006), 10.

3   A.K. Özcan, *Turkey's Kurds: A Theoretical Analysis of the PKK and Abdullah Öcalan* (New York: Routledge, 2006), 66.

4   Abdullah Öcalan, *Manifesto for a Democratic Civilization, Volume 2: Capitalism: The Age of Unmasked Gods and Naked Kings* (Porsgrunn, NO: New Compass Press, 2018), 26; 2nd revised edition will be published by PM Press in 2020.

5   Abdullah Öcalan, *Prison Writings: The PKK and the Kurdish Question in the 21st Century* (London: Transmedia Publishing, 2011), 95.

6   Abdullah Öcalan, *Democratic Confederalism* (Cologne: International Initiative, 2017), 31.

7   Ibid.

8   Abdullah Öcalan, *Manifesto for a Democratic Civilization, Volume 1*, 60.

9   Ibid., 61.

10 Öcalan, *Manifesto for a Democratic Civilization, Volume 1*, 91.

11 Douglas Burnham, *The Nietzsche Dictionary* (London: Bloomsbury, 2015), 102.

12 Öcalan, *Prison Writings*, 129.

13 Ibid., 130.

14 Ibid., 113.

15 Ibid., 53.

16 Paul White, *The PKK: Coming Down from the Mountains* (London: Zed Books, 2015), 30.

17 Ibid, 31.

18 Öcalan, *Prison Writings*, 54.

19 Ibid., 56.

20 White, *The PKK*, 44.

21 Murray Bookchin, *From Urbanization to Cities: Toward a New Politics of Citizenship* (London: Cassell, 1995); Murray Bookchin, *Re-enchanting Humanity: A Defense of the Human Spirit Against Antihumanism, Misanthropy, Mysticism, and Primitivism* (London: Cassell, 1995); Murray Bookchin, *The Ecology of Freedom: The Emergence and Dissolution of Hierarchy* (Palo Alto, CA: Cheshire Books, 2005).

22 Eric Wolf, *Europe and the People without History* (Berkeley: University of California Press, 1982).

23 Fernand Braudel, "History and the Social Sciences: The *Longue Durée*," in *The Longue Durée and World-Systems Analysis*, ed. Richard E. Lee, trans. Immanuel Wallerstein (New York: State University of New York Press, 2012); Immanuel Wallerstein, *World-System Analysis: An Introduction* (Durham, NC: Duke University Press, 2004).

24 V. Gordon Childe, "Changing Methods and Aims in Prehistory: Presidential Address for 1935," *Proceedings of the Prehistoric Society* 1 (1935): 1–15; V. Gordon Childe, *Man Makes Himself* (New York: New American Library, 1951).

25 Robert John Braidwood, "The Agricultural Revolution," *Scientific American* 203, no. 3 (September 1960): 130–152.

26 Melinda A. Zeder, "Animal Domestication in the Zagros: An Update and Directions for Future Research," *Publications de La Maison de l'Orient et de La Méditerranée* 8, no. 49 (2008): 243–77, accessed September 13, 2019, https://www.persee.fr/doc/mom_1955-4982_2008_act_49_1_2709.

27 Öcalan, *Manifesto for a Democratic Civilization, Volume 2*, 57.
28 Fernand Braudel, *The Structure of Everyday Life: The Limits of the Possible—Civilization and Capitalism*, vol. 1. (London: William Collins Sons & Co., 1981), 21.
29 Braudel, "History and the Social Sciences," 243.
30 Abdullah Öcalan, *The Political Thought of Abdullah Öcalan* (London: Pluto Press, 2017), 61, 63.
31 Ibid., 87.
32 Ibid., 89.
33 Michel Foucault, *Power/Knowledge: Selected Interviews and Other Writings 1972–1977*, ed. Colin Gordon, trans. Colin Gordon, Leo Marshall, John Mepham, and Kate Soper (New York: Pantheon Books, 1980).
34 Öcalan, *Manifesto for a Democratic Civilization, Volume 1*, 32.
35 Ibid., 33.
36 Mary Midgley, *The Myths We Live By* (London: Routledge, 2003), 1.
37 Ibid.
38 Foucault, *Power/Knowledge*; Cornelius Castoriadis, *The Imaginary Institution of Society*, trans. Kathleen Blamey, (Cambridge, MA: MIT Press, 1998); Roland Barthes, *Mythologies*, trans. A. Lavers (New York: Noonday Press, 1972); Max Horkheimer and Theodor Adorno, *Dialectic of Enlightenment*, ed. Gunzelin Schmid Noerr, trans. Edmund Jephcott (Stanford, CA: Stanford University Press, 2002 [1944]).
39 Öcalan, *Manifesto for a Democratic Civilization, Volume 1*, 39.
40 Peter Lassman, "The Rule of Man Over Man: Politics, Power and Legitimation," in *The Cambridge Companion to Weber*, ed. Stephen Turner (Cambridge, UK: Cambridge University Press, 2000), 95.
41 Max Weber, *The Vocation Lectures: "Science as a Vocation" "Politics as a Vocation,"* ed. David Owen and Tracy B. Strong, trans. Rodney Livingstone (Indianapolis: Hackett Publishing Company, 2004).
42 Öcalan, *Manifesto for a Democratic Civilization, Volume 2*, 237.
43 Bookchin, *The Ecology of Freedom*.
44 Bookchin, *From Urbanization to Cities*, 220.
45 Ibid., 221.
46 Bookchin, *Re-enchanting Humanity*, 232.
47 Öcalan, *Prison Writings*, 33.
48 Ibid., 24–25.
49 Stephen Toulmin, *Return to Reason* (Cambridge, MA: Harvard University Press, 2003).
50 John S. Mbiti, *African Religions and Philosophy* (London: Heinemann, 2nd edition, 1990), 106.
51 David Graeber, *The Democracy Project: A History, A Crisis, A Movement* (New York: Spiegel and Grau, 2013), 202.
52 Tim Sprod, *Philosophical Discussion in Moral Education: The Community of Ethical Inquiry* (London: Routledge, 2001), 14.
53 Anthony Simon Laden, *Reasoning: A Social Picture* (Oxford: Oxford University Press, 2012), vii.
54 Öcalan, *Manifesto for a Democratic Civilization, Volume 1*, 41.

55 Öcalan, *Prison Writings*, 21.
56 Ibid., 23.
57 Ibid., 24.
58 Öcalan, *Democratic Nation*, 25.
59 Öcalan, *Manifesto for a Democratic Civilization, Volume 1*, 80; Öcalan, *Manifesto for a Democratic Civilization, Volume 2*, 128; Theodor Adorno, *Minima Moralia: Reflections on a Damaged Life* (London: Verso, 2006 [1951]), 39.
60 Rahel Jaeggi, "No Individual Can Resist": Minima Moralis as Critique of Forms of Life," *Constellations* 12, no. 1 (March 2005): 65–82, accessed September 13, 2019, http://cef.pucp.edu.pe/wp-content/uploads/2014/08/Rahel-Jaeggi-_No-Individual-Can-Resist_-Minima-Moralia-as-Critique-of-Forms-of-Life.pdf.
61 Öcalan, *Democratic Nation*, 36.

NINETEEN

The Theology of Democratic Modernity: Labor, Truth, and Freedom

Nazan Üstündağ

When I think of the wave-particle dilemma, which is the cornerstone of the universe, I would without hesitation emphasize that energy is freedom. I believe that the material particle is a packet of imprisoned energy. Light is a state of energy. Can one deny the free flow of light? We must take into consideration that quanta are defined as energy's smallest particle state and are today almost seen as the factor that explains all diversity. Yes, quantum motion is the creative power of all diversity. I cannot resist asking whether this is the God that humanity has been searching for all along.
—Abdullah Öcalan

What needs to be elucidated here is not the metaphysical and dialectical dilemma but the distinction between good and beautiful metaphysical creations and bad and ugly metaphysical creations. Again, it is not the dilemma between religion and atheism or philosophy and science but religious, philosophical, and scientific beliefs, truth, and postulates that make life more endurable and attractive.
—Abdullah Öcalan[1]

İmralı as the Exact Opposite of Sovereignty

Island prisons play an important role in generating political fantasies that are based on relations of sovereignty.[2] Historically, penal colonies are the precursors of island prisons, and slave trading colonial powers like Britain and France, along with the Qing Empire in China and Imperial

Russia, have at times located their penal colonies on islands. With modernity, island prisons became a more common way of keeping the fiercest and most infamous lawbreakers physically and symbolically separated from society. Nation-states in places as diverse as Australia, Columbia, Indonesia, France, Senegal, Spain, apartheid South Africa, and the US have built island prisons.

As Michael Taussig noted in his brilliant book *My Cocaine Museum*,[3] the geography, history, memories, and myths surrounding island prisons offer an alternative trajectory for tracing the development of the modern state form. An island prison is like a quarantine: at an island prison, the political order that desires to control and constrain intimacies, routes, and mobility and that uses the allegory of "contagiousness" to understand rebellious thought and actions that dare to dream of a different world comes into being and solidifies.

The island, insofar as it is cut off from the mainland, is outside of society, the law, and culture. Isolation on a remote island places one beyond the outside. Isolation is how the state writes exile, exclusion, waste, disposal, and excess on the body of the prisoner and on the space in which s/he moves.

To be isolated on an island prison carves homelessness, disconnectedness, and loneliness onto the person's identity. In the case of Öcalan, the fact that he refuses to participate in the processes of nationalization, familization, and propertization,[4] which are the preconditions for individualization in modernity, means that he is not regarded as an individual by law and is, therefore, denied his rights.[5] Every time his lawyers are banned from visiting him, not only Öcalan but also belongings and becomings that fail to reproduce the relations of nation, family, and property are condemned and discounted. At the same time, however, any connections made with Öcalan, reminding the public of his name, and all collective orientations toward him point to potentialities beyond property, national, and family laws and call for politicization.

●

Island: a piece of land surrounded by water, disconnected from the mainland. A border on the sea? A limit? A threshold? Threshold: the front of a door. The in-between of a closure and an opening.

●

Contemporary social theory has shown that to live at the spatial margins of the nation-state is to live at the limit of the law, in the sense that at such margins life is equally vulnerable to either the application of law or its abandonment. Isolated regions, occupied areas, refugee camps, prisons, island prisons, places like Guantánamo or Imralı, are, for example, spaces where the law hurts and injures when it is applied. However, a hurt of equal intensity is produced when it is arbitrarily waived and impeded by executive power. Emergency rule is permanent in such places, and normality is the exception. These are also sites where the legislative, executive, and judicial power become undifferentiated as the authority of the police, the guards, and the camp management become absolute. At the margins of the nation-state and at the limit of the law, legality and violence become indistinguishable.

At the same time however, these spaces also testify to the fact that margins can become powerful thresholds that open toward radically transformative ways of becoming and belonging.

•

Threshold is one of those words that act; it transforms space into time.[6] A threshold erupts an enclosed spatiality and turns it into a harbinger of what might come, a messenger of potential and the before of a birth. The threshold is where memories assemble and hope fills the space; it is located in the in-between of what has happened long ago and what has never become.

•

Since the day of his imprisonment, the isolation of Abdullah Öcalan has been the terrain upon which the state and the Kurdish freedom movement have fought a battle. The state aimed at spatially and symbolically rendering İmralı exceptional and external, and thereby transforming it into a system where life and law would become obsolete.[7] The Kurdish freedom movement, the people, and Öcalan, on the other hand, struggled to turn it into a permanent threshold and source of potentiality. From this point of view, one can even argue that what has been written and said in İmralı is also the story of constituting and sustaining this potentiality. Abdullah Öcalan's historical uniqueness and success, moreover, is what he has built with his actions and writings in this threshold called İmralı, the exact opposite of sovereignty. In this essay I will discuss the last twenty years of Öcalan's writings and practice in the light of the theology of non-sovereignty that I believe he has constructed in İmralı and the key concepts of that theology.[8]

In political theory sovereignty is increasingly defined, in reference to Carl Schmitt and Giorgio Agamben, as the capacity and authority to decide on the state of exception: sovereignty is the power to declare emergency rule and to suspend the normal operation of law. The sovereign is the one who decides who, what, and where is situated within and outside of the normal law and when. The sovereign is responsible for protecting the legal order, and in the name of protecting that order can assert the need to override, suspend, or break the law. In that sense the sovereign is both within the law and beyond it; both inside and outside of society—located at its limit.

The sovereign is also always potentially violent, a potential that gives it its sacred and untouchable quality.[9] In capitalist modernity the nation-state is the only internationally recognized legitimate sovereign actor.[10] At its core, the state combines both the "rationality" of management and administration and a form of religiosity that demands that people die and/or become murderers for its sake. Those who struggle against the nation-state often reproduce this type of sovereignty, imitating the forms and styles of state-ness, thereby gaining also a sacred quality. Just like gods in mythology, the contemporary nation-state unleashes unspeakable violence against such enemies. It is, therefore, no wonder, for example, that whenever the Kurdish freedom movement develops the attributes of a sovereign power in the Kurdish regions, the Turkish state resists responding to this within the legal framework of crime or war. Instead, in such cases, its violence takes extreme forms, imitating the wrath of the gods (leaving dead bodies unburied, running over corpses with tanks, etc.). It is also no surprise that other states, which owe their existence to the common understanding that sovereignty should remain under the monopoly of the state—which is supposedly representing the nation—often remain silent about such events, if they don't loudly support them.

When writing about how power and sovereignty operate in the modern world, Agamben refers to a figure in Roman law: *homo sacer*. Homo sacer is someone who can be killed by anyone, without her/his death being seen as a sacrifice; hence s/he is the person over whom anyone can exercise sovereignty. In relation to homo sacer, normal law ceases to operate, and hence killing her/him would not qualify as murder. On the contrary, killing her/him is such an ordinary act that it is not even worth noting, remembering, or discussing. The encounter with homo sacer in that sense democratizes sovereignty and makes it available to all. While, according to Agamben, Jews in the Nazi camps is a key example of the production of homo sacer in modernity, Achille Mbembe argues that homo sacer is best understood by looking at how colonization and occupation treated its victims.[11]

One of the most important contributions of Agamben's contemporary political and social theory has been his proposal that membership to and exclusion from a group, which in modern world often takes a racial or ethnic form, are intrinsic to the modern state form and its sovereignty. In that sense, identities are much more than words on a list, such as Kurdish, Arabic, and Turkish, etc. Furthermore, they are not correctives to Marxist theory's failure to recognize their importance. They are constituted hierarchically and differentially within the matrix of biopolitics and sovereignty and are nodes through which the domination of capitalist modernity and the nation-state are accomplished.[12] African American scholars and theorists of decolonization have further developed these ideas by showing the intimate injuries that racial and ethnic management, power, and sovereignties cause and how these are generationally transmitted, giving rise to different communities with different memories and distinct subjectivities. For such communities, membership in the nation is foreclosed. The nation, meanwhile, is constituted as a sovereign entity intelligible to itself in relation to such communities. In its attempt to improve the "deviant" and "unruly minorities," it quantifies, quarantines, and manages them and, hence, along with sovereignty also acquires a purpose, direction, orientation, and administrative mechanism.

What all this means is that since a hierarchy between races and ethnicities is constitutive of the nation-state, in a radically pluralistic society the nation-state is a structural impossibility, or to put it in a more provocative and universal way: the state and the multitude are opposed to each other. Indeed, in his books, Öcalan stresses the inevitability of the state and society remaining in permanent antagonism and the contradictory processes of becoming society (collectivization) and becoming the state; one always grows at the expense of the other.[13] If the state is sacred—and it is indeed sacred and divine as long as it, like a god, is the only entity that has the right to make and unmake law—then identities that are reproduced without recourse to the state constitute sacrilege and blasphemy.[14]

In other words, the state and the multitude are not only structural opposites, they are also radically different as far as the political theology they support is concerned. However, this is not our current topic.

Exactly like the sovereign, the homo sacer is located both within and outside of the law. S/he is within the law, because it is through her/him that the inside of the law can be imagined, constituted, and organized. It is by denying her/him a social and political existence that we recognize who is included within law. Multiply layered encounters between the homo sacer and the sovereign enable people to learn how society is ordered, what memberships are necessary to possess rights, and the means and relations through which sovereignty is appropriated. On the other hand, the homo sacer points to an emptiness and lack (of identification and belonging) that is beyond the law and recognition. In that sense the homo sacer is also both an in-between and a limit. Within capitalist modernity the homo sacer and sovereignty are not in a dialectical relationship of mutual transformation but of continuity. Their relationship occurs in an ellipse and their encounters function to separate and divide space into its smallest cells. When the ellipse is folded in on itself, they become inseparable.

•

I will not argue that Abdullah Öcalan is a homo sacer in İmralı: the state feels the need to continuously perform its sovereignty for itself, society, and the world exactly because he is not. Indeed, there have been many instances when we witnessed the capacity of the Kurdish people, movement, and leadership to cut the ellipse from an unexpected point toward an opening. They have thereby rendered the İmralı system inoperative and transformed it into a threshold through which a different genealogy of political theology has become visible in the midst of the reified world of capitalist modernity.

Nor is Öcalan a sacred sovereign, as some observers claim.[15] He does not control any means of violence.[16] He is simultaneously imprisoned within the law and abandoned by it and has no physical autonomy or individual rights. The only way in which Öcalan can participate in the world is through his verbal and written gifts produced by mental labor under harsh conditions. Those who recognize him as their leader, on the other hand, relate to him by turning themselves into pure means, by putting their own bodies in the line of fire at protests or by hunger striking to end his isolation. The relationship between Öcalan and his followers is not one of property, family, or household and becomes most e/affective when it also transcends ethnicity and becomes something larger groups and communities can pursue.

Surely, such a relationship, whose orbit, direction, intensity, and contagiousness, as well as the values it generates, are interminable and inconsumable by the state and market is horrifying for the privileged. But not only for them. All actors who have a vested interest in and whose power is sustained by the reproduction of the law of capitalist modernity attribute to this relationship an archaism and hierarchy in order to devalue it and either reduce it to a relationship of exchange or make it unspeakable by interpreting it metaphysically. Yet at the very heart of this relationship resides a political imagination that has succeeded in remaining undefeated throughout history.

•

Walter Benjamin and Giorgio Agamben, both of them scholars who have contributed to deciphering the relationship of sovereignty, law, and violence, have also contemplated how to imagine what the opposites of the sovereign and violence would look like. For Benjamin, pure means is the opposite of violence. As opposed to violence, which always aims at making or sustaining law, pure means is a form of action that has no immediate end. It instead transforms the moment and the framework within which it unfolds. It thereby creates an exception and has the potential of evoking hidden memories, genealogies, and trajectories. For example, a general strike, different from other kinds of strikes, reminds the state and capital that they are neither immortal nor inevitable. Such is also the case for mass street protests and hunger strikes. While these acts might have an apparent primary demand, their more important achievement is the profanation of the state and the exposure of its dependency on consent and the limits of its capacity. In such instances the communal anger of the "people" takes a more concrete and absolute form than the state's wrath, and the state loses its lawmaking/suspending power. Instead of the law, such moments give rise to their own magical charms and spells in the form of symbols and slogans.[17]

In a similar vein, Agamben hints that a politics of sovereignty can only be overcome by profaning and making available to common use those things (means, goods, etc.) that the state monopolizes, and thereby reifies and transforms into a fetish, a taboo, and the sacred. The things that are profaned disconnect themselves from the names given to them by the state, the law, the market, and the household. They are transformed into thresholds and opened up to new names, processes, and meanings. In such instances, when the process of providing meaning is freed and becomes communal, all acts, including laboring, learning, and loving, shine in their true form. For Agamben, this is when the sacred and sovereign are replaced by magic and play. For Nejat, this is the moment of the commune.[18] It is the moment of Rojava, Cizre, and Gezi.

Benjamin also regards diplomacy (verbal negotiations) as nonviolence and pure means.[19] Diplomacy is in a way conversing and communing. It is open-ended and equalizing and forces partners to mutually recognize each other. Furthermore, its success relies on grace, style, and gesture, all of which introduce that which is beyond the topic at hand into the conversation and evoke other human histories, belongings, and heritages. In that sense, diplomacy oscillates between the short temporality of end-oriented negotiation and the eternal spiritual temporality of pure means.

From 2013 to 2015, many of us in Turkey lived in the space of nonsovereignty that Öcalan and the Kurdish movement built during the peace process. The transformation of İmralı into a threshold where peace negotiations were held had far-reaching consequences, enabling people in Turkey to engage in negotiation and diplomacy and to commune around different topics.[20] İmralı island also turned into a node of gift exchange, first, in 2012, with the hunger strike of thousands of imprisoned Kurdish activists around demands for peace and an end to Öcalan's isolation, and then with Öcalan's letter dedicated to the people that was read at the annual celebration of Newroz in Diyarbakır, declaring the beginning of a new post–armed struggle era. The non-sovereign political imagination performed on the island encapsulated the state and put people on equal footing, at least in terms of zikir [citing of memories and past events] and enabled the free circulation of ideas, ghosts, memories, and possibilities: orbits, orientations, and movements departed from their conventional paths. Taboo and fetishized words and means, such as PKK, Öcalan, communalism, radical democracy, democratic autonomy, confederalism, people's tribunal and justice, communal self-defense, and international solidarity, entered our lived world. They became toys in our hands, gained new meanings, and became the ground on which new relationships flourished and new dreams arose. We all became sorcerers of a sort, able to cast spells and do magic. In this period the harmony of the natural, social, and spiritual, its speed and excitement, was experienced as the other of capitalist modernity.

I should underline once again that the bases for what has happened from 2013 to 2015 were laid by the perspective, vocabulary, and analytical framework the opposition had gained from Öcalan's writings and the congresses, conferences, political alliances, and negotiations his proposals gave rise to. All of these have opened cracks in the spaces of stateness and capitalism in Kurdistan, simultaneously disrupting the traffic of goods, ideas, and affects in Turkey. Workshops, meetings, and visits organized by Kurdish political actors gave rise to a multicentered and multidirectional movement of intellectuals, journalists, youth, women, and leftists to Amed, Cizre, Mardin, Van, Suruç, and even to Hewlêr in Iraq and Qamishli in Syria and beyond. I guess revolution must be just this sort of multidirectional movement and the creation of the conditions that will reproduce it. It is the opening of social and individual bodies to each other, to different temporalities and spatialities, the rendering of property, nation, and family/household inoperative as a result of such a movement: revolution means that dreaming becomes the dominant mode of being and becoming.[21]

Before moving to the next section I should note that the theological imagination I will discuss here reflects only a fraction of the mental wrestling I have done with Öcalan's book to give meaning to the last few years forged by revolution and destruction.[22] When reading Friedrich Nietzsche, Georges Bataille says, one has to bleed, because Nietzsche himself bled when he wrote.[23] When reading Öcalan, one has to choose an equally difficult path and insist on believing in and being in love with the revolution, the universe, and humanity.

Capitalist Modernity as Theology

Walter Benjamin regards capitalism as a religion,[24] whereas Abdullah Öcalan believes that nationalism is the new religion of capitalist modernity. Given the intimate relationship between nationalism and capitalism and the fact that the notions of citizenship based on abstract rights and of the worker based on abstract labor became possible within the same world imaginary, one can conclude that both of these assertions are equally true.[25] In line with both Benjamin's and Öcalan's assertions, Agamben shows that it is not possible to understand the economic and political imagination of the modern world without understanding concepts that developed within

Christianity. In other words capitalist modernity is not only a system but also a cosmology and theology. It not only shapes people's everyday lives but establishes a universe where people's thoughts on happiness, agency, ethics, the meaning of life, love, sadness, and joy, as well as their feelings about intimacy, birth, death, power, crime, and punishment, are organized in line with capitalism's needs.

Nation, property, and family are the building blocks of capitalism as a system and a theology. They are constructs that shape belonging and embodiment and determine the significance of people, things, and events. They have also been rendered untouchable by an attributed holiness and placed beyond legal questioning. In capitalism, having a nation, property, and a family is almost like a form of worship.

What gives content to and injects constant life into property, nation, and family/household is progress: the motor of the operational system of capitalist modernity, which is kept outside of political debate and, hence, remains beyond challenge. Without the idea of progress most institutions of capitalist modernity—its factories, bridges, nuclear plants, buildings, and apartment complexes—would become hollow models. Indeed, Benjamin's work has brilliantly shown that as the fetishized objects of progress change and as progress disinvests itself of a formerly fetishized object, the latter rots and falls into ruin.

Finally, commodification is the interpretative grid of capitalist modernity and the glue that holds it together, rendering distinct spaces, temporalities, belongings, events, and experiences commensurate. Commodification enables the measurement, quantification, and exchange of value, and ensures that all relationships take place in real or symbolic markets, and that all feelings, life, and action can be replaced. Increasingly, more things are integrated into the market (including care, memory, and pain) and become meaningful on the basis of the price tags placed on them.

Scholars of postcolonialism and decolonization who have written on how capitalism and the nation-state have been coterminous with colonialism in terms of the violent transformations they cause testify that independence from colonial powers has often led to the emergence of a bureaucratic male elite that acts in the place and in the name of the "people" instead of bringing freedom to the latter. How then can a different path be pursued and a different future realized? During the insurgency against colonialism, different groups, including peasants and women, have rebelled for different reasons and attempted to take back the means

of production, reproduction, and defense from those who have monopolized them. However, in the aftermath of independence these means were
not distributed to the people but were re-monopolized by the centralized
nation-state. Moreover, despite the fact that each nation claimed uniqueness, what could be imagined within the borders of nationalism and the
nation-state remained derivative of Western thought and history, with the
triangle of nation/property/family seen as necessary for participating in
world history.[26]

On the other hand, neither capitalism nor state formation were ever
definitively complete. According to Chakrabarty the historical trajectory
of postcolonial societies was comprised of two conflicting and different
temporalities.[27] One could be characterized by the dominance of capital
and the process of commodification and the other by the communal and
the process of communing. During the insurgency against colonialism and its aftermath, communal and capitalist relations of production,
reproduction, and defense struggled against each other in certain places
and moments, with capitalist relations almost always prevailing. For
example, the fact that labor is always living and therefore resists abstraction becomes visible in India when factory machines and tools become
objects of religious rituals or when women work more slowly when they
are menstruating. Or, to give another example, carefree states of eroticism
contained neither by the family and household nor the market continued
to be experienced, moving and mobilizing people. In response to such
instances, capital increased factory discipline and encapsulated people's
insurgent and differentiating feelings, relations, and spaces, selling these
back to them as newness and progress, in much the same way as power
plunders language, decontextualizes words, and transforms the genuine
desire for freedom into propagandistic rhetoric. Still, the memory of
the encounter between capital and the communal, the fact that such an
encounter is imprinted in the material world (in the form of squatters,
for example), and the fact that it creates novel forms of friendship, love,
and collectivity, gives life to ideas and practices that play no role in the
reproduction of capital. It was crucial therefore that postcolonial theorists reveal these local ideas and practices—for example, peasant movements, anti-caste insurgencies, anti-colonial literature and debates—that
would later be appropriated by positions better aligned with capitalist
modernity. However, as crucial as it was, it was also melancholic, since
such practices and ideas didn't have a reliable consistency and unity, and

the horizon they pointed to could not be realistically reproduced as a future possibility. In short, most postcolonial and anti-colonial writers didn't see a viable path for collectives to become actors in the historical stage of modernity other than the one defined by the West as universal and believed that societies would eventually be imprisoned by a demand discourse that capitalism could contain. Even the most radical inevitably pledged loyalty to the Marxist framework, which centered the Western historical experience, terminologies, and interpretational grids. In other words, non-Western thought was condemned to fail to comprehensively theorize its own utopia, communality, and historicity based on the experience of living labor disrupting abstract labor from within in specific locations and periods.

Abdullah Öcalan also argues that capitalist modernity is never totally finalized. Capitalism, nationalism, and patriarchy, despite their violence and hegemony, cannot but create crises. There are always economies that produce, sustain, and distribute values outside of the spaces of marketization and commodification, distract and reorient people away from the dynamics of nationalization, familization, and propertization. There are always memories, insurgencies, beliefs, traditions, and relations that energize movements against the progressive path. Öcalan summarizes this with the concept of society's self-defense against state.[28] In Öcalan's framework, however, there is no space for melancholia. On the contrary, instead of feeling melancholia for lost or never realized communal forms and imaginations, we have to create ideas, relations, and practices here and now that will not be contribute to the reproduction of capital and commodification. This would only be possible using a comprehensive approach that endows people with the will and capacity to consistently and in relation to all subjects raise the question: "How can I be a force of intervention?" In my view, by discussing beliefs and metaphysics, by calling upon deep history and the Neolithic Age, by bringing together the natural and social sciences using concepts like social genes, second nature, and quantum, Öcalan searches out a theology that will guide people to collectively respond to questions about who they are ontologically, epistemologically, and politically and how they should live.

Before continuing with some aspects of this theology I would like to once again underline the historical importance of an approach that goes beyond deconstruction, criticism, insurgency, and remembering. In the last decade, all over the globe, we have witnessed moments when societies defended themselves against society-cide and performed democratic and communal modernities. This was largely the result of the intersection of the struggle of the oppressed, the rapid and contagious circulation of news and new ideas, and certain cracks that opened up within neo-liberal capitalism. Energy, intensity, and movement, along with reopenings, reorientations, and reconnections, characterized such moments. However, the movement and the love that surrounded the peoples of Egypt, Syria, Brazil, Indonesia, Turkey, and Greece, to name but a few, could not be raised to the level of theology. Instead, taking the forms of state violence and ISIS in the Middle East, drug wars in South America, racism and xenophobia in Europe, and primitive accumulation almost everywhere, organized crime reinstated capitalist modernity. Moreover, Islam, which the scholarship and theoretical debates of 1990s regarded as the only autonomous theology capable of challenging that of capitalist modernity, became a means for the latter's reproduction.[29] On the other hand, the Kurdish freedom movement, which in Rojava fought against one version of modernized capitalist Islam (or Islamized capitalist modernity) and in Bakur against another has succeeded in performing a different theology.[30] It is due to this theology, I would argue, that this struggle continues despite the destruction faced in both areas. In the next section, I will try to elaborate on this theology, which expresses itself in terms of freedom, truth, love, and movement.

Toward a New Theology
The Kurdish freedom struggle of the last forty years has been conducted at great cost and sacrifice. Nevertheless, it has gradually extended its horizon and its area of influence. Today the ambition of both Öcalan and the movement is to transform the world, starting with the Middle East. For a movement that was formed in the service of national liberation, over-coming its boundaries and becoming an actor for global change involves ideologically and materially addressing questions about the universe, humanity, and the meaning of life, along with questions concerning identity: Who are we, and where do we belong? Given that not only capitalist modernity but also Kurdish cultural traditions lay great emphasis on the family and fertility, and many Kurds, their enemies, and international forces define the Kurdish struggle as primarily nationalist and separa-tist,[31] acting against nationalism, patriarchy, and property requires Kurds to generate powerful new ideas and imaginaries that will mobilize people

and reorganize society. It necessitates that concepts such as "happiness," "relationship," "femininity," and "masculinity" are freed from the system, endowed with new meanings, and given alternative contents through new experiences. What gives Öcalan the status (and identity) of leadership, despite the fact that he has no sovereignty, is not only what he has produced for his movement and people through immense mental and affective labor (for no return) but the fact that he conceptualized his experiences in a dialogue with the books he has read in prison and conceived a new interpretative framework and theology. As such, whether in Kobane, Rojava, Bakur, Hewlêr, Istanbul, or Europe, those who look at the world through such an interpretative framework and theology define themselves as fighters for truth and assume responsibility not only for the establishment of justice and equality but also the revelation of truth. In that sense they are not only warriors and revolutionaries but also apostles.

The Universe and Humanity

Öcalan believes that capitalist modernity owes its success to division—of people, spheres of life, and knowledge. In terms of knowledge, Öcalan specifically argues that the divorce of the natural and the social sciences has caused both the destruction of nature and the failure of humans to understand themselves and the universe in a coherent and relevant manner. Therefore, in his writings, Öcalan brings together physics, biology, sociology, and history without privileging one over the other. For instance, quantum physics and a focus on subatomic particles shows the vitality of plurality, difference, and movement for existence. Observations of the "free" nature of the mobile and unruly subatomic particles or of the growth, multiplication, and death of organisms provides concepts, as well as senses and sensibilities, that can be used to understand society. This methodology also builds a bridge between the past and the present. In the past, knowledge was accumulated by watching and tending animals, the land, and plants, helping humans to discover truth, acquire wisdom, and affording them a language of metaphors, metonyms, and allegories. The same could be achieved by the democratization of the knowledge of physics, biology, and chemistry. Also, by integrating natural and social sciences, he aspires for a new sensibility and theology; when he writes that he wonders whether quantum motion is "the God that humanity has been searching for all along," he is trying to go beyond both science and religion; it is not because God created it that s/he can be found in quanta.

Nor should the fact that there is no creator per se erase the search for spirituality and deny the existence of metaphysics and the experience of the divine. The universe, the human, nature, and light abound with secrets, magic, and mysteries to be admired for their tendency to transcend, multiply, and differentiate, and quanta is what teaches us this truth.[32]

Natural sciences also inspire Öcalan to think about ethics. In his books Öcalan proposes ethics that are based on the idea that life is energy, and energy never disappears. If life is energy, then life is motion. Hierarchy emerges when motion is controlled. Repression and oppression stop movement and redirect it. When movement (of bodies, ideas, imaginations) is blocked, one is trapped and imprisoned. A moral life is only achieved by pouring and flowing in the right direction and in the right form.

Energy and life come from the light that the sun gives to the earth, for no return. The sun is the primary example of gift giving. The energy that the sun spreads across the earth takes many different forms. It does not disappear but changes and differentiates. Similarly, what is created and experienced in history won't disappear either. Values that are created by labor for no return are, in a particular way, similar to what the sun gives to the earth. Not only are they never completely gone, they also cannot be counted, calculated, and reciprocated. They can only become an inspiration for other ways of giving without receiving. History is not a succession of causal chains. Rather, like the relationship between sunlight and life on earth, it should be understood as a series of inspirations, contagions, visibilities and invisibilities, obscurations and revelations.

Each person is the singular product of the totality of the labor that contributed to the making of the natural and social worlds. Her/his biological and personal history cannot be grasped divorced from the history of universe, evolution, and civilization. Öcalan also argues that everything that has been constructed throughout history and the total production of labor constitute earth's second nature. In the contemporary world, first nature and second nature whose main actors are humans are in a dire conflict. In a moral political society these two natures must be brought into harmony. Moreover, one does not need to look far to find inspiration for building a moral society. The inspiration for a moral life resides in a person's constitution by history.

Once history and the products of labor are defined as second nature, it can be argued that just like biological evolution these have also been imprinted on and stored in the genes of humans and society. Humans must inevitably feel a central responsibility for the life, history, and labor invested in them, for these unique gifts for no return that they have received. Similarly, every person, to the extent that s/he contains all that comes before her/him and the values produced by the totality of universal and historical labor, is uniquely capable, resilient, and resolute. However, her/his qualifications are buried under the personalities that are forced on her/him by capitalism, nationalism, familialism, and religionism. In order for a human being to attain her/his full capacity and realize her/his role in universal history, s/he has to reveal her/his history, her/his social nature, her/his physical abilities, and the labor invested in her/him; s/he has to learn about and further develop her/his mind and her/his affective intelligence.

Every human being also contributes to making nature, life, history, and the universe through her/his choices, labor, movement, and the values s/he produces. It is, therefore, precisely the case that life is something for which one can die, and even at times kill.[33] The truth is not the individual, or, rather, the truth of the person is not divorced from the truth of the universe and life. At the moment of death, just like all other moments in life, one labors and produces value, which will then circulate and become part of the history and the genetic makeup of society. In the Kurdish freedom movement, therefore, dying in the struggle for freedom is defined as creating value, giving a gift to life, and laboring for society and the world.

Freedom

In his prison writings Öcalan makes different assertions about freedom and arrives at different conceptualizations. Freedom for Öcalan is closely associated with movement, the capacity to give meaning and love. I should note that within the scope of this article I have no intention of tracing the various trajectories of Öcalan's discussion of freedom. Instead, I will limit my comments to several aspects of Öcalan's understanding of freedom that directly affect his own practice and that of the Kurdish freedom movement.

As I have previously pointed out, for Öcalan, freedom is foremost about motion and energy. This can be seen both in his writings and in the suggestions he made regarding the organization of freedom and democracy within the Kurdish freedom movement and in the Middle East more broadly. Whenever he was able to communicate with the outside world Öcalan proposed that the Kurdish freedom movement, women, and other democratic forces in Turkey create new social and political bodies and that existing ones structurally transform their identities and their roles in the struggle. This was based in part on his constant consistent energetic and innovative search for the best possible form of social organization. However, another underlying reason is the fact that Öcalan aims to create movement and mobility in social and political life so politics will not be reduced to management and administration, dominated by habits and conventions, so that those who are at the core of existing organizations will be unsettled, and so that the way will be cleared to open new opportunities for those at the margins. The state, on the other hand, attempts to stop this movement by "capturing" and "arresting" its participants. Ironically, arrest only causes others to mobilize in order to take up the slack that are left behind and bring about the permanent circulation of bodies, labor, and speech in society.[34]

In my opinion, one further result of creating new organizations is non-sovereignty. The existence of a multiplicity of organizations operating in different and overlapping spaces and the complicated shifts in authority and in the relationships among them ensure that no single body will ever capture and monopolize the means of power and rule. On the contrary, the fact that a number of constantly changing institutions and administrators are simultaneously responsible for operating in a given field prevents each of them from remaining closed in on itself and forces all of them to remain in communication, without depriving any of them of their autonomy. It also guarantees that decisions made on the basis of the authority acquired by one organization can never be fully realized unless they are validated by the others. As such, multiplication, diversification, and differentiation—in other words, freedom—can be reproduced in a nonmechanical way.

For Öcalan, besides entailing mental and physical motion, freedom is also closely related to the capacity to make and give meaning. In other words, movement becomes freedom to the extent that people—individually and collectively—give meaning to it. On the other hand, in order to develop the capacity for meaning an individual or collective must first liberate and disconnect itself from the hegemonic sets of meaning. However, this alone is not enough. It is also necessary to produce explanations and stories in which an increasing number of people can recognize themselves and their experiences. For example, the historical narrative that Öcalan has developed based on the Neolithic Age provides a way for women to give meaning to their own lives, to their mothers' stories, to women's memories, myths, and tales, and to the suffering and resilience women have shown throughout history, while situating them in a holistic and sensible world.

In this context, I should also point to both the unique theoretical and daily vocabulary used by the Kurdish freedom movement. This vocabulary is in part created by Öcalan and encourages people to avoid language that will lead them to conceive of themselves in hegemonic ways. Allowing them instead to tell different stories about the universe, life, humanity, nature, etc., this vocabulary provides them with new ways of seeing and sensing. Here, the dialectical relationship of sacredness and profanation that I previously discussed comes into play. Having their own vocabulary for talking about different matters allows the movement and people to contribute to the production of knowledge in ways that were not previously possible.[35] Knowledge is profaned and democratized, depriving society of one of the means of creating hegemonic structures. Magic, as I have been using the term, drawing on Agamben's interpretation, becomes possible when different means (including those of knowledge making) are rescued from the hegemonic names given to them and limits imposed upon them, opening them up to multiple new names and stories.[36]

However, neither movement nor developing an autonomous capacity to create meaning are sufficient bases for freedom. Freedom also requires that people increase their power to actively build new things. Freedom is not doing what one wants to do. On the contrary, it demands the immense effort and willpower that allows a person to push her/himself to overcome her/his limits, to go against her/his habits, and to labor for and invest energy in her/himself and her/his relationships. For example, when women increase their physical capacity or acquire information and skills that are primarily the domain of men, they increase their power to "build," and they feel more independent and freer. Similarly, as Kurdish society builds its institutions and takes the means of production, reproduction, and self-defense back from the state, men, and the elite, they liberate themselves. Finally, the capacity to "build," just like the capacities of movement and meaning making, collectivizes the concept of freedom and makes clear that a person's freedom depends on the freedom and autonomy of the collective within which s/he lives, rather than being independent from it.

I would like to say something parenthetical here. Many cultures have produced narratives that connect love and freedom. Love, according to such narratives, is such a strong emotion that it may make people do things that are forbidden to them. Individuals recognize their core values and identity through love and rebel against structures that oppress and dominate them. Happiness, on the other hand, is achieved when a person can harmonize and create a balance between her/his own desires (love, sexuality, recognition, etc.) and social norms. In capitalist modernity such a balance will be attained through marriage and the nuclear family, ownership, and (gendered) citizenship. It seems like once these are attained, people run out of stories to tell. Love takes a central place in Öcalan's thought as well and is closely related to both freedom and truth. However, this love is not a form of love that can be sexually consummated, contained by household, property, and nation, or reproduce a lineage. Love and eroticism are lived in relation to nature, the world, and revolution, in people, living matter, and society—in other words, in all kinds of relationships—as a movement and a flow. As freedom is attained, one goes beyond what is currently possible and unlocks new secrets, acquiring sensibilities that will harmonize first and second nature.

Friendship and comradeship—"hevallik" in Kurdish—is one of the most important relationships that gives meaning to life and orients one toward truth. It is a form of loyalty that cannot be contained within nation, property, or household. It cannot be transformed into utility and cannot be exchanged. It involves both equality and differentiation. It develops through harmony as well as conflict, recognition as well as criticism. Friendship/comradeship/hevallik express themselves best in the Kurdish dance, halay: in an act where a collective made up of individuals leaning on each other flows in a single direction and becomes harmonious as the individuals differentiate themselves from one another in both style and gestures.

One aphorism that crystallizes Öcalan's thought and comprises both utopia and the epistemologies of heretical traditions of the past (i.e., Alevism, Sufism, mythology) is "Truth is Love; Love is Free Life." Therefore, "truth" is another concept that needs to be discussed to understand the theology of democratic modernity that Öcalan has in mind.

Truth
With Michel Foucault's work, which has greatly influenced Öcalan, it became impossible to talk about truth in itself without acknowledging that truth is produced by power and must be understood as a social and

political construct. Building upon these insights in his books, Öcalan comments that the greatest weapon of domination is the creation and circulation of truth, and that positive sciences are truth regimes that produce and are produced by power. However, acknowledging that truth is a construct does not lead Öcalan to relativism. Instead, he develops two different and complimentary approaches to truth and makes them the center of his theology. The different approaches are expressed in and associated with two diverse activities: "to build" and "to reveal."

For Öcalan, the goal of all historical action is freedom, hence movement. Truth, on the other hand, is the totality of the creations, sensations, and values that liberate life. Truth does not appear by itself. Neither is truth achieved through disclosure. Truth must be constructed with immense labor and ethical action. Truth is produced in relationships, efforts, and acts that liberate. What is opposed to truth is evil, withholding of one's labor, and disloyalty.[37] For example, whether one is right or wrong in an argument has little to do with the concept of truth, since if it does not contribute to collective freedom any line of argumentation can end up harming truth. In short, producing and constructing truth is about creating that which will contribute to freedom. In that sense, it is individual (the truths that the individual creates to make her/himself autonomous and free) and collective (the truths that are constituted to make society autonomous and free) and harmonizes the two.

On the other hand, one can also trace a metaphysical understanding of truth in Öcalan's writings. In this second register truth resides in the universe, society, and the individual and must be recovered. Truth is the totality of goodness, beauty, and integrity, the harmony between first and second nature, and the fact that "eternity is hidden in the now and intrinsic to occurrences in the moment." Truth is the wholeness of history and the universe and of the fact that all living things carry within themselves the totality of the labor spent and invested in the world. The responsibility and duty of revolutionary action and thought is to reveal this truth. The language Öcalan uses, which some consider hyperbolic and exaggerated at times, becomes meaningful in the framework of such an understanding of truth: one example is the way Öcalan links women and goddesses together. To the extent that Öcalan believes that the totality of women's histories is accumulated and embedded in each living women, he suggests that women should, in their lives and acts, in their worlds of meaning and sensuality, reveal the femininity they possessed during the Neolithic Age.

In that way, contemporary women can attain the power to make meaning and to construct that the goddesses described in Sumerian mythology once possessed, becoming free in the process and helping others to also gain their freedom. Women's passionate search for their truth in history, nature, and collective life, their experience of this search as both construction and revelation, and the immense labor, effort, and discipline, as well as dedication and love, they attach to their activities overall define the women's liberation process in the Kurdish freedom movement.

Conclusion

Öcalan's theology is empowering and emancipatory. However, it also points to a never-ending struggle and introduces criteria for living that many people would find daunting. Öcalan's narrative displaces melodrama, which has become popular in capitalist modernity, and organizes the relationship between the individual and society. It also rejects skepticism as a mode of opposition. Instead, he calls for life to be lived on epic terms and to be organized in a way that can serve as an example and provide a lesson. He thus invites the individual to contribute to making history by becoming a purveyor of collective liberation. What is interesting here is that Öcalan's narrative democratizes the epic: living an epic life is no longer a privilege reserved for the preordained but is something that is accessible to everyone. In the Kurdish freedom movement's theology every life can become epic in the struggle for truth and freedom and deserves to be recounted as mythology and legend. Telling the story of such lives will moreover multiply them, circulate the values produced, and evoke a sense of inspiration and loyalty.

If the building blocks of capitalist modernity are the nuclear family, property, and the nation-state, the building blocks of democratic modernity are movement, flexibility, and energy. Academies, communes, cooperatives, and the friendships that flourish within them are the structures that will produce and reproduce movement. What gives orientation, form, and content to democratic modernity is not progress but the search for truth. It is the desire to reveal and the capacity to build goodness and beauty that humans have inherited from their history. What brings together the different institutions, spaces, and directions of democratic modernity is love, giving without receiving, and creation.

This essay was written for this book.

Nazan Üstündağ received her PhD in 2005 from the Department of Sociology at Indiana University Bloomington. From 2005 to 2018, she worked as an assistant professor at Boğaziçi University Istanbul, Department of Sociology. Currently, she is an Academy in Exile and IIE-Scholar Rescue Fund fellow at Transregionale Studien. Üstündağ has written extensively on social policy, gendered subjectivities, and state violence in Kurdistan. She has also worked as a columnist for the journal *Nokta* and the newspaper *Özgür Gündem*, and her opinion pieces have appeared in Internet sites such as Bianet, T24, Roar Magazine, and Jadaliyya. Üstündağ is a member of both Women for Peace and Academics for Peace. She is currently wrapping up a book with the working title *Mother, Politician, and Guerilla: The Emergence of a New Political Cosmology in Kurdistan through Women's Bodies and Speech.*

Notes

1 Havin Guneser translated the Abdullah Öcalan quotes.
2 While I will not elaborate here, the controversy over Brexit, the example of Crimea, and the fact that refugees who try to reach Europe are held on various Mediterranean islands are further examples of the material and symbolic relationship of the nation-state to islands and isolation. I would like to thank Mustafa Emin Büyükcoşkun for reminding me of İbn Tufeyl's book *Hay Bin Yakzan*, written in the twelfth century. The book provides a different way of imagining islands, which offers an alternative way of interpreting Abdullah Öcalan's experience on İmralı. The relationship between Caliban and Prospero in Shakespeare's *The Tempest* is another potential source for tracing alternative social and political ways of imagining the trope of the island.
3 Michael Taussig, *My Cocaine Museum* (Chicago: Chicago University Press, 2004).
4 Familization and propertization are neologisms I will use in this article to denote the ways in which individuals are compelled to live their intimacies within heterosexual partnerships and nuclear families and feel that they matter and are accounted for by means of ownership (of houses, cars, and cell phones).
5 The role family plays in the acquirement of individual rights—specifically for the individual who lives a nonconforming life—is best displayed by the fact that while lawyers, politicians, and journalists are banned from the island, legal authorities have allowed Öcalan's brother to visit him three times, the first two times to end hunger strikes protesting Öcalan's absolute isolation, and most recently, in January 2019.
6 The influential French sociologist Michel de Certeau, *The Practice of Everyday Life*, trans. Steven Rendall (Berkeley: University of California Press, 3rd edition, 2011) has argued while space is at the disposal of the powerful, time is the tool of the oppressed, allowing them to use innovative tactics to interrupt the strategies of the powerful.
7 In the Kurdish freedom movement, İmralı is usually referred to as a "system" to denote the comprehensiveness of the policy of isolation and control exercised over Öcalan, including regulations and bylaws regarding his access to books,

letters, radio, and television, as well as visitors and national and international legal mechanisms. It is also called a "system" because people believe that what happens in İmralı cannot be understood independently of Turkey's overall policy toward the Kurds.

8   While theology is the science and study of the divine, I use the term here as the framework in which things like the universe, birth, death, the sacred, and truth are given meaning by reference to beyond the humanly visible and scientifically provable. Alternately, I could have used the term "spirituality" or, like Abdullah Öcalan himself, the term "metaphysics." The reason I use "theology" here is because, on the one hand, I want to underline the fact that the ideas that make capitalist modernity intelligible, comprehensible, and consistent are borrowed from monotheist religions. On the other hand, I want to emphasize that democratic modernity, as Öcalan constructs it, both poses a rupture from capitalist modernity and is based on a similarly comprehensive understanding of how to derive meaning and conduct life.

9   On the relationship between the sacred and violence, see Alphonso Lingis, *Violence and Splendor* (Evanston, IL: Northwestern University Press, 2011).

10 This is the case with the exception of some international organizations and, some would argue, some transnational companies. Another exception on the world political stage occurs when certain treaties involving security and peace are signed by humanitarian organizations or organizations fighting for the independence of a particular people.

11 Achille Mbembe, "Necropolitics," *Public Culture* 15, no. 1 (Winter 2003):15–40, accessed July 19, 2019, https://warwick.ac.uk/fac/arts/english/currentstudents/postgraduate/masters/modules/postcol_theory/mbembe_22necropolitics22.pdf.

12 These days it is common practice for political actors to use a rhetoric whereby different identities are addressed serially (such as Kurdish, Armenian, women, LGBTQI+, workers, etc.) and equivalently. Such an approach runs the risk of overlooking the fact that different identities have different genealogies shaped by the distinct relations of biopolitics and sovereignty they have been exposed to. I think it would be better to conceptualize women, Kurdish, or worker as nodes pointing to relations of exploitation, occupation, and violence, rather than as identities.

13 This is not to defend a liberal position. On the contrary, from a liberal perspective the state must manage and administer, as well as provide a common ground, to make societies, relations, goods, labor, etc. equivalent and interchangeable. I am here talking about the radical difference between the commune and the state.

14 For a community to reproduce itself without being recognized and contained by the state poses an ontological and theological problem for the state. That is why the state will not be satisfied with simply killing the insurgents of such a community but will engage in practices that destroy the body or prevent burial, an expression of the desire to rule over the otherworldly and the afterlife.

15 Many observers claim that there is an oppressive leadership cult surrounding Öcalan, without noting that the respect and love for Öcalan must be cultivated

every day and sustained with intense voluntary labor, since he has been in isolation for the last twenty years.

16 Öcalan has stated numerous times that he cannot make decisions on the part of the movement, since he is not the one with arms, and that the only role he could play would be in peace negotiations.

17 The Kobane events in Turkey were one such moment, with people in Kurdistan taking to the streets to protest Turkey's support of ISIS's invasion of the Kurdish city of Kobane in Northern Syria. In Europe, the Yellow Vests are an example of magical charm. In the Kurdish struggle, slogans such as *"edi bese"* [enough is enough], *"biji berxedane zindane"* (long live the resistance in prisons), *"kurtuluş yok tek başına"* (there is no personal salvation) operate like magical spells that give people strength, hope, rage, and courage.

18 In his anonymous book *Menkıbe*, which he finished before going to Kobane, Nejat Ağırnaslı—also known by his nom de guerre Paramaz Kızılbaş—focused on what the commune and communal are and how the communal has been plundered and commodified. For Nejat, the commune, besides being a historical social form, is a way of enjoyment and relating to things, people, names, society, and history. Gift giving, friendship, and a primary loyalty to friendship, imagination, and inspiration are all qualities that he associates with the communal. In his book, Nejat is also interested in how the commune and communing can be reproduced, and "play" is for him a form of living and relating that could provide a framework for the communal.

19 In Turkish, the Arabic word *müzakere* is used to refer to verbal negotiations. The root of the word is *zikir* [to remember] and *müzakere* is talking while remembering, and in that sense is intimately related with peacemaking, forgiveness, and resolution as much as commemoration.

20 I don't think that it is a coincidence that the Gezi events, with a million people in Turkey taking to the streets to protest the destruction of a park and occupying Istanbul's central neighborhood for two weeks, also occurred during this period; see Anthony Alessandrini, Nazan Üstündağ, and Emrah Yildiz, eds., *"Resistance Everywhere": The Gezi Protests and Dissident Visions of Turkey* (Washington, DC: Tadween Publishing, 2014). The peace process enabled contact and mutual tolerance among different groups, making such mass protests and actions thinkable and possible. Also, actors, such as women for peace, academics for peace, right to the city organizations, the LGBTQI+ movement, the health parliament for empowerment of people against professionalization of medical knowledge, and park and neighborhood forums became more influential than ever in shaping politics during this period, contributing to a widescale experiment with democratic autonomy. The boundary between the legal and illegal became porous in a way similar to a state of exception, however, this time in favor of inclusion, with, for example, guerrillas becoming more visible in Kurdistan and deceased leftist militants' photos and ideas becoming widespread in Turkey.

21 Nejat Ağırnaslı/Paramaz Kızılbaş, whose thought has influenced me greatly, defined revolution with the slogan *Hayalgücü iktidara!* [Imagination shall

come to power!] and vehemently defended the right and capacity to dream, imagine, and cast spells.

22 The period that followed the peace process in Turkey has been one of destruction and devastation. After the collapse of the negotiations, an urban asymmetrical war ensued in Kurdistan, pitting the youth backed by the guerrilla against the state and claiming hundreds of lives. During this war and its aftermath, the security forces destroyed several neighborhoods, forcing inhabitants out and replacing one-story houses with apartment complexes. Then a coup attempt in July 2016 offered an excuse for emergency law, giving the government the right to shut down organizations, publications, and universities, seize municipalities, and remove thousands of people from their positions. For a discussion of the urban war, see Nazan Üstündağ, "Democratic Autonomy in Kurdistan," *Roar Magazine* no. 6 (Summer 2017).

23 Georges Bataille, *On Nietzsche*, trans. Bruce Boone (Saint Paul, MN: Paragon House Press, 1996).

24 Walter Benjamin, "Capitalism as Religion" [1921], in *Selected Writings*, vol. 1, trans. Rodney Livingstone (Cambridge, MA: Belknap Press, 1996), 288–91.

25 Dipesh Chakrabarty, *Provincializing Europe: Postcolonial Thought and Historical Difference* (Princeton, NJ: Princeton University Press, 2000) shows the conceptual and historical relationship between the emergence of free labor and citizenship. Being a citizen and a worker are both achieved by subjection to particular disciplines and pedagogies. It should be noted that the capacity to operate according to abstract categories (worker, market, citizenship, etc.) was made possible by the spread of monotheist religions. The relationship between the emergence of the state and abstraction has been theorized in Pierre Clastres, *Society against the State*, trans. Robert Hurley (New York: Zone Books, 1989). Clastres shows that state formation and representation by abstraction is not an inevitable historical stage, and that so-called primitive societies have developed ways of defending themselves against it.

26 Partha Chatterjee, *Nationalist Thought and the Colonial World: A Derivative Discourse* (London: Zed Books, 1986).

27 Chakrabarty, *Provincializing Europe*.

28 While Öcalan does not say so, based on my reading of his writings, I would suggest that self-defense of the society is also the defense of magic and profanation against sacredness and sacrilization.

29 During 1980s and 1990s, a number of intellectuals argued that due to its capacity to organize public and private life, along with economy and morality, Islam, with its alternative ontology and epistemology, had the potential to be as powerful an ideology and imaginary as capitalist modernity. However, today, Islamic political parties such as the Adalet ve Kalkınma Partisi (AKP: Justice and Development Party) in Turkey not also reproduce but also expand the power of the state, patriarchy, and capitalism. ISIS, on the other hand, while instituting a very different law from the liberal West, also reproduces and expands capitalism, patriarchy, and state-ness, by claiming to be a state rather than a movement, by its use of marriage for organizing purposes (ISIS

brides), and by transforming genocide, occupation, and invasion into capital accumulation.

30 Bakur and Rojava refer to the northern and western parts of Kurdistan respectively and are within the borders of Turkey and Syria. The Yekîneyên Parastina Gel (YPG: Kurdish People's Defense Forces) has fought ISIS since 2013, losing thousands of fighters to this battle waged on multiple fronts. Meanwhile, after a brief period of peace negotiations from 2013 to 2015, the war between the *Partiya Karkerên Kurdistanê* (PKK: Kurdistan Workers' Party) and the Turkish army resumed, claiming hundreds of lives.

31 Despite the fact that PKK has numerous times officially stated that it gave up its separationist goals and instead pursues the creation of democratic autonomies without changing the borders of existing states, many academic and journalistic articles continue defining PKK as a separatist group.

32 This is remarkably reminiscent of the astronomy-based revolutionary theology that Blanqui developed by watching the stars from his window in the castle where he was imprisoned; see Louis-Auguste Blanqui, *Eternity by the Stars: An Astronomical Hypothesis*, trans. Frank Chouraqui (New York: Contra Mundum Press, 2013 [1872]).

33 The slogan "we love life so much we would die for it" is a slogan that needs to be understood in this context. Also, killing in combat in the Kurdish movement is understood as self-defense and as fighting for truth and humanity and, in that sense, is morally justifiable when it occurs in that context; see Nazan Üstündağ, "Self-Defense as a Revolutionary Practice in Rojava, or How to Unmake the State?" *South Atlantic Quarterly* 115, no. 1 (January 2016): 197–210.

34 I believe that when Öcalan refers to the possibility of Kurdish people changing the Middle East, he is not only basing this idea on their historical concentration in Mesopotamia but also on the fact that their existence in four different countries and in Europe gives them the unique capacity of multidirectional transcontinental movement.

35 One such example is "jineolojî" (women's science) and the vocabulary it has invented in thinking about women's history. Jineolojî makes it possible for women to write theoretically, conceptually, and politically outside of the academic language of women's studies and established feminist canons. On the other hand, it runs the risk of becoming an esoteric (to ordinary people) and sacred language, at times reducing people's use of this language to mere repetition.

36 Agamben uses the concepts of profanation and magic similarly. While profanation is overcoming social separations and freeing all that is reified by the state and capitalism for people's use, magic refers to how society will use this to create new meanings and practices. As such, what is reified or sacred takes its place in the everyday world.

37 Despite the fact that Öcalan probably didn't read Badiou, the similarities (as much as the differences) in their approaches to truth are striking. One difference, for example, is that based on Öcalan's teachings before he was arrested; the PKK conceptualized loyalty literally and saw taking revenge when comrades were killed as one form of it.

TWENTY

Power and Truth: Analytics of Power and Nomadic Thought as Fragments of a Philosophy of Liberation

Michael Panser

In my study of the intersection of the philosophical systems of Michel Foucault and Abdullah Öcalan, I focus on three central terms or ideas that can help us to widen our understanding of the current social situation, of movements of thought, and of possibilities for action. I believe that a few mechanisms of thinking addressed in Foucault's work could be critical to understanding the new paradigm and thinking of the Kurdish freedom movement.

The three terms are:

a) system of thought—which Öcalan describes as organized thinking and a regime of truth;

b) analytics of power—an understanding of systems and societies;

c) the principle of guidance as practiced by the Kurdish movement— the *rastiya serokatî*, or *governmentality*, as Foucault describes it, through which we can develop a basic understanding of central fragments of the Kurdish movement regarding education, organization, and the practice of a democratic autonomy.

Any thinking takes place within a specific system of thought, with reason forming the pattern of our perception, the way we grasp the world, and the way we organize our daily lives. It creates meaning, through which it inspires decisions and shapes standards in an ongoing game of experience, criticism, and change. Whether we talk about individuals, collectives, or societies—every subject carries her/his experiences with her/him and by reflecting on her/his life is able to effect change. This means that each of our actions is based on a certain kind of awareness, on the ability to perceive ourselves in the context of reality. Öcalan calls this "regimes of truth." What we perceive and constantly analyze to find a basis for our actions is an approach to truth; fragments of reality that we experimentally interact with, filter, interpret, and then deem true. The differentiation of societies over the past centuries has led to a diversity in the human standards and ways of thinking that form the basis of action. Within society this plays out as a complex game of ongoing negotiation between different regimes of truth. This means that the various approaches to truth and the ways in which subjects structure and change their realities provide the basis for social diversity and creativity.

What is political theory, then? An attempt to question one's own subjective and collective framework of meaning, to move it, if necessary, and to reveal possibilities for action: a toolbox, experimental and always connected to one's intentions. This more or less summarizes Öcalan's approach to the different ways of interpreting history and writing a creative and fragmentary history of our present.

Every kind of thinking—and the resultant political theory—that dedicates itself to the necessity of social change is strategic. Our thinking cannot be separated from our power to act or from our ability to change reality through purposeful action. So there is a connection, a triangular reciprocity, and a field of tension between knowledge, power, and truth. This is one of the central arguments developed by Foucault. Based on a particular understanding of a given situation we are able to act in a variety of ways. We can use our own power to act to shift our own relationship with reality and to effect movement and change. Every subject has the ability to act purposefully within her/his own perceptual framework. S/he can change the situation within her/his own system or can move the framework of her/his own perception and, thereby, her/his own potential to act through critical and theoretical reflection: a transcendent way of thinking that shifts one's position—nomadic thinking. Organized thinking—on this principal issue, Foucault and Öcalan complement each other: every approach to truth is subjective, and every attempt to evade reality is critical and must be met with consistent criticism and innovation.

That means (and here we are moving on to the second idea) that we have to give up an old notion that weighs heavily on the intellectual horizon of the West: power as something negative, as purely suppressive, as the pole of evil, and as sovereign rule from above. Here, I refer to some of Foucault's central ideas, which often underlie Öcalan's thinking, albeit implicitly rather than as something detailed in his writing. Nonetheless, the objective that Öcalan suggests with his new paradigm of democratic confederalism runs in parallel the system Foucault's methodology gives rise to. At different points he refers directly to concepts that are part of Foucault's understanding of power—for instance, the concept of biopower as one of the most important pillars of capitalist rule. Part of Öcalan's thinking is based on an equivalent analysis of power. This kind of thinking also underlies other similar worldviews, including the Indigenous cosmovisions in Latin America (e.g., the Zapatistas), Zoroaster's conclusions, and Far Eastern worldviews, which do not recognize the object: focusing instead on heterogeneity, change, connectedness, and subjectivity.

So what is power? Power is not simply the great Other that is facing us, the king, the police(wo)man, God. All those are effects of a concentration of power, more or less symbolic, with different ways of interpreting reality. Power is neither good nor evil, as such. Generally, power, on the one hand, denotes a subject's capacity to move within a system, to create frameworks of meaning, and to act on them—thus, agency. On the other hand, today's societies are fundamentally marked by power; they organize themselves along lines of hegemonic ambition, accumulation of power, access, and the structural ability to shift meaning. Every subject has the capacity to act. Power evolves in every part of society; it pervades and structures society. To cite Foucault—power is the field of lines of force that populate and organize an area. Power is not something you gain, take away, share, keep, or lose; power is something that is implemented from innumerable points in the play of unequal and flexible relations: power is omnipresent. Power is above all the name given to a complex strategic situation in a society. It is the meta-understanding of mechanisms of power relations that Foucault provides when analyzing society that reveals possibilities for action.

This allows us to grasp dominance as a concentration of power at a certain point within a system. A part of or point in the system—the human being, a party, a state, a man, or any institution—creates a framework of meaning, which, if not accepted, might be answered with exclusion and/ or aggression. Dominance denies the other parts of the society the power to act, partly or entirely, or to violently deprive them of this power by force, thereby making them objects, victims of their own decision without further discussion. Imposing dominance requires means and tactics that effectively separate the subject from her/his own truth and her/his own vitality, thereby gaining control over her/him. Dominance develops when the power of definition held by Others regarding their own way of life and their own decisions—their ability to define their own necessities—is effectively disrupted. Dominance means divesting the dominated of their power. But because power is never separable from one's knowledge—and the ability to act is closely connected to one's consciousness of the world and one's access to truth—a project of dominance must strive to implement its own regime of truth as an absolute, normative, and uniformly acceptable standard of truth. This is the essence of the state project and the patriarchal gesture. The way of interpreting history Öcalan proposes tries to name this project of disempowering societies, to create ways to access truth and make resistance strategically feasible. To use Foucault's words: Society Must Be Defended.

Where there is power, there is resistance. Resistance always forms a part of power relations, because no kind of dominance can become absolute, even though its claims may be real. Power is strictly relational, which means it only exists between subjects. The game of power, resistance, negotiation, and fighting is a process, a steady flow of ascendency and decline. This game cannot come to an end, except through the extinction of the Other—which would mean the collapse of the system. And as dominance—like the state—depends on the control and organization of power relations, the strategic codification of points of resistance can lead to revolution.

We are not located outside of the power dynamic. Our consciousness and our way of life represent attempts to pursue our demands and become an acknowledged part of society; we become subjects through power, within the social matrix of various powers.

A society without dominance doesn't need to fight a war of liberation against an enemy (although self-defense might be necessary) but to empower itself. Here we find a central argument of Öcalan's new paradigm.

So what is in the way? We have to confront the issue of governance, my third point. What is a state? The state only exists in practice—in other words, through the people who act according to its principles. This is where Öcalan's conclusions about the process of civilization and Foucault's understanding of subjectivization—i.e., turning into a self—converge, both from a macro and a micro point of view. The state is not a single institution; it is not one large machine that consists of administration, police, justice, and the military. These are forms that the state has adopted, effects of truth or strategic measures, so to speak. Rather, and above all, the state is an idea by which human beings act and relate to reality. The state is ideology, "Weltanschauung." This view of the state is the basis of Öcalan's proposals for a democratic socialism and of his perspective on societies that oppose the state and fight a defensive war against its hold.

How does the state approach work—what is its access to reality? Foucault identified strategies and dispositives that provide the framework of state power and control and explained how the state constructed this framework in the first place, applying his concept of governmentality—the art of governing. Earlier, I mentioned the complex of power, knowledge, and truth. It is within this complex that we must imagine the state shaping and establishing its principle of guidance.

First, as a system of thought, the state's regime of truth—its relation to reality—leads to reification, control, and mobilization: creating hierarchies, restriction, separation, scarcity, dominance of rationality, and functionality, as well as the great systems of dichotomy: homogenization and exclusion, normality and state of emergency, private and public. The state is mobilization, organization through pressure, and external guidance—alien leadership.

Second, centralization of power. The state rests on an idea of a great central power around which everything else is organized and structured. For a long time, this was God, later a king, and with the development of capitalism it was transformed into the principle of "practical constraint," which mobilizes and manifolds the center; a totally unified system in place of God. It is the central mechanism embraced by any movement that acts on the basis of the state.

Third, the state rules through the effects of truth that permeate and structure everything: state architecture, strategic dispositives, including the prison system, the medical complex, bureaucratic administration, police control systems, and the public. In PKK ideology, this overall state technique that serves to reduce society is called *şerê taybet*, which means *special warfare*. These are war tactics that establish the state's regime of truth and attempt to destroy all other possible ways of thinking. This works through the introduction of influential paradigms: consumerism, nationalism, militarism, hostility, and liberal and feudal personal behavioral patterns—widely implemented forms of socialization. These are mechanisms by which the system of thought called "statehood" works in society.

So we can conclude that the state is a certain way of regarding the world via absolutist thinking, dogma, law, and reified regimes of truth in the form of epistemic monopolies. The state represents the centralization and organization—meaning control—of social negotiations through subjugation of the Other. The state is leadership through disempowerment—relinquished leadership. In this setting, capitalism and the state don't oppose each other. Capitalism is a version of state-led governmentality, the extension of both the state's dominance and efficiency throughout the most basic sectors of society. Today, lines of power penetrate our bodies and principles of state leadership have been consolidated in our consciousness and our actions. Capitalist modernity, coming from the West, has, through the imperial extension of its own conception of state leadership, managed to establish an all-encompassing leadership over societies and individuals—over their ways of thinking, their ways of acting, their desires, and the ways in which they become subjects.

What does all this mean in terms of social practice for a project of liberation from capitalist modernity? A society that wants to free itself from the state has to create a genuine socialist governmentality in opposition to the state-led one. This is what in Öcalan's philosophy is called rastiya serokatî: the principle of right guidance.

In Foucault's sense, we can interpret this on multiple levels: as a process of social organization, in which democratic mechanisms of decision-making and tools of mediation are created based on a recognition of plurality, participation, and social ethics. Guidance also implies a self-empowering way of living, a development and evolution of one's perception and one's power to act.

The new paradigm—the utopia of democratic confederalism—is just such a project of socialist governmentality, one that offers a real possibility to wrest social life from the hands of capitalist modernity. Similar in principle to the Zapatista project in Mexico, it is about the "good government" that was lacking in past socialisms—self-government and self-administration of society beyond the state.

Socialist governmentality, as Foucault says, is not reflected in the socialist writings of the nineteenth and twentieth centuries—it still has to be invented. The truth about leadership, as Öcalan puts it, and the practice of democratic autonomy are an attempt to conduct this experiment.

Those who want to lead themselves need to philosophize; those who want to philosophize need to address the truth. This I believe, summarizes the essence of mobility and the strength of the movement and the philosophy of Abdullah Öcalan. It is a form of nomadic thinking, as Foucault puts it, a critical, subjective, self-reflective approach to truth based on multiplicity, solidarity, and social ethics. Most importantly, the new paradigm leads to a socialization and collectivization of philosophy and the tools for self-awareness. Impressively, Rojava shows us a highly functional academy system. Each social group organizes itself based on its concerns, area of work, or identity and has its own academy, with Öcalan's epistemology playing an important role. In this way, a society creates its own framework of the significant beyond the reach of a state. The struggle for self-liberation through an understanding of one's own situation and history, one's own possibilities, hopes, and desires, is a fundamental component of the socialist project. In societies in Western and Central Europe in particular, this awareness is of central importance, as the dominance of the state is more deeply anchored in the collective worldview of the citizenry, and the resistance is less effectively organized. All the aspects of state-centered thinking need to be systematically exposed and opposed: organized thinking requires flexible methods, self-awareness, and ideology; it means becoming aware of your own room to maneuver, creativity, and power to act—and self-guidance through deindividualization of meaning and the organization of decision-making.

This essay was originally delivered as a speech at the Network for an Alternative Quest conference Challenging Capitalist Modernity II: Dissecting Capitalist Modernity—Building Democratic Confederalism, April 3–5, 2015, Hamburg.

Michael Panser (1988–2018), a former history student, took up the autodidactic study of philosophy and political theory in 2011, with a focus on nomadic thinking, internationalism, and revolutionary liberation movements. In 2015, he traveled to Rojava, where, in 2017, he joined the Partiya Karkerên Kurdistanê (PKK: Kurdistan Workers' Party), taking the nom de guerre Bager Nûjiyan. Michael lost his life during a December 14, 2018, Turkish bombing raid in southern Kurdistan (Northern Iraq).

Afterword

Abdullah Öcalan

Dear editors and the contributors to the *Building Free Life: Dialogues with Öcalan*,

I have recently learned that you contributed to a book of essays in dialogue with my views titled *Building Free Life: Dialogues with Öcalan*. My lawyers gave a copy of the book to the prison administration, but I have not had an opportunity to read it, because the administration has yet to give it to me. After reviewing the book, I hope to offer a more detailed response.

I would like to take this opportunity to express some of my views regarding socialism and its practice, a subject I have addressed extensively in previous writings. If I have the opportunity, I may return to this subject in the future. I also have a specific analysis and evaluation of real socialism. There have clearly been errors stretching back to the time of Marx. Many people have evaluated them, including some renowned European social scientists, and I have also dealt with these issues in my writings.

I took into consideration the treatment of real socialism by the "French school." Foucault, for example, has addressed many of these issues. I consider Sartre's existentialist philosophy particularly important and take existence as my point departure. Although the French school has much to offer that is of profound importance, in my view, existence, existentialism, and constructivism are important reference points. I also considered the Russian school, but in that case the dogmatism stands out more glaringly. In my opinion, existence and construction are two indispensable concepts in opposition to dogmatism. While the French school is trying to adapt socialism to French society, I am trying to adapt it to the Middle East. I develop my concept of socialism from the perspective of the Middle East as a counterweight to real socialism.

As I have noted throughout my writings, I have benefited—and continue to benefit—to a great extent from your work and assessments. I have already mentioned several people specifically. Alongside these contributions and historical overviews, I present my own distinct approach. As you have also recognized, there exists a situation in which epistemologies cannot escape becoming part of the power apparatus. For example, Karl Marx is one of the most erudite of thinkers and undoubtedly the person with the most profound insight into the nature of capital. Unfortunately, even this crucial quality was not enough to allow his system of thought to escape the grasp of capitalist modernity. My intent is not to criticize but to clarify. Similar problems also arise with Lenin and Mao. The systems they envisaged were dependent on capitalist modernity in numerous ways (particularly its knowledge structures and the way modern life is understood). But while, on the one hand, I try to develop socialism from the perspective of the Middle East, an area that lies at the heart of the hegemonic crisis, I also aim to transcend capitalist modernity and its institutions to build its alternative: democratic modernity.

Of course, I do this by embracing the legacy of all previous truth travelers as an expression of this search for truth. Some of them sought truth in the form of religion, while others are the women and men of thought and action who have left their mark on history.

In this sense, it is an honor for me that you have shared your evaluations of my writings, which are an expression of my quest for truth. At the same time, you have made a valuable contribution to the collective production of universality from the point of view of the Middle East—the core of our paradigm. As truth seekers of universality, I salute you with deep respect.

Abdullah Öcalan
İmralı Island Prison

Abdullah Öcalan is the founder of the Partiya Karkerên Kurdistanê (PKK: Kurdistan Workers' Party). Since his abduction in 1999, he has been imprisoned on the island of İmralı under aggravated isolation conditions. In prison, he wrote more than ten books that revolutionized Kurdish politics. He writes extensively about history, philosophy, and politics and is considered a key figure for the political solution of the Kurdish question. Öcalan makes contributions to the discussion about the search for freedom and developed democratic confederalism as a non-state political system. His main work is the five-volume manifesto of the democratic civilization. His writings have been translated into more than twenty languages.

Index

"Passim" (literally "scattered") indicates intermittent discussion of a topic over a cluster of pages.

Publications by Abdullah Öcalan in English

Books

Declaration on the Democratic Solution of the Kurdish Question (Neuss: Mesopotamia Publishers, 1999).

The Third Domain (Cologne: International Initiative Edition, 2003).

Prison Writings I: The Roots of Civilisation (London: Pluto Press, 2007).

Prison Writings II: The PKK and the Kurdish Question in the 21st Century (London: Pluto Press, 2011).

Prison Writings, Volume 3: The Road Map to Negotiations (Cologne: International Initiative Edition, 2012).

The Political Thought of Abdullah Öcalan (London: Pluto Press, 2017).

Beyond State, Power, and Violence (Oakland: PM Press, 2020).

Building Free Life: Dialogues with Öcalan (Oakland: PM Press, 2020).

Manifesto of the Democratic Civilization newly edited and published by PM Press

> *Volume I: Civilization: The Age of Masked Gods and Disguised Kings* (2nd revised edition, 2021).

> *Volume II: Capitalism: The Age of Unmasked Gods and Naked Kings* (2nd revised edition, 2020).

> *Volume III: The Sociology of Freedom* (2020).

> *Volume IV: The Civilizational Crisis in the Middle East and the Democratic Civilization Solution* (2020).

> *Volume V: The Manifesto of the Kurdistan Revolution* (2021).

> (Volumes I and II previously published by the Norwegian collective New Compass Press.)

Pamphlets Compiled from the Prison Writings

War and Peace in Kurdistan (Cologne: International Initiative Edition, revised edition, 2017).

Democratic Confederalism (Cologne: International Initiative Edition, revised edition, 2017).

Liberating Life: Woman's Revolution (Cologne: International Initiative Edition, 2013).

Democratic Nation (Cologne: International Initiative Edition, 2016).

ABOUT PM PRESS

PM Press is an independent, radical publisher of books and media to educate, entertain, and inspire. Founded in 2007 by a small group of people with decades of publishing, media, and organizing experience, PM Press amplifies the voices of radical authors, artists, and activists. Our aim is to deliver bold political ideas and vital stories to all walks of life and arm the dreamers to demand the impossible. We have sold millions of copies of our books, most often one at a time, face to face. We're old enough to know what we're doing and young enough to know what's at stake. Join us to create a better world.

PM Press
PO Box 23912
Oakland, CA 94623
www.pmpress.org

PM Press in Europe
europe@pmpress.org
www.pmpress.org.uk

FRIENDS OF PM PRESS

These are indisputably momentous times—the financial system is melting down globally and the Empire is stumbling. Now more than ever there is a vital need for radical ideas.

In the years since its founding—and on a mere shoestring— PM Press has risen to the formidable challenge of publishing and distributing knowledge and entertainment for the struggles ahead. With over 450 releases to date, we have published an impressive and stimulating array of literature, art, music, politics, and culture. Using every available medium, we've succeeded in connecting those hungry for ideas and information to those putting them into practice.

Friends of PM allows you to directly help impact, amplify, and revitalize the discourse and actions of radical writers, filmmakers, and artists. It provides us with a stable foundation from which we can build upon our early successes and provides a much-needed subsidy for the materials that can't necessarily pay their own way. You can help make that happen—and receive every new title automatically delivered to your door once a month—by joining as a Friend of PM Press. And, we'll throw in a free T-shirt when you sign up.

Here are your options:

- **$30 a month** Get all books and pamphlets plus 50% discount on all webstore purchases

- **$40 a month** Get all PM Press releases (including CDs and DVDs) plus 50% discount on all webstore purchases

- **$100 a month** Superstar—Everything plus PM merchandise, free downloads, and 50% discount on all webstore purchases

For those who can't afford $30 or more a month, we have **Sustainer Rates** at $15, $10 and $5. Sustainers get a free PM Press T-shirt and a 50% discount on all purchases from our website.

Your Visa or Mastercard will be billed once a month, until you tell us to stop. Or until our efforts succeed in bringing the revolution around. Or the financial meltdown of Capital makes plastic redundant. Whichever comes first.

DEPARTMENT OF ANTHROPOLOGY & SOCIAL CHANGE

Anthropology and Social Change, housed within the California Institute of Integral Studies, is a small innovative graduate department with a particular focus on activist scholarship, militant research, and social change. We offer both masters and doctoral degree programs.

Our unique approach to collaborative research methodology dissolves traditional barriers between research and political activism, between insiders and outsiders, and between researchers and protagonists. Activist research is a tool for "creating the conditions we describe." We engage in the process of co-research to explore existing alternatives and possibilities for social change.

Anthropology and Social Change
anth@ciis.edu
1453 Mission Street
94103
San Francisco, California
www.ciis.edu/academics/graduate-programs/anthropology-and-social-change

Beyond State, Power, and Violence

Abdullah Öcalan
with a Foreword by Andrej Grubačić
Edited by International Initiative

ISBN: 978-1-62963-715-0
$29.95   800 pages

After the dissolution of the PKK (Kurdistan Workers' Party) in 2002, internal discussions ran high, and fear and uncertainty about the future of the Kurdish freedom movement threatened to unravel the gains of decades of organizing and armed struggle. From his prison cell, Abdullah Öcalan intervened by penning his most influential work to date: *Beyond State, Power, and Violence*. With a stunning vision of a freedom movement centered on women's liberation, democracy, and ecology, Öcalan helped reinvigorate the Kurdish freedom movement by providing a revolutionary path forward with what is undoubtedly the furthest-reaching definition of democracy the world has ever seen. Here, for the first time, is the highly anticipated English translation of this monumental work.

Beyond State, Power, and Violence is a breathtaking reconnaissance into life without the state, an essential portrait of the PKK and the Kurdish freedom movement, and an open blueprint for leftist organizing in the twenty-first century, written by one of the most vitally important political luminaries of today.

By carefully analyzing the past and present of the Middle East, Öcalan evaluates concrete prospects for the Kurdish people and arrives with his central proposal: recreate the Kurdish freedom movement along the lines of a new paradigm based on the principles of democratic confederalism and democratic autonomy. In the vast scope of this book, Öcalan examines the emergence of hierarchies and eventually classes in human societies and sketches his alternative, the democratic-ecological society. This vision, with a theoretical foundation of a nonviolent means of taking power, has ushered in a new era for the Kurdish freedom movement while also offering a fresh and indispensible perspective on the global debate about a new socialism. Öcalan's calls for nonhierarchical forms of democratic social organization deserve the careful attention of anyone interested in constructive social thought or rebuilding society along feminist and ecological lines.

"Öcalan's works make many intellectuals uncomfortable because they represent a form of thought which is not only inextricable from action, but which directly grapples with the knowledge that it is."
—David Graeber author of *Debt: The First 500 Years*

The Sociology of Freedom: Manifesto of the Democratic Civilization, Volume III

Abdullah Öcalan
with a Foreword by John Holloway
Edited by International Initiative

ISBN: 978-1-62963-710-5
$28.95   480 pages

When scientific socialism, which for many years
was implemented by Abdullah Öcalan and the Kurdistan Workers' Party (PKK),
became too narrow for his purposes, Öcalan deftly answered the call for a radical
redefinition of the social sciences. Writing from his solitary cell in İmralı Prison,
Öcalan offered a new and astute analysis of what is happening to the Kurdish
people, the Kurdish freedom movement, and future prospects for humanity.

The Sociology of Freedom is the fascinating third volume of a five-volume work
titled The Manifesto of the Democratic Civilization. The general aim of the two earlier
volumes was to clarify what power and capitalist modernity entailed. Here, Öcalan
presents his stunningly original thesis of the Democratic Civilization, based on his
criticism of Capitalist Modernity.

Ambitious in scope and encyclopedic in execution, The Sociology of Freedom is a
one-of-a-kind exploration that reveals the remarkable range of one of the Left's
most original thinkers with topics such as existence and freedom, nature and
philosophy, anarchism and ecology. Öcalan goes back to the origins of human
culture to present a penetrating reinterpretation of the basic problems facing the
twenty-first century and an examination of their solutions. Öcalan convincingly
argues that industrialism, capitalism, and the nation-state cannot be conquered
within the narrow confines of a socialist context.

Recognizing the need for more than just a critique, Öcalan has advanced what is
the most radical, far-reaching definition of democracy today and argues that a
democratic civilization, as an alternative system, already exists but systemic power
and knowledge structures, along with a perverse sectarianism, do not allow it to be
seen.

The Sociology of Freedom is a truly monumental work that gives profuse evidence
of Öcalan's position as one of the most influential thinkers of our day. It deserves
the careful attention of anyone seriously interested in constructive thought or the
future of the Left.

Capitalism: The Age of Unmasked Gods and Naked Kings (Manifesto of the Democratic Civilization, Volume II), Second Edition

Abdullah Öcalan
with a Preface by Radha D'Souza

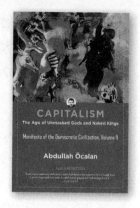

ISBN: 978-1-62963-787-7
$26.95   384 pages

Capitalism: The Age of Unmasked Gods and Naked Kings is the second volume of Abdullah Öcalan's definitive five-volume work *The Manifesto of the Democratic Civilization*. For years he has unraveled the sources of hierarchical relations, power, and the formation of nation-states that has led to capitalism's emergence and global domination. He makes the convincing argument that capitalism is not a product of the last four hundred years but a continuation of classical civilization.

Unlike Marx, Öcalan sides with Braudel by giving less importance to the mode of production than to the accumulation of surplus value and power, thus centering his criticisms on the capitalist nation-state as the most powerful monopoly of economic, military, and ideological power. He argues that the fundamental strength of capitalist hegemony, however, is the competition in voluntary servitude that a market economy has given rise to—not a single worker would reject higher wages—resulting in an unprecedented ability to convince people to surrender their individual power and autonomy. Öcalan further contends that the capitalist phase of city-class-state-based civilization is not the last phase of human intelligence; rather, the traditional morals upon which it is based are being exhausted and the intelligence of freedom is rising in all its richness. That is why he prefers to interpret capitalist modernity as the era of hope—but only insofar as we are able to develop a sustainable defense against it.

"Öcalan builds upon the past insights to provide what is, in my opinion, the most succinct and most elaborate definition of democracy."
—Andrej Grubačić, coauthor of *Wobblies and Zapatistas: Conversations on Anarchism, Marxism and Radical History*

"Öcalan presents himself as an outstanding expert on European intellectual history as well as the history and culture of the Near and Middle East. Against this background he reflects on the state of the international system and the conflict region of the Middle East after the collapse of real socialism as well as—very self-critically—the history of the PKK and his own political actions."
—Werner Ruf, political scientist and peace researcher

The Battle for the Mountain of the Kurds: Self-Determination and Ethnic Cleansing in the Afrin Region of Rojava

Author: Thomas Schmidinger with a Preface by Andrej Grubačić

ISBN: 978-1-62963-651-1
$19.95   192 pages

In early 2018, Turkey invaded the autonomous Kurdish region of Afrin in Syria and is currently threatening to ethnically cleanse the region. Between 2012 and 2018, the "Mountain of the Kurds" (Kurd Dagh) as the area has been called for centuries, had been one of the quietest regions in a country otherwise torn by civil war.

After the outbreak of the Syrian civil war in 2011, the Syrian army withdrew from the region in 2012, enabling the Party of Democratic Union (PYD), the Syrian sister party of Abdullah Öcalan's outlawed Turkish Kurdistan Workers' Party (PKK) to first introduce a Kurdish self-administration and then, in 2014, to establish the Canton Afrin as one of the three parts of the heavily Kurdish Democratic Federation of Northern Syria, which is better known under the name Rojava.

This self-administration—which had seen multiparty municipal and regionwide elections in the summer and autumn of 2017, which included a far-reaching autonomy for a number of ethnic and religious groups, and which had provided a safe haven for up to 300,000 refugees from other parts of Syria—is now at risk of being annihilated by the Turkish invasion and occupation.

Thomas Schmidinger is one of the very few Europeans to have visited the Canton of Afrin. In this book, he gives an account of the history and the present situation of the region. In a number of interviews, he also gives inhabitants of the region from a variety of ethnicities, religions, political orientations, and walks of life the opportunity to speak for themselves. As things stand now, the book might seem to be in danger of becoming an epitaph for the "Mountain of the Kurds," but as the author writes, "the battle for the Mountain of the Kurds is far from over yet."

"Preferable to most journalistic accounts that reduce the Rojava revolution to a single narrative. It will remain an informative resource even when the realities have further changed."
—Martin van Bruinessen, Kurdish Studies on *Rojava: Revolution, War and the Future of Syria's Kurds*

The Art of Freedom: A Brief History of the Kurdish Liberation Struggle

Havin Guneser with an Introduction by Andrej Grubačić and Interview by Sasha Lilley

ISBN: 978-1-62963-781-5
$15.95   192 pages

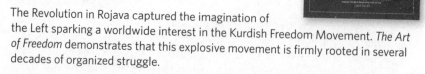

The Revolution in Rojava captured the imagination of the Left sparking a worldwide interest in the Kurdish Freedom Movement. *The Art of Freedom* demonstrates that this explosive movement is firmly rooted in several decades of organized struggle.

In 2018, one of the most important spokespersons for the struggle of Kurdish Freedom, Havin Guneser, held three groundbreaking seminars on the historical background and guiding ideology of the movement. Much to the chagrin of career academics, the theoretical foundation of the Kurdish Freedom Movement is far too fluid and dynamic to be neatly stuffed into an ivory-tower filing cabinet. A vital introduction to the Kurdish struggle, *The Art of Freedom* is the first English-language book to deliver a distillation of the ideas and sensibilities that gave rise to the most important political event of the twenty-first century.

The book is broken into three sections: "Critique and Self-Critique: The rise of the Kurdish freedom movement from the rubbles of two world wars" provides an accessible explanation of the origins and theoretical foundation of the movement. "The Rebellion of the Oldest Colony: Jineology—the Science of Women" describes the undercurrents and nuance of the Kurdish women's movement and how they have managed to create the most vibrant and successful feminist movement in the Middle East. "Democratic Confederalism and Democratic Nation: Defense of Society Against Societycide" deals with the attacks on the fabric of society and new concepts beyond national liberation to counter it. Centering on notions of "a shared homeland" and "a nation made up of nations," these rousing ideas find deep international resonation.

Havin Guneser has provided an expansive definition of freedom and democracy and a road map to help usher in a new era of struggle against capitalism, imperialism, and the State.

"Havin Guneser is not just the world's leading authority on the thought of Abdullah Öcalan; she is a profound, sensitive, and challenging revolutionary thinker with a message the world desperately needs to hear."
—David Graeber author of *Debt: The First 500 Years* and *Bullshit Jobs: A Theory*

We Are the Crisis of Capital: A John Holloway Reader

John Holloway

ISBN: 978-1-62963-225-4
$22.95   320 pages

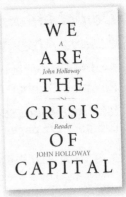

We Are the Crisis of Capital collects articles and excerpts written by radical academic, theorist, and activist John Holloway over a period of forty years.

Different times, different places, and the same anguish persists throughout our societies. This collection asks, "Is there a way out?" How do we break capital, a form of social organisation that dehumanises us and threatens to annihilate us completely? How do we create a world based on the mutual recognition of human dignity?

Holloway's work answers loudly, "By screaming NO!" By thinking from our own anger and from our own creativity. By trying to recover the "We" who are buried under the categories of capitalist thought. By opening the categories and discovering the antagonism they conceal, by discovering that behind the concepts of money, state, capital, crisis, and so on, there moves our resistance and rebellion.

An approach sometimes referred to as Open Marxism, it is an attempt to rethink Marxism as daily struggle. The articles move forward, influenced by the German state derivation debates of the seventies, by the CSE debates in Britain, and the group around the Edinburgh journal Common Sense, and then moving on to Mexico and the wonderful stimulus of the Zapatista uprising, and now the continuing whirl of discussion with colleagues and students in the Posgrado de Sociología of the Benemérita Universidad Autónoma de Puebla.

"Holloway's work is infectiously optimistic."
—Steven Poole, the Guardian (UK)

"Holloway's thesis is indeed important and worthy of notice."
—Richard J.F. Day, Canadian Journal of Cultural Studies

Don't Mourn, Balkanize!
Essays After Yugoslavia

Andrej Grubačić with an introduction by
Roxanne Dunbar-Ortiz

ISBN: 978-1-60486-302-4
$20.00   272 pages

Don't Mourn, Balkanize! is the first book written from the radical left perspective on the topic of Yugoslav space after the dismantling of the country. In this collection of essays, commentaries and interviews, written between 2002 and 2010, Andrej Grubačić speaks about the politics of balkanization—about the trial of Slobodan Milošević, the assassination of Prime Minister Zoran Djindjic, neoliberal structural adjustment, humanitarian intervention, supervised independence of Kosovo, occupation of Bosnia, and other episodes of Power which he situates in the long historical context of colonialism, conquest and intervention.

But he also tells the story of the balkanization of politics, of the Balkans seen from below. A space of bogumils—those medieval heretics who fought against Crusades and churches—and a place of anti-Ottoman resistance; a home to hajduks and klefti, pirates and rebels; a refuge of feminists and socialists, of anti-fascists and partisans; of new social movements of occupied and recovered factories; a place of dreamers of all sorts struggling both against provincial "peninsularity" as well as against occupations, foreign interventions and that process which is now, in a strange inversion of history, often described by that fashionable term, "balkanization."

For Grubačić, political activist and radical sociologist, Yugoslavia was never just a country—it was an idea. Like the Balkans itself, it was a project of inter-ethnic co-existence, a trans-ethnic and pluricultural space of many diverse worlds. Political ideas of inter-ethnic cooperation and mutual aid as we had known them in Yugoslavia were destroyed by the beginning of the 1990s—disappeared in the combined madness of ethno-nationalist hysteria and humanitarian imperialism. This remarkable collection chronicles political experiences of the author who is himself a Yugoslav, a man without a country; but also, as an anarchist, a man without a state. This book is an important reading for those on the Left who are struggling to understand the intertwined legacy of inter-ethnic conflict and inter-ethnic solidarity in contemporary, post-Yugoslav history.

"These thoughtful essays offer us a vivid picture of the Balkans experience from the inside, with its richness and complexity, tragedy and hope, and lessons from which we can all draw inspiration and insight."
—Noam Chomsky

Yugoslavia: Peace, War, and Dissolution

Noam Chomsky. Edited by Davor Džalto
with a Preface by Andrej Grubačić

ISBN: 978-1-62963-442-5
Price: $19.95   240 pages

The Balkans, in particular the turbulent ex-Yugoslav
territory, have been among the most important world
regions in Noam Chomsky's political reflections and
activism for decades. His articles, public talks, and
correspondence have provided a critical voice on political and social issues
crucial not only to the region but the entire international community, including
"humanitarian intervention," the relevance of international law in today's politics,
media manipulations, and economic crisis as a means of political control.

This volume provides a comprehensive survey of virtually all of Chomsky's texts
and public talks that focus on the region of the former Yugoslavia, from the 1970s
to the present. With numerous articles and interviews, this collection presents a
wealth of materials appearing in book form for the first time along with reflections
on events twenty-five years after the official end of communist Yugoslavia and the
beginning of the war in Bosnia. The book opens with a personal and wide-ranging
preface by Andrej Grubačić that affirms the ongoing importance of Yugoslav
history and identity, providing a context for understanding Yugoslavia as an
experiment in self-management, antifascism, and mutlethnic coexistence.

*"Chomsky is a global phenomenon. . . . He may be the most widely read American voice
on foreign policy on the planet."*
—New York Times Book Review

*"For anyone wanting to find out more about the world we live in . . . there is one simple
answer: read Noam Chomsky."*
—New Statesman

*"With relentless logic, Chomsky bids us to listen closely to what our leaders tell us—and
to discern what they are leaving out. . . . Agree with him or not, we lose out by not
listening."*
—Businessweek

Re-enchanting the World: Feminism and the Politics of the Commons

Silvia Federici

with a Foreword by Peter Linebaugh

ISBN: 978-1-62963-569-9
$19.95   240 pages

Silvia Federici is one of the most important contemporary theorists of capitalism and feminist movements. In this collection of her work spanning over twenty years, she provides a detailed history and critique of the politics of the commons from a feminist perspective. In her clear and combative voice, Federici provides readers with an analysis of some of the key issues and debates in contemporary thinking on this subject.

Drawing on rich historical research, she maps the connections between the previous forms of enclosure that occurred with the birth of capitalism and the destruction of the commons and the "new enclosures" at the heart of the present phase of global capitalist accumulation. Considering the commons from a feminist perspective, this collection centers on women and reproductive work as crucial to both our economic survival and the construction of a world free from the hierarchies and divisions capital has planted in the body of the world proletariat. Federici is clear that the commons should not be understood as happy islands in a sea of exploitative relations but rather autonomous spaces from which to challenge the existing capitalist organization of life and labor.

"Silvia Federici's theoretical capacity to articulate the plurality that fuels the contemporary movement of women in struggle provides a true toolbox for building bridges between different features and different people."
—Massimo De Angelis, professor of political economy, University of East London

"Silvia Federici's work embodies an energy that urges us to rejuvenate struggles against all types of exploitation and, precisely for that reason, her work produces a common: a common sense of the dissidence that creates a community in struggle."
—Maria Mies, coauthor of *Ecofeminism*